The Legitimacy of Use of Force in Public and Islamic International Law

Mohammad Z. Sabuj

The Legitimacy of Use of Force in Public and Islamic International Law

palgrave
macmillan

Mohammad Z. Sabuj
Law and Social Sciences
Royal Holloway, University of London
Egham, UK

ISBN 978-3-030-77297-0 ISBN 978-3-030-77298-7 (eBook)
https://doi.org/10.1007/978-3-030-77298-7

This Palgrave Macmillan imprint is published by the registered company Springer Nature Switzerland AG.
The registered company address is: Gewerbestrasse 11, 6330 Cham, Switzerland

To my wife Hosneara
And my children
Jemina and Umar
This Book
Is
Affectionately Dedicated

Preface

Authority to use force has been a subject of contentious debate among academics, politicians, and lawyers. This debate has developed a fundamental question of 'the legitimacy of the use of force' by states and armed non-state actors based on Muslim states. In the twenty-first century most international and non-international armed conflicts have involved Muslim states, and these conflicts raised the question of the legitimacy of use of force, namely where does the legitimacy of the use of force lie—Public or Islamic international law? This question is being asked in the context of the use of force against Muslim states and armed non-state actors functioning from those states. The question of the legitimacy of use of force following the 9/11 terrorist attack, invasion of Afghanistan, and the Iraq War has turned towards a new direction, where Muslim states and armed non-state actors approach this question in the context of the legal-political legacies of the use of force at the domestic and international levels. This book addresses the legitimacy question from the context of the legal and political legacies created by the extraterritorial and internal use of force. Hence it offers a different way of understanding and interpreting the use of force. It examines the legal and political accounts given by state authorities and leaders of armed non-state actors to justify internal and extraterritorial use of force. This examination includes the legal position of the use of force in Public and Islamic international law and the political legacies developed by these potentially two conflicting legal systems. During this examination, this book addresses the necessity of political authority as an argument for the legitimate use of force. It argues that Public international law on the use of force suffers from legitimacy deficits, which can be overcome by taking a coherent approach to the use of force in conjunction with Islamic law.

Egham, UK Mohammad Z. Sabuj

Note on Periodization

There are many ways to periodize various developments of Islamic law. This book has adopted the following periodization scheme:

The formative period of Islam	Starts with the birth of Islam and ends with the rise of schools of thought around the early tenth century.
The Classical period of Islam	Begins from the start of the rise of schools of thought (*Madhahib*) and continues until the end of the twelfth and early thirteenth centuries.
The post-Classical period	From the early thirteenth century until 1500 CE.
Early Modern period	From 1500 CE to modernity.
The Modern period	Marked by the establishment of the Egyptian army and the institutions of administrative and social control put into its service in the 1820 CE.

Acknowledgements

This book is the result of many years of research on the legitimacy of use of force in Public and Islamic international law. During these years, conversations with and feedback from many colleagues about this project have had a significant impact on the shape and content of this book. I would like to take this opportunity to thank Kevin Barker (Kingston University, UK), Paul Andell, and Stephen Coleman (University of Suffolk, UK). All of them have provided valuable suggestions, support, and encouragement, which influenced my thinking about the project from different angles and perspectives. I also offer my gratitude to my students and mentors, who have provided valuable feedback on chapters. I am particularly grateful to several scholars who read and offered very helpful feedback on early draft chapters, notably Professor Sue Farran (Newcastle Law School), Professor Esin Orucu (University of Glasgow), Professor Anton Cooray (City Law School), and Alexander Gilder (Royal Holloway, University of London).

I would like to express my gratitude to my teachers, who have encouraged me to be a student of law and always given me their valuable advice when needed most. I am very grateful to Professor Muhammad Ekramul Haque (University of Dhaka, Bangladesh), Tanvir Parvez (Advocate, Supreme Court of Bangladesh), and Professor Abu Mohammad (School of Law, City University, Bangladesh). I would also like to extend my thanks to Professor Hakeem Yusuf (University of Derby) and David McGrogan (Northumbria law School) for their invaluable comments on the draft chapters and encouragement for publication of this book.

At Palgrave Macmillan, I would like to thank Rebecca Roberts and Charanya Manoharan for their assistance at the editorial and production stages. I am particularly grateful to Nick Barclay, who sourced very helpful anonymous reviews for the book, and I benefited significantly from their feedback. I also thank my good friend and colleague Dimitris Xenos for his valuable guidance and support.

I thank my research supervisor Professor Mohamed Badar (University of Northumbria) for his academic guidance. I also thank my research supervisor Lee McConnell (University of Bristol) for his assistance and concern for my wellbeing during doctoral studies at Northumbria Law School and beyond. Thanks to the University of Northumbria, University of Suffolk, Institute of Advanced Legal Studies (IALS), and Royal Holloway, University of London, Library staff for their assistance, especially for helping with many inter-library loan requests. I am also grateful to Professor Matthew Humphreys and Mr Robert Jago (Department of Law and Criminology, Royal Holloway, University of London) for giving me the space to complete the writing of this book.

Portions of the article 'The Islamic Law of Rebellion and Its Potential to Complement Public International Law on the Use of Force' are reprinted in this book with kind permission of the co-author Mohamed Badar, and the co-editor of the *Journal of International and Comparative Law* (*JICL*) Anton Cooray. This was first published in 2019 at 6(2) of the *JICL*. I thank the journal for permission to reuse the relevant passages.

Finally, I thank and especially acknowledge the valuable support, love, and co-operation from my wife, Hosneara, who rallied and encouraged me when I needed it most. The interregnum between the start of this project and final publication has seen our family welcome our son Umar. Our daughter Jemina has been wonderfully patient and understanding throughout the research and writing of the book.

Egham, UK
Spring 2021

Mohammad Z. Sabuj

Contents

List of Figures

Table of Cases

Application of the Convention on the Prevention and Punishment of the Crime of Genocide (*Bosnia and Herzegovina v. Serbia and Montenegro*) ICJ Rep 2007

Application of the Obligation to Arbitrate Under Section 21 of the UN Headquarters Agreement [1988] ICJ Rep 34

Armed Activities on the Territory of the Congo (*DRC v. Uganda*) Judgment, ICJ Rep 2005

Caroline Case, UN Docs. S/PV (1981) 2285–88

Case Concerning Military and Paramilitary Activities in and Against Nicaragua (Merits) (*Nicaragua v. United States*) [1986] ICJ Rep 14

Case Concerning the Gabcikovo-Nagymaros Project (*Hungary/Slovakia*), ICJ Rep 1997

Corfu Channel (*UK v. Albania*) Judgment of 9 Apr 1949, ICJ Rep 1949

Fisheries case (*Spain v. Canada*) ICJ Rep 1998, 466

Guyana v. Suriname, Award of the Arbitral Tribunal, 17 Sept 2007

Legal Consequences of the Construction of the Wall in the Occupied Palestinian Territory, 9 July 2004, ICJ, Advisory Opinion, General List No 131

North Sea Continental Shelf (Federal Republic of Germany/Denmark) ICJ Rep. 1969

Oil Platform (Iran v. US) Judgment, ICJ Rep 2003

Prosecutor v. Al Mahdi (2017) 17 International Criminal Law Review 486–516

Prosecutor v. Dusko Tadic, Judgment in Appeal, ICTY, Case IT-94-1-A (15 July 1999)

Questions of Interpretation and Application of the 1971 Montreal Convention Arising from the Aerial Incident at Lockerbie (Libyan Arab Jamahirya v US), 1992 ICJ 114 (Apr 14, 1992)
The M/V Saiga (Saint Vincent and the Grenadines v. Guinea) Judgment of 4 Dec 1997, ITLOS
United States Diplomatic and Consular Staff in Tehran (US v Iran), 1980 ICJ at 40 (May 24, 1980)
Western Sahara, 1975 ICJ at 42–44.

Introduction

Public international law has always understood the use of force as a challenge. This challenge has seen the controversial claim to support the application of Public international law as objective, neutral, and universal irrespective of the nature of its subject. As a result, Public international law claims its scope of application in both Muslim and non-Muslim states alike. Since the formation of nation-states following decolonization and the end of the Ottoman Empire in 1922 many Muslim states had been striving to establish Islamic Shari'a as the main source of law. However, following the Second World War, the Muslim states prioritized their national interest and identity over the Islamic recognition of all Muslims as a single community (ummah). This strategic shift saw the popularity of building a secular state in many Muslim states in South Asia, Africa, and the Middle East. Also, the continued influence of Western power in deciding the legal and political directions of Muslim states in the post-war world with an added emphasis on the application of Public international law in those states has proven to be a huge challenge. The challenge was to secure legality of the application of Public international law in Muslim states that often accepted Islam as the main source of law. This challenge became more acute when Muslim and non-Muslim states used inter-state force between them. In the absence of legality of the use of force Muslim states often confronted the Western states and demanded to justify such use of force. As a result, Public international law needed to search for its legality in the context of the Muslim states. Moreover, the economic and political instability of the Muslim states following the two World Wars prompted those countries to become state parties to key international legal treaties such as the UN Charter. Once the Muslim states became member states of the UN Charter, they supplied the Western states with their highly desired legality of extraterritorial use of force. An-Na'im called for the necessity of a secular state in Muslim territories without imposing Shari'a as a state legal system.[1] He proffered a political analysis of the secular nature of Muslim states in the modern Muslim world. However, Islamic political leaders often held the West responsible for imposing secularism on them. They treated Western law and culture as a threat to Islam.[2] This political position became very persuasive in convincing the Muslim population to question the legality of any recourse to force by the West. This political position also paved the way to make the population believe that Public international law is a purely pro-Western legal system that the West often used as a weapon against the Muslims. This situation gave rise to turmoil in Muslim states, which led to the installation or reinstation of Islamic legal order, which the states and armed non-state actors often explained and applied to confront rather than complement Public international law on the use of force. Baderin has given an excellent account of this situation in his book but in the context of human rights law.[3] In addition, his book did not discuss the underlying challenges posed on Public international law that triggered the question of the legitimacy of use of force between Muslim and non-Muslim states.

Scope of the Book

The legitimacy question concerning the use of force came across as a contentious issue in Public international law when NATO bombed Kosovo to protect civilians against the Serbian forces in 1999. The NATO claimed legitimacy of the use of force, as opposed to legality, as it had not obtained authorization from the Security Council before the use of force which it was legally bound to. As a result, the legitimacy of use of force became a political tool and a successful method to bypass the legality. However, the scope of the legitimacy argument has expanded since then. State authorities have argued for an extended legitimacy of the use of force against armed non-state actors to tackle the threat to national security that the latter posed. Similarly, armed non-state actors claimed the legitimacy of

[1] An-Na'im, *Islam and the Secular State*, 30.

[2] Shah, *Self-Defence in Islamic and International Law*, ix.

[3] Baderin, *International Human Rights Law and Islamic Law*.

use of force against their government and foreign states that colluded with the former to administer such force. Shah has dealt with these challenges of Public international law very well in his book *Self-Defence in Islamic and International Law*.[4] He highlighted the politically motivated interpretation of Islamic and International law to justify the use of force in self-defence proffered by armed non-state actors like Al-Qa'ida and state authorities such as the UK and US while justifying the invasion of Iraq. Although he preferred a modernist approach to self-defence in Islamic law to show that it is compatible with International law, this approach was purely based on the US policies on the 'war on terror' and the Qur'anic concept of jihad. As a result, Shah has not dealt with the legitimacy of the legal-political legacies generated by various interpretations of 'jihad', which this book has done. Also, Shah did not address the legitimacy question and its scope of application to understand the growing challenges posed to Public and Islamic international law in relation to use of force, that is justification of the use of force when the 'war on terror' no longer satisfies the legitimacy of use of excessive force after the invasion of Afghanistan and the Iraq War by the US-led coalition. Similarly, Al-Dawoody offered an excellent analysis of Islamic law to clarify misconceptions on the Muslim calls for recourse to jihad in international and domestic armed conflicts with reference to the teachings of Islam.[5] But his analysis does not include 'legitimacy' as a threat to the legality of use of force in Public international law, which is the focus of this book. He developed the analysis surrounding the rules of warfare under the heading 'Islamic international humanitarian law' and classical Muslim jurisprudence on terrorism, and its punishment under the heading 'Internal Hostilities and Terrorism'. Likewise, Bakircioglu's book focused on the use of force in Public and Islamic international law, but he limited the discussion to just war tradition in Islam and the West.[6] In addition, he gave a good account of the modernist approach to Islamic law on the use of force and considered its compatibility with Public international law. However, his book did not assess the legitimacy of the use of force in Islamic and Public international law in a systematic manner. For example, Bakircioglu does not explain why his argument would convince the non-Muslim states that are claiming the universal and neutral application of

[4] Shah, *Self-Defence in Islamic and International Law*.
[5] Al-Dawoody, *Islamic Law of War: Justifications and Regulations*.
[6] Bakircioglu, *Islam and Warfare: Context and Compatibility with International Law*.

Public international law in both Muslim and non-Muslim states. Similarly, Vanhullebusch's book is more focused on international law rather than Islamic law, but his contribution stood out for outlining the conduct of war (*jus in bello*) under International humanitarian law in comparison to Islamic law.[7] For instance, Vanhullebusch has given a naturalist analysis of the laws of war. He discussed the use of force in Islamic and International law in a historical context such as colonialism, nationalism, and sovereignty. However, this book drives these scholarships in a new direction. The author of this book contributes to continuing the current scholarships concerning the use of force to address the legitimacy question from the legal and political perspectives. As a result, this book offers an interdisciplinary approach to address the challenges of the use of force in Public and Islamic international law in the twenty-first century.

This book discusses the role of states and armed non-state actors based in Muslim states in claiming the legitimacy of use of force at the state level and the inter-state level. The reason for which this book does this is to acknowledge the current challenges posed by the Muslim states and armed non-state actors to Public international law on the use of force. The nature and scope of these challenges have transformed with the turn of the twenty-first century. In the years since the 9/11 terrorist attacks, most use of force by states and armed non-state actors, which involved one or more Muslim states, have been categorized as acts of terrorism.[8] This categorization has been made without any scrutiny, rational or sound, of such use of force.[9] This is because categorization of the use of force is often being made to deliver rapid responses to particular incidents rather than to contextualize such use of force. A popular example of such rapid response is the invasion of Iraq in 2003 by the coalition force of the UK and USA without any authorization from the Security Council. The coalition force claimed the legality of their use of force in Iraq based on the security threats posed by the states and armed non-state actors. Since then, there has been a meteoric rise in the making of similar claims by or on behalf of the elite and militarily powerful states. These claims are often being made under the auspices of self-defence, national security, and humanitarian crises.[10] However, most of these claims are being questioned by states,

[7] Vanhullebusch, *War and Law in Islamic World*.
[8] Blair, A Battle for the Global Values, 79, 82; see also Wedeen, Beyond the Crusades, 56.
[9] Ryan, 'Framing September 11', 19; see also Jabara, 'September 11' (2001), 136.
[10] Steenberghe, The Law of Self-Defence, 43.

non-state actors, lawyers, and scholars due to their inconsistency with the proscriptions of the United Nations Charter.[11] As a result, these claims of legitimacy of extra-Charter use of force have been subject to contentious debate among academics, politicians, lawyers, and the public at large. For instance, while it is arguable that all extra-Charter uses of force are illegal it is also conceivable that such uses of force are legitimate. As a result, it is necessary to understand the distinguishing features of the legal and legitimate use of force in terms of Public international law. This book evaluates this distinction to make a potential contribution to settle the debate on the legitimacy of use of force.

Challenges Posed to Public International Law on the Use of Force

Article 2(4) of the United Nations Charter has imposed a general prohibition of extra-Charter use of force with a couple of exceptions, namely (a) defensive use of force in response to an armed attack under article 51 and (b) under the authority of the Security Council according to Chapter VII of the Charter. This position has been also supported by customary international law.[12] However, few scholars, known as 'the expansionists', have argued that the UN Charter is not fit and proper in the modern world to deal with extensive security crises and challenges posed by extensive threats of terrorism.[13] In this regard, the expansionists have claimed the legitimacy of using defensive force before an 'armed attack' by invoking anticipatory, pre-emptive, and preventive self-defence.[14] This claim has also been supported by a group of scholars known as 'the realists'.[15] Moreover, the current state practice indicates a strong proposition for the legitimacy

[11] Dinstein, *War, Aggression and Self-Defence*, 208; see also Gardam, *Necessity, Proportionality and the Use of Force by States*, 148.

[12] Ruys, *'Armed Attack' and Article 51 of the UN Charter*, 377; see also Banks and Criddle, Customary Constraints on the Use of Force, 67.

[13] Steenberghe, The Law of Self-Defence, 43; see also Martineau, Concerning Violence, 95.

[14] Deeks, 'Taming the Doctrine of Pre-Emption' in Weller (ed), *The Oxford Handbook of the Use of Force*, 661; see also Hamid, The Legality of Anticipatory Self-Defence in the 21st Century, 441; Murphy, The Doctrine of Pre-emptive Self-Defence, 699.

[15] Crawford and Nicholson, 'The Continued Relevance of Established Rules and Institutions' in Marc Weller (ed), *The Oxford Handbook of the Use of Force*, 97; see also Glennon, Why the Security Council Failed, 16.

of defensive use of force before an 'armed attack'.[16] Although no state has denied the legality of the prohibition of use of force under the UN Charter, many attempts have been made to legitimize such use of force on different grounds, namely exception, expansion, and explanation. For instance, the operation to Provide Comfort in 1991, aimed at the protection of Kurds in northern Iraq and the Shi'ites in the south; the NATO action in Kosovo in 1999 under the name Operation Allied Force in response to the suppression of the Albanians in Kosovo by the Serbs; invasion of Iraq in 2003; and the use of force in Syria since 2014. Contrary to this argument for the legitimacy of extra-Charter use of force, a group of scholars known as 'the Restrictivists' have argued that allowing pre-emptive, anticipatory, and preventive use of force will result in not only a violation of the prohibition of the use of force proscribed by article 2(4) of the UN Charter but also an unreasonable extension of the article 51 requirement of an 'armed attack'.[17] The unreasonableness lies in the fact that such extension would allow states to use aggressive force under the banner of 'self-defence' against their enemy states. On this footing, elite and powerful states often claim the legitimacy of extensive use of force beyond the proscriptions of the UN Charter based on their preferential treatment of national security and geopolitical interests. As a result, the views of the Expansionists and Restrictivists often reflect on different and competing feelings, expectations, and interpretations of the UN Charter and pose huge challenges to Public international law on the use of force.

Public international law faced further challenges when the powerful states and regional organizations professed legitimacy of extra-Charter use of force based on the security threats imposed by few states and armed non-state actors. The extra-Charter use of force by the militarily powerful states often involved one or more Muslim states and armed non-state actors functioning from those states.[18] For example, since the 9/11 terrorist attack, most extraterritorial use of force resorted against a considerable number of Muslim states such as Iraq in 2003, Libya in 2011, Syria between 2014 and 2020, and the currently ongoing conflict in Yemen. Moreover, unequal and arbitrary exercise of military power by the

[16] Trapp, 'Can Non-State Actors Mount an Armed Attack?' in Weller (ed), *The Oxford Handbook of the Use of Force in International Law*, 693.

[17] Sofaer, On the Necessity of Pre-emption, 211; see also Kammerhofer, Introduction, 13; Martineau, Concerning Violence, 95.

[18] Thomas, The Uses and Abuses of Legitimacy in International Law, 729.

powerful states and regional organizations at the international level in comparison to Muslim states has given rise to political and ideological conflicts. On the one hand, the highly politicized armed non-state actors functioning in Muslim states claim the legitimacy of their violent act of extremism to tackle extra-Charter use of force by the powerful states and regional organizations. On the other hand, the latter claim legitimacy of such use of force on a controversial basis, namely anticipatory or preventive self-defence, intervention by invitation, humanitarian intervention, and responsibility to protect. These controversial claims of legitimacy have been feeding those armed non-state actors with a strong sense of justification in their use of force at the state level and inter-state level.[19] Moreover, those non-state actors claimed legitimacy of asymmetrical use of force against their government and allies who have shown allegiance to remain silent on the extra-Charter use of force by or on behalf of the Western states and regional organizations. As a result, armed non-state actors have been involved in violent use of force at the state and inter-state levels, and hence playing a key role in the debate of the legitimacy of use of force in Public international law. This debate is very contentious and remained unsettled. Existing scholarly responses to this debate are either insufficiently comprehensive or out of date as they do not address this legitimacy debate between the powerful states and Muslim states as well as non-state actors. This lack of comprehensive and contemporary scholarly responses on issues surrounding 'the legitimacy of use of force' in Public international law has created a gap in the existing literature. This book fills that gap by adopting an in-depth analysis of the scope of the legitimate use of force in Public international law and a thorough examination of the legitimacy of use of force in Islamic international law as claimed by the armed non-state actors and state authorities based on Muslim states.

Why Comparative Approach?

Unlike Public international law, there is no general prohibition of the use of force in Islamic international law. Islamic international law allows the use of force in exceptional circumstances and as a last resort but within the strict guidance as provided in the sources of law such as the Qur'an, Sunna, Ijma (consensus), and Qiyas (analogy). As a result, Islamic international law is a source-oriented legal framework. The legitimacy of use of force in

[19] Kennedy, *Muslim Rebels*, 109.

Islamic law lies in the sources which the Shari'a has supplanted. The Shari'a is a living mechanism that has been developing since the formative period of Islam. Muslim scholars have been actively engaged in the exertion of intellectual and jurisprudential efforts such as Ijtihad to keep the Shari'a up to date and fit in modern times. In Ijtihad, the scholars have also considered the practices of four rightly guided Caliphs, the juristic opinions of the different schools of legal thought (*Madhhab, pl. Madhahib*), and the treaties concluded between Muslims and non-Muslims.[20] However, the Muslim states and armed non-state actors have made the legitimacy argument subject to a significant influx of political agenda. This has resulted in a controversial interpretation of the Shari'a from the perspective of the use of force which eventually transformed the meaning of legitimate use of force in Islamic international law. On the contrary, the legitimacy of use of force in Public international law is based on the process that it follows in the making of laws. Although the origin of Public international law is rooted in the classical natural law tradition, it has moved further from its source and developed through the law-making process. The legitimacy of use of force has questioned Public international law based on the inequality of sovereign power of the member states at the Security Council, where most of the decisions on the use of force are made. Moreover, this book argues that the side-lining of Islamic law by Public international law as its valid source and rejecting application of the former in the resolution of an inter-state dispute has resulted in legitimacy deficits of the latter. Furthermore, Public international law has left the treatment of armed non-state actors in the hands of their rulers or governments which often use violent force against them. They often use such force in collusion with foreign powers. The non-state actors have argued that the collusion of their rulers with foreign powers and the resulting persecution are illegal in Islamic law. They have also argued that this situation has given rise to their legitimate right of defensive use of force against their rulers as well as the foreign powers. This is a strong claim made by the non-state actors in Muslim states, which questioned the legitimacy of the political doctrine of 'sovereignty of states' and blurred the distinction made in Public international law between international and internal armed conflicts. This book shows that the controversy between Public and Islamic international law reaches a vantage point where both states and armed non-state actors make conflicting claims of the legitimate use of force. These conflicting

[20] Al-Shaybani, *The Islamic Law of Nations*, 5.

claims of legitimacy on the use of force have given rise to the legitimacy question, that is 'where does the legitimacy lie – Public or Islamic international law?'

Contribution of the Book

The author of this book discusses the legitimacy question from the perspectives of Public and Islamic international law on the use of force. He argues that it is time for Public international law, as a global legal framework, to overcome its legitimacy deficits by recognizing Islamic international law as its valid source of law and applying the latter in the decision-making process, whether judicial or political, involving one or more Muslim states and non-state actors. This book argues that overcoming the legitimacy deficits of Public international law will enhance its descriptive legitimacy among the people of Muslim states and beyond through their realization that Public international law does not disregard Islamic international law but complements it. The book concludes that descriptive legitimacy deficits of Public international law on the use of force, as one of the major shortcomings, are a result of weak cohesion of international society. The incorporation of Islamic law will fulfil this major shortcoming by creating a stronger cohesion between Public and Islamic international law.

This book offers a different way of understanding and interpreting the use of force. It gives a detailed account of the legality of use of force in both legal systems. It also examines the significance of the legitimacy arguments made in the practices and ideologies of states and armed non-state actors. It discusses the legitimacy question in the context of the legal-political legacies of the use of force and history of the evolution of Islamic law since the formative period through to modern times. It outlines the source-oriented legitimacy of Public and Islamic international law, the process legitimacy of the same, and the descriptive legitimacy of Public international law. In doing so this book suggests a coherent approach between these two conflicting legal systems to overcome the legitimacy deficits on the use of force. While answering the legitimacy question this book makes further suggestions as to how Public international law can overcome the existing legitimacy deficits. This book conducts a philosophical inquiry into the 'spirit' of the law in question rather than the 'letter'. This philosophical inquiry finds the legitimacy of use of force when the law-making process stands for the cultural and religious values of the subjects. It also finds that the legitimacy is specifically concerned with the forms of use of force justified by the belief of the people. This belief emanates from their cultural, political, and religious values. For example, whereas popular Western cultural and political values do not believe that the Security Council may retain its legitimacy when it struggles to confront the threat of force directed to the West, the Muslim states and most third world states believe that the Security Council may retain its legitimacy by effectively regulating the use of force as provided by the UN Charter, for instance, all uses of force must be authorized by the Security Council. Based on these methods, this book aims to (a) conduct an in-depth philosophical inquiry into Public international law on the use of force and (b) analyse the scope of the legitimate use of force in Public and Islamic international law as claimed by states and armed non-state actors. The central philosophical inquiry and analysis of the use of force, at both inter- and intra-state levels, focus on various phenomena including the main challenges which Public international law confronts. This book answers the legitimacy question by engaging in scholarly and systematic responses to the challenges posed to the use of force.

Structure of the Book

The chapters are concerned primarily with the law and state practice of the use of force in Public and Islamic international law. The chapters offer an analysis of the challenges posed to both legal systems to find the scope of the legality of use of force as claimed by the armed non-state actors and state authorities. The analysis contextualizes the underlying principles of the legitimacy of use of force in Public and Islamic international law by outlining the legal principles that regulate internal as well as extraterritorial use of force. For this purpose, the chapters examine the legitimacy of use of force by applying the criteria such as source-oriented, process, and descriptive legitimacy. Moreover, this book offers a coherent approach between these two potentially conflicting legal systems that may lead to overcoming the legitimacy deficits of Public international law on the use of force.

Chapter 1 outlines the law of the use of force in Public international law. It examines the United Nations Charter framework in regulating the use of force in the modern world such as the general prohibition of the use of force under article 2(4), use of force in self-defence under article 51, and by the Security Council under Chapter VII of the Charter. It discusses the legality of use of force in Public international law from the perspective of innovative approaches by states concerning the use of force such as humanitarian intervention, intervention by invitation, and responsibility to protect. It explains the customary international law on the use of force and the challenges posed by contemporary state practices and scholarly arguments on the Charter framework. An understanding of the law on the use of force is central to answer the 'legitimacy question' asked by states and armed non-state actors. It is also particularly important to answer this question because the charter framework on the use of force consists of the key peremptory norms of Public international law. This chapter sets out the context in which the state authorities, non-state armed actors, and scholars have asked the legitimacy question. Moreover, it discusses the legal status of state practices of elite and militarily powerful states about their exercise of force without obtaining authorization from the Security Council or following the proscriptions of the UN Charter. The chapter concludes by arguing that Public international law has failed to regulate the use of force in the modern world. It shows that Public international law on the use of force has partially answered the legitimacy question by recognizing the legitimacy of pre-emptive defensive force. As a result, the claims of the legitimacy of foreign intervention, anticipatory and preventive self-defence, pose huge challenges to Public international law on the use of force. This chapter suggests that the current political and social perspectives, which shape the legal-political legacies on the use of force in the modern world, should assess the legitimacy of these uses of force.

Chapter 2 discusses the meaning and significance of the legitimacy of use of force. It offers a critical analysis of the legitimacy of extra-Charter use of force under the banner of anticipatory and preventive self-defence. It then turns on the challenges posed on Public international law on the use of force by the extent of the threat to national security and pursuing geopolitical interests. This chapter emphasizes the legitimacy of anticipatory and preventive use of force and foreign intervention by states as well as regional organizations such as the NATO (North American Treaty Organization), which had assumed the responsibility to protect on few occasions. In addition, to assess the legitimacy of extra-Charter use of force this chapter scrutinizes the decision-making process at the Security Council, where most decisions concerning the use of force are made. It examines the nature and extent of the use of force as argued to be legitimate by states and non-state actors at the state level and inter-state level. The examination focuses on the social and political perspectives of the challenges posed on Public international law on the use of force. In this setting, this chapter answers the key question such as 'whether Public international law on the use of force can answer the legitimacy question and regulate armed violence in the modern world?' It concludes that the elite and powerful states, which often relegate the interests of those who suffer the impact of such uses of force, claim the legitimacy of use of force in pursuance of their political interests. In other words, this chapter shows that these claims of the legitimate use of force lack justification in the descriptive sense. This chapter also finds the lack of descriptive legitimacy in the biased political management of the powerful states and continuation of the colonial trend to exercise dominance both inside and outside of the Security Council.

Chapter 3 discusses the use of force provisions in Islamic international law. It outlines the origin and development of Islamic international law on the use of force. It shows that the main provision of the use of force, which is jihad, has developed and subjected to different meanings and significances. This chapter gives examples of the use and abuse of 'jihad' in claiming the legitimacy of use of force by states and armed non-state actors at the state level and inter-state level. It gives a detailed account of the legitimacy of use of force and their politicization by these actors. This account includes a discussion about the sources of Islamic international law on the use of force and its development from the formative through classical to the Modern period. It argues that the law is rooted in the Shari'a that has been developing from the sources such as the Qur'an, Sunna, Ijma (consensus), Qiyas (analogy), and through juristic methods such as Ijtihad (exertion of intellectual reasoning of Muslim jurists and exegetes). It shows that Islamic law of treaties has also contributed to the formation of the legal framework while interacting with other Muslim and non-Muslim territories. This chapter also offers a historical, legal, and political account of the fundamental principles of use of force in Islamic international law with reference to aggression, the responsibility to protect, humanitarian intervention, and intervention by invitation. It concludes that a ruler or government can exercise the legal authority to use force at the state and inter-state levels in exceptional circumstances, that is in pursuance with the 'right authority' and 'just cause'. It suggests that the legitimacy of use of force in Islamic international law lies in the legal-political legacies that can pave the way for any legitimate use of force to become the law.

Chapter 4 reviews the legitimacy of use of force by Muslim states and armed non-state actors that function from those states. The review includes an in-depth analysis of the claims of the legitimate use of force from the perspectives of Islamic law, religion, and politics. The analysis from these perspectives leads to answering the legitimacy question. This chapter shows that the claims of the legitimate use of force in Islamic international law are being made from the perspectives of Shari'a. It also shows that religiopolitical interests also motivated the actors to claim the legitimacy of use of force. This chapter argues that these claims of the legitimate use of force must be scrutinized from the legal-political legacies created by Islamic law. It suggests that the religiopolitical interests and arguments must be separate from the law when the legal-political legacies of Islamic law support this. The chapter discusses a vantage point where the legitimacy question generates conflicting claims of the legitimate use of force by states and armed non-state actors such as (a) the non-state actors' claim of the legitimate use of force in Islamic international law against their rulers and foreign powers that collude with the former; and (b) the state's claim of the legitimate use of force against another state and armed non-state actors alike in Public international law under the banner of intervention by invitation, the responsibility to protect, and humanitarian intervention. It concludes that Public international law must adopt a coherent approach on the use of force in Islamic international law to overcome its legitimacy deficits.

Chapter 5 answers the legitimacy question. It shows that the legitimacy of use of force lies in neither Public nor Islamic international law but in a coherent approach where these two conflicting legal systems can reconcile the legitimacy deficits. In this setting, the legitimacy debate reaches a vantage point where the key issue is 'whether the justifications based on the religion and institutional political position as proffered by Islamic and Public international law on the use of force respectively can adopt a coherent approach.' This chapter argues that, while the justifications challenge each other's legitimacy of the use of force, a coherent approach can reconcile the justifications and overcome the legitimacy deficits. It outlines the coherent approach as a combination of source-oriented and process legitimacy of the use of force in Public and Islamic international law. It suggests that these two legal systems can obtain source-oriented legitimacy by showing their roots in the religion and natural law tradition. It also suggests that the process legitimacy of Islamic international law can be obtained by exercising Ijtihad as a justified method of exercising intellectual reasoning in line with the Shari'a. It shows that Ijtihad is a legitimate method that can facilitate the continuous development of the Shari'a by deducing and interpreting legal principles from the sources of Islamic law, the purpose of the Shari'a (*maqāsid al-Shari'a*), pragmatic eclecticism, and public welfare (*masalahah*). It also suggests that Public international law can obtain the process legitimacy by securing sovereign equality in the decision-making process at the Security Council, recognizing Islamic law as a valid source of Public international law on the use of force, and applying Islamic law in matters involving one or more Muslim states and armed non-state actors. This chapter argues that implementation of article 2(1) of the UN Charter, article 38 of the Statutes of the International Court of Justice, and appointment of judges from the experts in Islamic law in the international courts and tribunals can overcome the legitimacy deficits of Public international law. This chapter concludes that while Islamic international law has supplied the basis for regulating the use of force in the modern world through its progressive methods of jurisprudence and legal-political legacies, it is time for Public international law to adopt and apply Islamic international law. This coherent approach of Public international law on the use of force will secure legitimacy in the descriptive sense and lead to its recognition as more objective, neutral, and universal.

The author concludes the book by drawing together the analysis in previous chapters which cumulatively answers the legitimacy question, that is where does the legitimacy of use of force lie—Public or Islamic international law? The concluding chapter shows that a coherent approach would overcome the currently existing legitimacy deficits of Public international law on the use of force. The author suggests that overcoming the legitimacy deficits of Public international law will enhance its descriptive legitimacy of the use of force among the people of Muslim states who are often being affected by such use of force in current times. The author argues that the descriptive legitimacy deficit of Public international law, as one of the major shortcomings, is a result of the weak cohesion of international society. This chapter concludes with a cogent argument of the author that the recognition and incorporation of Islamic law on the use of force will fulfil this major shortcoming of Public international law by creating a stronger cohesion between Public and Islamic international law. The author suggests that to overcome the legitimacy deficits Public international law must recognize Islamic international law on the use of force as its source particularly in those situations where any decision to use force involves one or more Muslim states and armed non-state actors of those states.

References

Al-Dawoody A., *Islamic Law of War: Justifications and Regulations* (Palgrave Macmillan 2011).

Al-Shaybani, *The Islamic Law of Nations: Shaybani's Siyar* (Majid Khadduri tr, Baltimore: Johns Hopkins Press, 1966).

An-Na'im A., *Islam and the Secular State* (Harvard University Press, 2009).

Baderin M., *International Human Rights Law and Islamic Law* (Oxford University Press, 2003).

Bakircioglu O., *Islam and Warfare: Context and Compatibility with International Law* (Routledge, 2014).

Banks W.C., and Criddle E.J., 'Customary Constraints on the Use of Force: Article 51 with an American Accent' (2016) 29 Leiden Journal of International Law 67.

Blair T., 'A Battle for the Global Values' (2007) Foreign Affairs 79.

Crawford J. and Nicholson R., 'The Continued Relevance of Established Rules and Institutions Relating to the Use of Force' in Marc Weller (ed), *The Oxford Handbook of the Use of Force in International Law* (1st edn, Oxford University Press, 2015).

Deeks A. S., 'Taming the Doctrine of Pre-Emption' in Marc Weller (ed), *The Oxford Handbook of the Use of Force in International Law* (Oxford University Press, 2015).

Dinstein Y., *War, Aggression and Self-Defence* (fifth edn, Cambridge University Press, 2011).

Gardam J., *Necessity, Proportionality and the Use of Force by States* (Cambridge University Press, 2004).

Ghafur Hamid A.G., 'The Legality of Anticipatory Self-Defence in the 21st Century World Order: A Reappraisal' (2007) 54 Netherlands International Law Review 441.

Glennon M., 'Why the Security Council Failed' (2003) Foreign Aff. 16.

Jabara A., 'September 11: Doesn't it Have a Political and Historical Context?' (2001) 58 Guild Practitioner 136.

Kammerhofer J., 'Introduction; The Future of Restrictivist Scholarship on the Use of Force' (2016) 29 Leiden Journal of International Law 13.

Kennedy J.T., *Muslim Rebels: Kharijites and the Politics of Extremism in Egypt* (Oxford University Press, 2006).

Martineau A-C., 'Concerning Violence: A Post-Colonial Reading of the Debate on the Use of Force' (2016) 29 Leiden Journal of International Law 95.

Murphy S.D., 'The Doctrine of Pre-emptive Self-Defence' (2005) 50 Villanova Law Review 699.

Ruys T., *'Armed Attack' and Article 51 of the UN Charter: Evolutions in Customary Law and Practice* (Cambridge University Press, 2010).

Ryan D., 'Framing September 11: Rhetorical Device and Photographic Opinion' (2004) European Journal of American Culture 19.
Shah N., *Self-Defence in Islamic and International Law* (Palgrave Macmillan, 2008).
Sofaer A.D, 'On the Necessity of Pre-emption' (2003) 14 European Journal of International Law 209.
Steenberghe R., 'The Law of Self-Defence and the New Argumentative Landscape on the Expansionists' Side' (2016) 29 Leiden Journal of International Law 43.
Thomas C., 'The Uses and Abuses of Legitimacy in International Law' (2014) 34 Oxford Journal of Legal Studies 729.
Trapp K.N., 'Can Non-State Actors Mount an Armed Attack?' in Marc Weller (ed), *The Oxford Handbook of the Use of Force in International Law* (Oxford University Press 2015).
Wedeen L., 'Beyond the Crusades: Why Huntington and Bin Laden are Wrong' (2003) X Middle Eastern Policy 56.
Vanhullebusch M., *War and Law in Islamic World* (Brill, 2015).

CHAPTER 1

The Legitimacy of Public International Law on the Use of Force

1.1 Introduction

This chapter approaches the use of force in Public international law from a distinct perspective. It offers the benchmark for the legitimacy argument which has been made throughout this book. It argues that Public international law is suffering from legitimacy deficits due to the challenges posed on this. It shows that the 9/11 terrorist attack and the use of force that followed from this in the Muslim world have given rise to the challenges. Understanding the challenges is central to answer the 'legitimacy question' (where does the legitimacy of use of force lie—Public or Islamic international law?) asked by states and armed non-state actors.[1] It offers an analysis of the use of force provisions in the United Nations Charter (UN Charter) to show how states and non-state actors view any use of force beyond the proscriptions of the Charter (extra-Charter use of force). This analysis includes recent state practice and scholarly positions that call for the legitimacy of extra-Charter use of force on grounds such as to protect the national security of states and to safeguard, restore other people's fundamental rights, and maintain international order and stability. These grounds include humanitarian intervention, intervention by invitation, and use of force in response to an 'armed attack' by armed non-state

[1] For an outline of the legitimacy question please see 'Introduction'.

M. Z. Sabuj, *The Legitimacy of Use of Force in Public and Islamic International Law*,
https://doi.org/10.1007/978-3-030-77298-7_1

actors. This chapter also discusses the effect of the legitimacy argument on the UN Charter and customary international law on the use of force.

This chapter begins with an outline of the legitimacy issue in Public international law on the use of force (Sect. 1.2). This outline includes the reason for the issue and how the author addresses this. The chapter develops with an examination of the legitimacy arguments made by scholars such as expansionists and realists (Sect. 1.3). It shows how these scholars pose challenges by claiming the legitimacy of extra-Charter use of force. This examination develops an analysis of the effect of the challenges on the UN Charter and customary international law (Sect. 1.4). This chapter concludes by arguing that the legitimacy of use of force in Public international law is a contentious issue for states and armed non-state actors, who are the primary subjects of use of force. It also argues that legitimacy is a political argument that is necessary for Public international law to evolve with the time and acceptance by those who are the subjects of use of force, that is state authorities, its population, and armed non-state actors.

1.2 The Legitimacy Issue in Public International Law on the Use of Force

Some thirty years ago, Thomas Franck observed that no one seemed to be asking fundamental questions about the legitimacy of international law.[2] However, his observation no longer holds at least concerning the use of force that followed since the 9/11 terrorist attacks. The legitimacy of use of force has become the central concern among states and armed non-state actors since then.[3] The Muslim world has witnessed and has been subject to the use of force by militarily powerful states from the West, which raised the question of the legitimacy of such use of force. The question is 'legitimacy', as opposed to legality. This is because willing and able Western states used extra-Charter force against the Muslim states on a political basis such as securing themselves from perceived threats to national security.[4] Although this claim may be politically legitimate it is not legal according to the UN Charter. The charter explicitly prohibits extraterritorial use of force except when such force is necessary for

[2] Franck, 'Why a Quest for Legitimacy?', 535.

[3] Gray C., *International Law and the Use of Force*, 5.

[4] O'Connell M. E., 'Self-Defence, Pernicious Doctrines, Peremptory Norms' in O'Connell M. E., Tams C. J., and Tladi D. (eds), *Self-Defence against Non-state actors*, 174.

self-defence in response to an armed attack or a collective security measure authorized by the Security Council.[5] The International Court of Justice (ICJ) has clarified that an 'armed attack' must be sufficiently sustained by using military means at a certain level of intensity.[6] Moreover, to exercise defensive use of force under article 51 a state must satisfy that all other alternatives had been considered and proven insufficient.[7] Therefore, defensive use of force is legal only when it is used as a 'last resort' in response to an 'armed attack'.[8] Furthermore, the extent to which an 'armed attack' can be defended is determined by the necessity to repel the attack, but not to retaliate or in any way take revenge against the aggressor.[9] Scholars have claimed that any force used under the right of self-defence should be 'proportionate' to the actual armed attack.[10] As a result, the UN Charter requires that the 'armed attack' must occur before triggering to exercise of the right to self-defence. However, since 9/11 militarily powerful states have claimed legitimacy of defensive use of force before the occurrence of an armed attack. This is a clear violation of the UN Charter.

States have claimed that the self-defence provision of the UN Charter cannot address the serious threat of force that exists in the modern world.[11] They feel that a state may not have the military capacity to use force in self-defence if it waits for an 'armed attack' to occur.[12] As a result, those states claim the legitimacy of use of force in the forms of pre-emptive, anticipatory, and preventive self-defence.[13] However, these forms of use of force are not recognized by the UN Charter as they are beyond the

[5] UN Charter, art 2(4), 51 and chapter VII; *Oil Platform (Iran v. US)* Judgment, ICJ Rep 2003, para 51; see also the Articles on the Responsibility of States, Report of the International Law Commission (ILC), art 50; for a discussion about the UN Security Council's power to authorize the use of force as an exception see Chap. 2.

[6] *Nicaragua v. United States*, 103.

[7] Steenberghe, The Law of Self-Defence, 61.

[8] Akande D. and Liefländer T., 'Clarifying Necessity, Imminence, and Proportionality in the Law of Self-Defence', 563.

[9] Gray, *International Law and the Use of Force*, 25.

[10] Schachter, *International Law in Theory and Practice*, 152-55; see also Gardam, *Necessity, Proportionality and the Use of Force by States*, 148–53; Dinstein, *War, Aggression and Self Defence*, 208–10.

[11] O'Connell M. E., 'Self-Defence, Pernicious Doctrines, Peremptory Norms' in O'Connell M. E., Tams C. J., and Tladi D. (eds), *Self-Defence against Non-state actors*, 174.

[12] Shah, 'Self-defence, Anticipatory Self-defence and Pre-emption', 95.

[13] For an analysis of these forms of self-defence see Sect. 1.3 (below).

parameters of defensive use of force. To justify these extra-Charter uses of force militarily powerful states proffered the claim of legitimacy. They claimed that although the nature of force is extra-Charter they are legitimate. Thus, the legitimacy of use of force is a political argument. On the contrary, those Muslim states which have become the subject of extra-Charter use of force refused to accept this argument proffered by the powerful states. The Muslim states argued that legitimacy cannot provide the necessary justification for extra-Charter use of force.[14] As a result, a great deal of tension has been created between the Muslim and non-Muslim states. The armed non-state actors added further tension in this relationship by bringing the claim of the legitimate use of force against the states (Muslims and non-Muslims) to gain recognition for a cause (however portrayed) or seek out international recognition or pursue state leadership.

Traditionally, the principle of state sovereignty had not included armed non-state actors as a subject of Public international law but within the authority of a state.[15] This was the position up until 9/11 as it was generally assumed that only states could mount an 'armed attack'. However, the UN Security Council decided that the events of 11 September 2001 amounted to an 'armed attack'—a use of force so sustained that it triggered a right of self-defence on the part of the United States.[16] Also, the International Court of Justice (ICJ) has observed, albeit, in a dissenting opinion, that armed non-state actors can mount an 'armed attack' under article 51 of the UN Charter.[17] On the contrary, few scholars have observed that the response of the Security Council and the ICJ was merely positive to the pressures for momentous and situational changes but never demonstrated the actual legal position.[18] Besides, there is no conceptual or

[14] Heydar, *Islamic Peace Ethics: Legitimate and Illegitimate Violence in Contemporary Islamic Thought*, 13.

[15] The General Assembly (GA) has made a declaration on the protection of state independence and sovereignty in A/RES/2131 (XX) (21 Dec 1965); see also O'Connell M. E., 'Presumption of Peace: Illegal War, Human Rights, and Humanitarian Law', 526.

[16] SC Resolutions 1368 (2001) and 1373 (2001).

[17] *Legal Consequences of the Construction of the Wall in the Occupied Palestinian Territory*, Advisory Opinion, Separate Opinion of Judge Higgins, para 33; Separate Opinion of Judge Kooijmans, para 35; Declaration of Judge Buergenthal, para 6; see also *Armed Activities on the Territory of Congo (DRC v Uganda)*, Judgment, Separate Opinion of Judge Kooijmans, paras 28 ff; Separate Opinion of Judge Simma, para 11.

[18] Wilmshurst, *Principles of International Law on the Use of Force*, 66; see also Gray, *International Law and the Use of Force*, 164; Myjer and White, The Twin Towers attack: An Unlimited Right to Self-Defence, 5.

normative link between 'armed attack by non-state actors' and 'automatic trigger of self-defence'.[19] However, article 51 of the UN Charter does not specify the source of an 'armed attack' to trigger the right of self-defence. Hence, it is arguable that an 'armed attack' by non-state actors can trigger a right of self-defence in certain circumstances. For example, where the nature of the attack is so grave that it can amount to an 'armed attack'. In this respect the ICJ observed that 'armed attack' for self-defence included:

> Not merely action by regular forces across an international border, but also 'the sending by or on behalf of a state of armed band, groups, irregulars or mercenaries, which carry out acts of armed force against another State of such gravity as to amount to' (*inter alia*) an actual armed attack conducted by irregular forces, 'or its substantial involvement therein'.[20]

Therefore, states are responsible for an 'armed attack' launched by armed non-state actors who are operating within their territory, and the attack is attributable to those states.

The author of this book assesses these conflicting claims of legitimacy made by states and armed non-state actors by adopting a coherent approach between the politics of legitimacy and the legitimacy of politics. In other words, when the powerful states claim the legitimacy of extra-Charter use of force against Muslim states and armed non-state actors, they claim the legitimacy of their political arguments (the politics of legitimacy) to extend the proscription of the UN Charter on the use of force. On the contrary, Muslim states and armed non-state actors question such claims to be illegitimate for bringing a political claim (the legitimacy of politics) to justify the use of force without considering Islamic law. Moreover, armed non-state actors claim the legitimacy of use of force in the furtherance of Islamic law and politics. They claim that Islam and politics are inseparable from each other, and both must be considered to understand the legitimacy of use of force in Islamic law (the politics of legitimacy). However, the author assesses this argument under the lens of the legal-political legacies that have evolved from the Islamic political practices but within the proscriptions of the Islamic Shari'a (the legitimacy of politics). Therefore, the legitimacy question reaches a vantage point where the author assesses this question by adopting a coherent approach.

[19] Orakhelashvili, 'Changing Jus Cogens through State Practice?', 173.

[20] *Nicaragua v. US*, para 195.

This approach facilitates both Public and Islamic international law on the use of force to evolve consistently under the auspices of the politics of legitimacy and the legitimacy of politics. In this setting 'the politics of legitimacy' makes the scope for the development of law, and 'the legitimacy of politics' controls such development by taking into account how the subjects of use of force perceive this to be legitimate in line with their respective legal-political legacies.

1.3 The Legitimacy Arguments Made by the Expansionists and the Realists

The Charter framework has been subject to challenges for being too restrictive and incapable of dealing with the use of force in the modern world.[21] This section offers an examination of these challenges to assess the legitimacy of Public international law on the use of force. The current challenges posed on the Charter framework include arguments for the expansion of the law and its legitimacy to regulate the use of force in current world affairs. These challenges are overwhelming in nature, and the extent of such challenges can be an immensely powerful factor to question the ability of the Charter system in regulating the use of force in the modern world. The fundamental provision of the Charter system is the prohibition of the use of force, and if it is questioned then the system is a substantial risk of failure. These challenges are the core concerns of Public international law on the use of force. Moreover, diverse groups of scholars and state authorities are posing these challenges such as realists, expansionists, and governments. They question the legitimacy of the Charter system as a global legal framework to control the use of force in the modern world.[22]

1.3.1 Challenges Posed by the Realists' Attack on the Prohibition of the Use of Force

Despite the general prohibition of inter-state use of force imposed by article 2(4) of the United Nations Charter, such force has been used under the auspices of self-defence, collective security, and humanitarian

[21] Berman, *Passion and Ambivalence*, 84.

[22] O'Connell, 'Self-Defence, Pernicious Doctrines, Peremptory Norms' in O'Connell, Tams, and Tladi (eds), *Self-Defence against Non-state actors*, 174.

crises.[23] Such use of force has brought challenges to Public international law regarding its ability to control the use of force in the modern world. Although no state has denied the validity of prohibition of the use of force as provided in the UN Charter, many attempts have been made to claim the legitimacy of extra-Charter use of force on different grounds such as exception, expansion, and explanation.

The Realists have made the most serious attack on the prohibition of the use of force. The scholars and state authorities from this group argue that the UN Charter is incapable of regulating the use of force in the current world as it is unable to address the challenges posed to the state parties.[24] Scholars from within Public international law, who do not claim themselves as Realists, have also argued that the prohibition of the use of force has been violated so often that it no longer represents the law.[25] The Realists have acknowledged that state parties may sometimes seem to have complied with the rules on the use of force, but that is only because the rules happened to coincide for the time being with the underlying geopolitical interests that shape their behaviour.[26] Andreas Paulus has summed up this approach of the Realists' to Public international law on the use of force in the following words:

> When the basic interests of states are at stake, in 'high politics', international law is considered marginal to international politics. In this topic, international law is merely a superstructure, a Marxian Uberbau that masks the real forces of international law—above all, power and military capabilities. This 'search for the actual laws' in political reality, not legal norms, characterizes realism. At the heart of international relations, it is power relationships that count: at the personal level, at the state level, at the interstate level.[27]

A conflict of interest has been seen between 'state necessity' and 'prohibition of the use of force'.[28] The national security strategies adopted by the powerful states purely focused on their national security interests rather

[23] Chapter VII, UN Charter.

[24] Glennon, Why the Security Council Failed, 16.

[25] Crawford and Nicholson, 'The Continued Relevance of Established Rules and Institutions' in Weller M. (ed), *The Oxford Handbook of the Use of Force*, 97.

[26] Crawford, Chance, Order, Change, Ch 1.

[27] Paulus, Realism and International Law, 269.

[28] Akande D. and Liefländer T., 'Clarifying Necessity, Imminence, and Proportionality in the Law of Self-Defence', 563.

than showing respect and compliance with Public international law on the use of force. For example, the US National Security Strategy in 2002 supported the use of pre-emptive and even preventive self-defence that was adopted in the 2010 strategy.[29] Moreover, the Realists have attacked, directly or indirectly, the rule *pacta sunt servanda*, on which all else depends on Public international law.[30] They have done this in the name of humanitarian intervention and preventive measures against terrorism, both very modern issues high on almost everyone's list of concerns which, they believe, cannot any longer be met with the old rules and processes of the UN Charter.[31]

1.3.2 Challenges Posed by the 'Expansionists' on the Prohibition of the Use of Force

Further challenges have been posed by the 'Expansionists' on article 2(4) prohibition of the use of force as well as its exception under article 51 of the UN Charter. They claim that the use of defensive force after an 'armed attack' is not a sufficient mechanism to confront the current threats posed on the national security of state parties.[32] In this regard, the Expansionists claim the legitimacy of using defensive force before an 'armed attack' by invoking anticipatory, pre-emptive, and preventive self-defence. For example, Israel's attack on the Osirak nuclear reactor in Iraq in 1981, which the Security Council condemned in Resolution 487 (1981).[33] The Council's position at that point essentially signified the opposition of the community of states to acts such as this, with the effect that state practice leading to the relevant change in the Charter-based legal framework would be difficult to consolidate.[34]

Pre-emptive self-defence denotes to use of defensive force to halt an imminent threat of an armed attack from a state or non-state actor.[35] This approach adheres to the *Caroline principle* that a state may respond to an

[29] The National Security Strategy of the United States; see also Henderson, 'The 2010 United States National Security Strategy', 403.

[30] Franck, The Power of Legitimacy and the Legitimacy of Power, 95.

[31] Ibid.

[32] Martineau, 'Concerning Violence, 98.

[33] Orakhelashvili, 'Changing Jus Cogens Through State Practice?', 170.

[34] Hamid, The Legality of Anticipatory Self-Defence, 441.

[35] Deeks, 'Taming the Doctrine of Pre-Emption' in Weller M. (ed), *The Oxford Handbook of the Use of Force*, 661.

armed attack before it is completed, but only where the need to respond is 'instant, overwhelming, and leaving no choice of means, and no moment for deliberation'.[36] Moreover, anticipatory self-defence denotes defensive use of force to halt a particular tangible course of action that the potential victim state perceives will shortly evolve into an armed attack against it.[37] The potential attack appears more distant in time than an attack forestalled by pre-emptive self-defence, but the potential victim state has good reasons to believe that the attack is likely, is near at hand, and, if it takes place, will result in significant harm.[38] Furthermore, preventive self-defence signifies the defensive use of force to halt a serious future threat of an armed attack, without clarity about when or where the attack may emerge.[39]

1.3.3 Challenges Posed by the Extra-Charter Practices of the Powerful States

The influence of the great powers in the Security Council in pursuing their geopolitical interests is a case in hand to name the challenges posed by the elite and powerful states who are militarily capable of using force. The institutional inequality between members of the Security Council takes the conflict of interests between states to enhanced controversy. The permanent members' rights were always prevailed over the rights of other non-permanent members due to the former's exercise of veto power.[40] For instance, where Security Council resolutions authorized the use of force, they were in the best interest of the great powers, and such resolutions were vetoed when they were against their geopolitical interests.[41] Moreover, hegemony amongst the great powers often makes the powerful states exercise influence over other members to carry out their collective

[36] *Caroline Case*, 2285–88.

[37] Murphy, The Doctrine of Pre-emptive Self-Defence, 704.

[38] Deeks, 'Taming the Doctrine of Pre-Emption' in Marc Weller M. (ed), *The Oxford Handbook of the Use of Force*, 663.

[39] The National Security Strategy of the United States.

[40] Westra, *International Law and the Use of Armed Force*, 8; see also Krisch, 'The Security Council and the Great Powers' in Lowe V., Roberts A., Welsh J. and Zaum D. (eds), *The United Nations Security Council and War*, 136.

[41] *Nicaragua v. United States*, para 268; see also Krisch, 'The Security Council and the Great Powers' in Lowe V., Roberts A., Welsh J. and Zaum D. (eds), *The United Nations Security Council and War*, 136.

goals.[42] Furthermore, powerful states and their allies often disregard the charter requirement of obtaining authorization from the Security Council before unilaterally intervening in the affairs of another state.[43] Examples include but are not limited to the invasion of Iraq in 2003,[44] and Russia's actions in Ukraine in 2014.[45] As a result, if there is a conflict of interest between powerful and non-powerful states, the interests of the former often prevail over the latter.[46] Gerry Simpson has articulated this asymmetrical power practice by distinguishing the two groups of states:

> An elite group of states, commonly referred to as the 'Great Powers', and a large mass of middle and smaller powers who defer to these larger powers in the operation and constitution of an international legal order. These Great Powers occupy a position of authority within each of the legal regimes that have arisen since 1815. Sometimes these regimes are constructed around loose affiliations of interested Great Powers (the Vienna Congress), at other times the role of the Great Powers is laid out in the detailed provisions of an originating document (The United Nations Charter). In each instance, these powers have policed the international order from a position of assumed cultural, material, and legal superiority. A key prerogative of this position has been a right to intervene in the affairs of other states in order to promote some proclaimed community goal.[47]

Therefore, it is arguable that the powerful states are in an advantageous position in terms of influencing the decision-making process at the Security Council. As a result, the ability of the Security Council to regulate the use of force in the modern world has been questioned. Moreover, the challenges posed to the Charter framework by the Realists and Expansionists by claiming pre-emptive, anticipatory, and preventive self-defence in response to serious and imminent threats could be an option for the powerful states with the military capacity to launch such attack to promote their self-interests. These challenges have resulted in crucial legitimacy issues which included the ability of Public international law to regulate the use of force in the modern world. Furthermore, the powerful states have

[42] Simpson, *Great Powers and Outlaw States*, 192; see also Warren A. and Bode I. (eds), *Governing the Use of Force*, 145.

[43] Corfu Channel (*UK v. Albania*) Judgment of 9 Apr 1949, ICJ Rep 1949, 35.

[44] Taft and Buckwald, Pre-emption, Iraq, and International Law, 557.

[45] Weller, 'Introduction' in Weller M. (ed), *The Oxford Handbook of the Use of Force*, 25.

[46] Westra, *International Law and the Use of Armed Force*, 8.

[47] Simpson, *Great Powers and Outlaw States*, 5.

claimed the state practices of extra-Charter use of force as legitimate under the auspices of a threat to national security and violation of human rights. However, these claims illustrate that geopolitical interests such as hegemony and national security are the main driving force behind them. As a result, these claims of legitimacy must be examined.

If Public international law tolerates extra-Charter use of force, the Charter system is likely to be under a potential threat of failure.[48] This is because stretching defensive use of force beyond article 51 of the UN Charter would allow states to use aggressive force in the name of self-defence against their enemy states.[49] In response to such use of force, the enemy state may use defensive force and accuse the first state to have used force in aggression.[50] An example is Israel's attack on Egypt in 1967 after the Egyptian government unilaterally had ordered the withdrawal of the United Nations Emergency Force, which since 1956 had served as a buffer between the two enemies, and had redeployed its forces to occupy the buffer zone in a threatening posture.[51] This situation would also result in the aggressive use of force by those states who are militarily able and politically willing against their enemy states. Therefore, the current legal framework, according to the Restrictivists, of the UN Charter in regulating inter-state force is proper.[52]

Despite the strength of the argument of the Restrictivists against stretching the current Charter proscription of defensive use of force, the Expansionists and Realists have triumphed over the former based on their support for such stretch, namely imminent threat to national security. The challenges posed on national security by the risk of imminent and intensive terrorist attacks in the contemporary world have given rise to several claims of legitimacy of extra-Charter use of force made by scholars and state parties.[53] However, there are possibilities of abuse of the trajectory of use of force in self-defence if it is allowed where an 'armed attack' has not

[48] Tucker, The Interpretation of War, 13.

[49] Martineau, Concerning Violence, 98.

[50] Sofaer, On the Necessity of Pre-emption, 211.

[51] Franck, The Power of Legitimacy and the Legitimacy of Power, 104.

[52] Kammerhofer, Introduction; The Future of Restrictivist, 13; see also Martineau, Concerning Violence, 95.

[53] Greenwood, 'International Law and the Pre-Emptive Use of Force' 14–15 (listing Franck, Waldock, Fitzmaurice, Bowett, Schwebel, Jennings, Watts, and Higgins as supporting anticipatory self-defence) cited in Deeks, 'Taming the Doctrine of Pre-Emption', in Weller M. (ed), *The Oxford Handbook of the Use of Force*, 665.

occurred.[54] Certainly, the states that claim legitimacy of the extra-Charter use of force would argue that there were certainties or likelihood that an 'armed attack' would have occurred had they taken no action in self-defence. Perceived threats can create pre-emptive, anticipatory, and preventive responses that may not have any real basis but are based upon presumed or projected future capabilities of the rival side—if not *threat-obsessed hyperrationality*.[55]

In these circumstances, a solution is on offer to balance the conflicting but strong views of the Restrictivists on the one hand and Expansionists and Realists on the other. From the case-by-case interpretation, the Security Council has qualified the meaning of 'armed attack' to include instances of an imminent attack.[56] However, the ICJ has been reluctant to deal with this issue despite having the opportunity to do so in the *Nicaragua Case*. Whereas the ICJ had declined to give an opinion on the lawfulness of a pre-emptive, anticipatory, or preventive self-defence,[57] the Secretary-General's High-Level Panel on Threats, Challenges, and Change has stated the possibility of pre-emptive self-defence to respond to an imminent armed attack.[58] This view has also been endorsed by the then secretary-general.[59] As a result, the legality of defensive use of force has been arguably extended to include pre-emptive use of force. There is no basis in Public international law for going further than this. In particular, as far as a right of pre-emptive self-defence implies a departure from the requirement of 'imminence', it has no basis in the law as Hans Blix said in his third Hersch Lauterpacht Memorial Lecture on 24 November 2004:

> Although 'imminence' may be a severe time requirement, 'a growing threat' would be an unacceptably lax criterion and would not tally with the generally accepted position that force should be used only as a last resort.[60]

[54] Brownlie, *International Law and the Use of Force by States*, 259; see also Corten O., 'A Plea against the Abusive Invocation of Self-Defence as a Response to Terrorism', EJIL Talk!, (14 July 2016) cited in O'Connell, 'Self-Defence, Pernicious Doctrines, Peremptory Norms' in O'Connell, Tams, and Tladi (eds), *Self-Defence against Non-state actors*, 174.

[55] Gardner, Alienation and the Origins and Prevention of War' in Gardner H. and Kobtzeff O. (eds.) *The Ashgate Research Companion to War*, 35.

[56] Franck, *Recourse to Force*, 97.

[57] *Nicaragua v. US*, 102–6.

[58] In Larger Freedom: Towards Development, para. 124.

[59] Ibid.

[60] Hans Blix, Third Hersch Lauterpacht Memorial Lecture.

Therefore, the right to use defensive force without reference to the Security Council is limited to instances of actual or imminent armed attack.[61] This is a stretch of the Charter system to an extent that adopted the *Caroline* principle to transform pre-emptive use of force into customary international law.

1.4 The Effect of Extra-Charter Use of Force on the UN Charter and Customary International Law

As discussed above, although most states in the modern world are members of the United Nations, they do not strictly observe the use of force provisions of the UN Charter. In practice, member states maintain international relations according to their arguments for legitimacy, which could come into conflict with each other due to diverse cultural and religious values.[62] As a result, a conflict of state practices prevails which eventually threatens the legitimacy of use of force in Public international law. In these circumstances, state practice needs scrutiny in line with the nature and scope of the charter framework and customary international law. This section does this by outlining the effect of extra-Charter use of force on the UN Charter, comparing the state practices with that law, and giving an account of customary international law on the use of force.

1.4.1 The Effect of Extra-Character Use of Force on the UN Charter

Despite a general prohibition on inter-state use of force and the restriction to use defensive force to respond to an actual and pre-emptive attack in the UN Charter,[63] the legitimacy argument to extend this restriction by the powerful states has posed a huge challenge on the charter system. It raises the question of the effectiveness of the charter system to regulate the use of force in the modern world.[64] The state practices suggest that the

[61] Franck, 'The Power of Legitimacy and the Legitimacy of Power, 104.

[62] For a discussion about the tension between state practices in relation to use of force see Sect. 1.4 (below).

[63] UN Charter, art 2 (4), 51; see also *Case Concerning Military and Paramilitary Activities in and against Nicaragua* (Merits) (*Nicaragua v. United States*) [1986] ICJ Rep.14, 99.

[64] Orford A., *International Authority and the Responsibility to Protect*, 8.

justification to use extra-Charter force has been offered by the Realists, Expansionists, and militarily powerful states.[65] These show that force was used under the banner of self-defence when it was not necessary to do so. For example, the US in the Dominican Republic in 1965 (referring first to the protection of nationals and then to the spreading of communist threat) and Grenada in 1983 (referring first to the invitation from the government and then to the approval by the Organisation of Eastern Caribbean States [OECS] and the need to combat the regional threat consisting in the spread of armaments).[66] Also, the Iraq War in 2003 witnessed another articulation of a claim in state practice that force was used as an anticipatory measure.[67] The coalition initially claimed pre-emptive self-defence against the threats caused by Iraq but later it changed its course. The legal basis, as claimed by the coalition, was the revival of the Security Council Resolutions 678 (1990), 687 (1991), and 1441 (2002), which never authorized the use of force against Iraq in 2003.[68] A new Resolution authorizing the use of force against Iraq was necessary to legalize the invasion.[69] But without such a Resolution the coalition forces attacked Iraq. Such change of course is fatal to the international law on the prohibition of the use of force.[70] These instances resemble more to reprisals than self-defence,[71] and armed reprisals are prohibited.[72] Although there are doctrinal attempts to subsume armed reprisals within self-defence, it is acknowledged that reprisals are essentially aimed at retaliating and forestalling recurrence, mostly well after the initial attack has taken place, as opposed to responding to an ongoing armed attack.[73]

In addition to the above, the use of force to protect vulnerable populations from governments that expose the people to war crimes, genocide, or crimes against humanity, or governments that refrain from protecting

[65] See Sect. 1.3 (above).

[66] Orakhelashvili, 'Changing Jus Cogens Through State Practice?', 169.

[67] Gray, *International Law and the Use of Force*, 170, 190.

[68] Ibid., 273.

[69] Habermas, 'Interpreting the Fall of a Monument', 21; see also Applbaum, 'Forcing a People to be Free', 271; Davis, 'The Legitimacy of War', 178.

[70] Murphy, 'Assessing the Legality of Invading Iraq', 173.

[71] Rehman and Ghosh, '"International Law, US Foreign Policy and Post 9/11 Islamic Fundamentalism: The Legal Status of the "War on Terror"', 87, 94.

[72] Art 50, ILC's Articles on State Responsibility, ILC Report 2001, UN GOAR, 56th Sess, Supp No 10, A/56/10 http://www.un.org/documents/ga/docs/56/a5610.pdf accessed 18 August 2020.

[73] Dinstein, *War, Aggression and Self-Defence*, 249.

them from such atrocities has become a contentious issue.[74] The perpetrators claimed such use of force as legitimate under the banner of 'Humanitarian Intervention' and 'Responsibility to Protect'.[75] However, such use of force turned out to be suffering from legitimacy deficits. For example, NATO's use of force in Kosovo to protect Kosovo Albanians in 1999 and in Libya to protect the civilian population in 2011 has been condemned by the international community. NATO's use of force in Kosovo was instantly condemned by India, China, and a group of Latin American states as unlawful.[76] The statement of the Non-allied Movement (NAM), backed by 132 states, 'reject[ed] the so-called "right" of humanitarian intervention, which has no legal basis in the UN Charter or the general principles of international law'.[77] These examples show that no legal entitlement to humanitarian intervention or responsibility to protect has ever emerged in state practice. The following words of Alexander Orakhelashvili are the true indicators of the current legal status of the state practices:

> Claims in favour of the extra-Charter exceptions have always been incoherent to constitute valid state practice for the purposes of customs-generation, and fallen far short of commanding the support of states to produce an amending peremptory norm under Article 53 VCLT. All this practice has either been fragmented and not general; or inconsistent in relation to the same state, same incident, or as between multiple states; or it has consolidated within a group of states but been rebuffed by the rest of the community of states. The whole practice in relation to anticipatory self-defence, pre-emption, humanitarian intervention, or self-defence against non-state actors has attempted to gain higher ground by professing to follow the UN Charter framework of *jus ad bellum*, and is therefore subsumable within the previous dictum from Nicaragua that unilateral claims reinterpreting the established legal framework are generally counterproductive.[78]

[74] Orford, *International Authority and the Responsibility to Protect*, 184.

[75] Orford, 'Lawful Authority and Responsibility to Protect', 248.

[76] Statement by the Rio Group, 26 Mar 1999, A/53/884, S/1999/347. 2 http://repository.un.org/bitstream/handle/11176/35671/A_53_884%3bS_1999_347-EN.pdf?sequence=21&isAllowed=y accessed 18 August 2020.

[77] Statement by the Non-Aligned States (132 states), 24 Sept 1999, cited in Brownlie, *Principles of Public International Law*, 744; see also Bennouna, 'Non-Aligned Movement (NAM)', Max Planck Encyclopaedia of Public International Law (May 2018).

[78] Orakhelashvili, 'Changing Jus Cogens Through State Practice?', 175.

Furthermore, states and regional organizations have claimed the ineffectiveness of the prohibition of the use of force provision for being too strict.[79] For example, article 2(4) and its exceptions do not give lawful authority to intervene in humanitarian crises. However, the Security Council can authorize a humanitarian intervention under Chapter VII of the Charter, but without such authorization, any unilateral intervention on any grounds would raise the question of legitimacy. Hence, the question is whether the effectiveness of the Charter is limited by the fact that intervention on humanitarian or other grounds is permissible only under Chapter VII? The limitation of intervention on humanitarian grounds is in place within the Charter system to prevent unjustified and biased intervention where the sole purpose of the intervention is upholding the interests of the intervening state.[80] States must obtain authorization from the Security Council to avoid any contestation in terms of the legitimacy of such questionable and controversial intervention.

1.4.2 *Use of Force in Customary International Law*

Customary international law plays a significant role in the development of the law of the use of force. It provides the basis for the legitimacy of use of force beyond the charter framework. Hence, any use of force beyond the charter framework but within the ambit of customary international law can generate a legitimate basis for the use of force. In addition, the legal-political legacies that develop over time by states and armed non-state actors concerning the use of force can show the need for the legitimacy arguments view from the purview of customary international law.

Extra-Charter use of force has been the subject of customary international law for an exceptionally long time. In the *Caroline case* pre-emptive use of force was recognized as legitimate only where the need to respond was 'instant, overwhelming, and leaving no choice of means, and no moment for deliberation.'[81] This argument is compatible with the Realists who argued that any instant threat of force must trigger the right to use defensive force when such threat is overwhelming and there is no choice

[79] Banks and Criddle, 'Customary Constraints on the Use of Force: Article 51 with an American Accent', 67.

[80] Orford, *Reading Humanitarian Intervention*, 88; see also Barnett, *The International Humanitarian Order*, 69.

[81] *Caroline Case*, UN Docs. S/PV (1981) 2285–88.

of deliberation due to the imminent nature of the threat.[82] Moreover, the Expansionists claimed legitimacy of use of force to end humanitarian crises in situations where such force can be used without authorization from the Security Council. These claims are legitimate as they promote the political interest of the powerful states which are militarily willing and able to use inter-state force where necessary. However, they pose a huge challenge to customary international law. Those states make a politically strong legitimate basis for stretching the proscriptions of the UN Charter or for including extra-Charter use of force in the sphere of customary international law by creating the legal-political legacies of use of force in inter-state affairs. Although the militarily willing and able states have claimed legitimacy of these legal-political legacies, they have not made any extra-Charter use of force to transform into customary international law beyond the pre-emptive self-defence as shown in the above section.

Although these legacies are very convincing political arguments to support the legitimacy of use of force, they are not legal but justified under the politically oriented international community of states. Muslim states and armed non-state actors, which have been the most targeted territories for exercising the use of force in the twenty-first century by the powerful states based on legitimacy, do not accept such use of force as legitimate. They argue that such use of force is repugnant to the UN Charter and Islamic international law.[83] As a result, the legitimacy question reaches a vantage point where it is necessary to adopt a coherent approach between the legitimacy arguments made by states and armed non-state actors based on 'the politics of legitimacy' and 'the legitimacy of politics'.

1.5 Conclusion

The use of force in Public international law faces many challenges. These challenges are built on the claim of the legitimacy of extra-Charter use of force to pursue self-defence. Public international law jurisprudence has recognized the challenges to address an imminent threat to an armed attack and the national security of states. As a result, it has recognized the legitimacy of pre-emptive use of force in self-defence and accordingly adopted this in the legal framework as a principle of customary

[82] Realists' argument has been discussed in Sect. 1.3 of this chapter (above).

[83] Shah, 'The 'Unwilling' and 'Unable' Test in International Law: The Use of Force against Non-State Actors, 109.

international law. In other words, the recognition of the legitimacy of pre-emptive use of force has been facilitated by customary international law that provided the platform for an extension of defensive use of force beyond the provisions of the UN Charter framework. A further extension, although strongly argued on political grounds, has been rejected due to their lack of legitimacy.[84] However, this extension to the defensive use of force added objectivity to the judgement. As a result, it has become a new addition to the use of force in Public international law.[85] This new addition has paved the way for pre-emptive self-defence to become a principle of Public international law on the defensive use of force.

The challenges posed on the charter framework about its ability to regulate the use of force in international affairs are based on political considerations which have found that Public international law, as it stands, can do only extraordinarily little to answer the legitimacy question. Whereas legitimacy has been offered as a primary source of justification, Public international law has answered the legitimacy question only partially by recognizing the legitimacy of pre-emptive self-defence in response to an imminent armed attack. As a result, it is necessary to answer the legitimacy question by examining the claims of the legitimate use of force outside of the charter framework and beyond pre-emptive self-defence. The legal-political legacies created by the claims of legitimacy of extra-Charter use of force have generated the need to address the legitimacy question from the political and social perspectives of Muslim states and armed non-state actors. This is because such use of force has specifically targeted them since the turn of the twenty-first century. The author does this in the next chapter (Chap. 2).

References

A/RES/2131 (XX) (21 Dec 1965) http://www.un-documents.net/a20r2131.htm accessed 2 September 2020.

Akande D. and Liefländer T., 'Clarifying Necessity, Imminence, and Proportionality in the Law of Self-Defence' (2013) 107 (3) American Journal of International Law 563.

Applbaum A. I., 'Forcing a People to be Free' in Lukas Meyer (ed), *Legitimacy, Justice and Public International Law* (Cambridge University Press, 2009).

[84] O'Connell argued that this extension is against the principle of jus cogens and peremptory norm of Public international law—see O'Connell, Tams, and Tladi (eds), *Self-Defence against Non-state actors*, 174.

[85] Henderson, 'The Bush Doctrine: From Theory to Practice', 3.

Attorney General Lord Goldsmith, 'Statement to the House of Lords' (*Hansard*, 21 April 2004, column 370) https://publications.parliament.uk/pa/ld200304/ldhansrd/vo040421/text/40421-07.htm accessed 22 September 2020.

Attorney General Lord Goldsmith, 'Statement to the House of Lords' (*Hansard*, 17 March 2003, column WA3) https://publications.parliament.uk/pa/ld200203/ldhansrd/vo030317/text/30317w01.htm accessed 4 October 2020.

Aust H. P., *Complicity and the Law of State Responsibility* (Cambridge University Press, 2011).

Banks W. C. and Criddle E. J., 'Customary Constraints on the Use of Force: Article 51 with an American Accent' (2016) 29 Leiden Journal of International Law 67.

Barnett M., *The International Humanitarian Order* (Routledge, 2010).

BBC News Desk, 'Yemen Crisis: Who Fights Whom?' (28 March 2017) http://www.bbc.co.uk/news/world-middle-east-29319423 accessed 28 September 2020.

Bellamy A.J., 'Feature—Legality of the Use of Force Against Iraq—International Law and the War Within Iraq' (2003) MelbJlIntLaw 6.

Bennouna M., 'Non-Aligned Movement (NAM)', Max Planck Encyclopaedia of Public International Law (May 2018).

Berman N., *Passion and Ambivalence: Colonialism, Nationalism, and International Law* (Martinus Nijhoff, 2012).

Blix H., 'Third Hersch Lauterpacht Memorial Lecture' (24 November 2004) http://lcil.law.cam.ac.uk/lectures/hersch_lectures_2004.php accessed 2 September 2020.

Brunee J. and Toope S., 'The use of force: International law after Iraq' (2004) 53 International and Comparative Law Quarterly 785.

Brownlie I., *Principles of Public International Law* (Oxford University Press, 2008).

———, *International Law and the Use of Force by States* (Oxford: Clarendon Press, 1963).

Cassese A., 'The Nicaragua and Tadic Tests Revisited in Light of the ICJ Judgment on Genocide in Bosnia' (2007) 18 European Journal of International Law 649, 654.

Charter of the United Nations, 1945, 9 Int. Leg., 332, http://www.un.org/en/documents/charter/ accessed 3 September 2020.

Crawford J., *State Responsibility* (Cambridge University Press, 2013a).

———, 'Chance, Order, Change: The Course of International Law' (2013b) 365 Recueil des Cours de l'Academic de Droit International, Ch 1.

d'Asperont J. (ed), *Participants in the International Legal System: Multiple Perspectives on Non-State Actors in International Law* (Oxford: Routledge, 2011).

Davis T., 'The Legitimacy of War—Toward a New Principle for Intervention, with its application to Iraq War of 2003' in Gardner H. and Kobtzeff O. (eds), *The Ashgate Research Companion to War: Origins and Prevention* (Ashgate 2012).

Dinstein Y., *War, Aggression and Self-Defence* (fifth edn., Cambridge University Press, 2011).

Doswald-Beck L., 'The Legal Validity of Military Intervention by Invitation of the Government' (1985) 56 British Yearbook of International Law 189.

Evera S., *Causes of War* (Cornell University Press, 1999).

Foreign Affairs Select Committee (2004, para. 429) https://publications.parliament.uk/pa/cm200304/cmselect/cmfaff/441/441.pdf accessed 26 September 2020.

Franck T., 'Why a Quest for Legitimacy?' (1987) 21 UC Davis L Rev 535.

———, *Recourse to Force: State Action Against Threats and Armed Attacks* (Cambridge University Press, 2002a).

———, *Fairness in International Law and Institutions* (Oxford University Press, 2002b).

———, 'The Power of Legitimacy and the Legitimacy of Power: International Law in an Age of Power Disequilibrium' (2006) 100 America Journal of International Law 88.

General Assembly, 'Declaration on Principles of International Law concerning Friendly Relations and Co-operation among States in accordance with the Charter of the United Nations' A/RES/2625 (XXV) (24 Oct 1970) Principle 1 http://www.un-documents.net/a25r2625.htm accessed 25 September 2020.

Gardam J., *Necessity, Proportionality and the Use of Force by States* (Cambridge University Press, 2004).

Gardner H., 'Alienation and the Origins and Prevention of War' in Gardner H. and Kobtzeff O. (eds.), *The Ashgate Research Companion to War: Origins and Prevention* (Ashgate Publishing Limited, 2012).

Glennon M., 'Why the Security Council Failed' (2003) Foreign Aff. 16.

Gray C., *International Law and the Use of Force* (Oxford University Press, 2018).

Habermas J., 'Interpreting the Fall of a Monument' in Max Pensky (ed), *Globalising Critical Theory* (Lanham, MD: Rowman & Littlefield Publishers, 2005).

Hamid A.G., 'The Legality of Anticipatory Self-Defence in the 21st Century World Order: A Reappraisal' (2007) 54 Netherlands International Law Review 441.

Heydar S., *Islamic Peace Ethics: Legitimate and Illegitimate Violence in Contemporary Islamic Thought* (Nomos Verlagsgesellschaft, Baden-Baden, Germany 2017) 13.

Henderson C., *The Persistent Advocate and the Use of Force* (Routledge, 2016).

———, 'The 2010 United States National Security Strategy and the Obama Doctrine of Necessary Force' (2010) 15 (3) Journal of Conflict & Security Law 403.

———, 'The Bush Doctrine: From Theory to Practice' (2004) 9(1) Journal of Conflict and Security Law 3.

Hoerauf D., 'The Status of the Libyan Rebels under the Laws of War: A Litmus Test for the Lawfulness of NATO's Libyan Engagement under UN Resolution 1973' (2012) 6 Phoenix Law Review 93.

Implementing the Responsibility to Protect: Report of the Secretary-General, 12 January 2009, A/63/677 and GA Res 63/308 (2009) https://unispal.un.org/DPA/DPR/unispal.nsf/0/EEF9DE1F698AA70D8525755100631D7C accessed 16 August 2020.

In Larger Freedom: Towards Development, Security and Human Rights for All, Report of the Secretary-General, UN Doc. A/59/2005, http://ww.un.org/largerfreedom/contents.htm accessed 17 November 2020.

International Commission on Intervention and State Sovereignty, The Responsibility to Protect (Ottawa: International Development Research Centre for ICISS, 2001) http://responsibilitytoprotect.org/ICISS%20Report.pdf accessed 14 August 2020.

International Law Commission, 'Responsibility of States for Internationally Wrongful Acts' (12 December 2001) http://legal.un.org/ilc/texts/instruments/english/draft_articles/9_6_2001.pdf accessed 25 September 2020.

Jamnejad M. and Wood M., 'The Principle of Non-Intervention' (2009) 22 Leiden Journal of International Law 345.

Jenkins B. M., *The Dynamics of Syria's Civil War* (Rand Corporation, 2013).

Johnson J.T., 'Threats, Values and Defense' in Elshtain J.B. (ed), *Just War Theory* (Blackwell, 1992).

Kammerhofer J., 'Introduction; The Future of Restrictivist Scholarship on the Use of Force' (2016) 29 Leiden Journal of International Law 13.

Kelsen H., *The Law of the United Nations: A Critical Analysis of its Fundamental Problems* (London: Stevens and Sons, 1950).

Ki-moon B., 'Address to Stanley Foundation Conference on the Responsibility to Protect', New York, 18 July 2012 (UN News Centre, 18 Jan 2012) http://www.un.org/apps/news/infocus/sgspecches/statements_full.asp?statID=1433 accessed 14 September 2020.

Krisch N., 'Unilateral Enforcement of the Collective Will: Kosovo, Iraq, and the Security Council' (1999) 59 Max Planck Yearbook of United Nations Law 81.

Lackey D.P., *The Ethics of War and Peace* (Englewood Cliffs, NJ: Prentice Hall, 1988).

Lauterpacht H., *The Function of Law in the International Community* (Oxford: Clarendon Press, 1933).

Lowe V., *International Law* (Clarendon Law, 2007).

Lowe V., Roberts A., Welsh J. and Zaum D. (eds), *The United Nations Security Council and War: The Evolution of Thought and Practice Since 1945* (Oxford University Press, 2008).

Lubell N., *Extraterritorial Use of Force Against Non-State Actors* (Oxford University Press, 2010).

Malone D. and Ugarte B. (eds), *The UN Security Council in 21st Century* (Lynne Rienner Publishers, 2016).
Malone D. (ed), *The UN Security Council: From the Cold War to the 21st Century* (Lynne Rienner Publishers, 2004).
Martineau A-C., 'Concerning Violence: A Post-Colonial Reading of the Debate on the Use of Force' (2016) 29 Leiden Journal of International Law 95.
Meyer L. (ed), *Legitimacy, Justice and Public International Law* (Cambridge University Press, 2009).
Myjer E. and White N., 'The Twin Towers attack: An Unlimited Right to Self-Defence' (2002) 7 Journal of Conflict and Security Law 5.
Murphy S., 'Assessing the Legality of Invading Iraq' (2004) 92 Georgetown Law Journal 173.
———, 'The Doctrine of Pre-emptive Self-Defence' (2005) 50 Villanova Law Review 699.
O'Connell M. E., Tams C. J., and Tladi D. (eds), *Self-Defence against Non-state actors* (Cambridge University Press, 2019).
O'Connell M. E., 'Presumption of Peace: Illegal War, Human Rights, and Humanitarian Law' in Sadat L. N. (ed), *Seeking Accountability for the Use of Force* (Cambridge University Press, 2018).
Orford A., *Reading Humanitarian Intervention: Human Rights and the Use of Force in International Law* (Cambridge University Press, 2003).
———, *International Authority and Responsibility to Protect* (Cambridge University Press, 2011).
———, 'Lawful Authority and Responsibility to Protect' in Falk R. and Juergensmeyer M. (eds), *Legality and Legitimacy in Global Affairs* (Oxford University Press, 2012).
Orakhelashvili A., 'Changing Jus Cogens Through State Practice? The Case of the Prohibition of the Use of Force and Its Exceptions' in Marc Weller (ed), *The Oxford Handbook of the Use of Force in International Law* (OUP 2015).
Paliwal S., 'The Primacy of Regional Organisations in International Peacekeeping: the African Example' (2011) 51 Virginia Journal of International Law 185.
Paulus A., 'Realism and International Law: Two Optics in Need of Each Other' (2002) 96 American Society of International Law Proceedings 269.
Pensky M. (ed), *Globalising Critical Theory* (Lanham, MD: Rowman & Littlefield Publishers, 2005).
Ramsay P., *The Just War: Force and Political Responsibility* (University Press of America, 1983).
Randelzhoefer A., 'Article 51' in Bruno Simma (ed), *The Charter of the United Nations: A Commentary* (Oxford University Press, 1994).
Regan R., *Just War: Principles and Cases* (The Catholic University of America Press, 1996).

Rehman J. and Ghosh S., '"International Law, US Foreign Policy and Post 9/11 Islamic Fundamentalism: The Legal Status of the "War on Terror"' (2008) 77 Nordic Journal of International Law 87.

Report of the International Law Commission (ILC) on the work of its 53rd session, UN GAOR, 56th Sess, Supp No 10, A/56/10, ch IV.E.1.

Reschke B., '*Use of Force', Prohibition of', A Concise Encyclopaedia of the United Nations* (2nd edn, Helmut Volger, Brill: Martinus Nijhoff, 2009).

Responsibility to Protect: Report of the International Commission on Intervention and State Sovereignty (International Development Research Centre 2001) 13–18 https://www.idrc.ca/en/book/responsibility-protect-report-international-commission-intervention-and-state-sovereignty accessed 14 August 2020.

Russett B., *The Prisoners of Insecurity* (San Francisco: Freeman, 1983).

Ruys T., *'Armed Attack' and Article 51 of the UN Charter: Evolutions in Customary Law and Practice* (Cambridge University Press, 2010).

Sands P., *Lawless World: America and the Making and Breaking of Global Rules* (Allen Lane: Penguin Books 2005).

Schachter O., *International Law in Theory and Practice* (Leiden: Martinus Nijhoff, 1991).

SC Resolutions 1368 (2001) and 1373 (2001) http://www.un.org/Docs/scres/2001/sc2001.htm accessed 11 September 2020.

Schroeder E., 'The Kosovo Crisis: Humanitarian Imperative versus International Law' (2004) 28 Fletcher F Wld Aff 179.

Shah N. A., 'Self-defence, Anticipatory Self-defence and Pre-emption: International Law's Response to Terrorism' (2007) 12 (7) Journal of Conflict & Security Law 95.

———, 'The 'Unwilling' and 'Unable' Test in International Law: The Use of Force against Non-State Actors in Pakistan and Afghanistan' (2020) 4 Asian Yearbook of Human Rights and Humanitarian Law 109.

Shaw M., *International Law* (6th edn, Cambridge University Press, 2008).

Simma B. (ed), *The Charter of the United Nations: A Commentary* (2nd edn, Oxford University Press, 2002).

Simpson G., *Great Powers and Outlaw States: Unequal Sovereigns in the International Legal Order* (Cambridge University Press, 2004).

Sofaer A.D., 'On the Necessity of Pre-emption' (2003) 14 Eur. J. Int'l L. 209.

Statement by the Rio Group, 26 Mar 1999, A/53/884, S/1999/347. 2 http://repository.un.org/bitstream/handle/11176/35671/A_53_884%3bS_1999_347-EN.pdf?sequence=21&isAllowed=y accessed 28 October 2020.

Steenberghe R., 'The Law of Self-Defence and the New Argumentative Landscape on the Expansionists' Side' (2016) 29 Leiden Journal of International Law 43.

Taft W. H. and Buckwald T. F., 'Preemption, Iraq, and International Law' (2003) 93 American Journal of International Law 557.

Tanca A., *Foreign Armed Intervention in Internal Conflict* (Martinus Nijhoff Publishers, 1993).

Thakur R., 'It's Time to Redefine a "just war"' UNU Update 27 (September–October 2003) http://update.unu.edu/archive/issue27_2.htm accessed 5 September 2020.

The Daily Mail, 'US Airstrikes Destroy ISIS Targets in Syria' (4 October 2014) http://www.dailymail.co.uk/video/news/video-1122157/New-video-U-S-launches-airstrikes-against-ISIL-Syria.html accessed 21 September 2020.

The Indian Representative to the Security Council: S/PV.6508 (30 Mar 2011) https://digitallibrary.un.org/record/700207/files/S_PV.6508-EN.pdf?version=1 accessed 17 September 2020.

The National Security Strategy of the United States, Washington DC, Sept 2002 http://www.whitehouse.gov/nsc/nss/pdf accessed 23 October 2020.

Trapp K.N., 'Back to Basics: Necessity, Proportionality, and the Right of Self-Defence against Non-State Terrorists Actors' (2007) 56 International and Comparative Law Quarterly 141.

Tucker R. W., 'The Interpretation of War under Present International Law' (1951) 4 ILQ 11.

Walzer M., *Just and Unjust War* (New York: Basic Books, 1977).

Warren A. and Bode I. (eds), *Governing the Use of Force in International Relations* (Palgrave Macmillan, 2014).

Weller M. (ed), *The Oxford Handbook of the Use of Force in International Law* (Oxford University Press, 2015).

Westra J.H., *International Law and the Use of Armed Force* (Routledge, 2007).

Wheeler N. J., *Saving Strangers: Humanitarian Intervention and International Society* (Oxford University Press, 2002).

White N. and Ölgen Ö., 'The Security Council and the Decentralised Military Option: Constitutionality and Function' (1997) 44 Netherlands International Law Review 388.

Wilmshurst E., *Principles of International Law on the Use of Force by States in Self-Defence* (Chatham House: Royal Institute of International Affairs, 2005).

World Summit Outcome Document (2005a), paras 138–9 http://www.un.org/womenwatch/ods/A-RES-60-1-E.pdf accessed 16 August 2020.

'World Summit Outcome Document' A/RES/60/1 (2005b) para 5 http://www.un.org/en/development/desa/population/migration/generalassembly/docs/globalcompact/A_RES_60_1.pdf accessed 25 September 2020.

Yearbook of the International Law Commission, 2001, Vol II (2), 84, para 21 http://legal.un.org/ilc/publications/yearbooks/english/ilc_2001_v2_p1.pdf accessed 11 September 2020.

CHAPTER 2

Responses to the Legitimacy of Use of Force

2.1 Introduction

This chapter focuses on the responses to the legitimacy arguments made by the Realists, Expansionists, and militarily powerful states.[1] As discussed in Chap. 1, the powerful states used extra-Charter force against the Muslim states on a political basis, such as securing themselves from perceived threats to national security. As a result, the claims for the legitimate use of force beyond the scope of the United Nations Charter by states and regional organizations alike are mainly based on geopolitical interests and national security.[2] The geopolitical interests and national security measures have posed substantial challenges for Public international law regarding its ability to regulate the use of force in international affairs. Although the recognition of legitimate recourse to defensive force to include pre-emptive self-defence in response to an armed attack partially addresses the challenges, it does not answer the legitimacy question.[3] It does not address the challenges posed by the claims of legitimacy of anticipatory and

[1] The legitimacy argument has been discussed in Chap. 1.

[2] Markowitz, Jonathan, Fariss, 'Power, Proximity and Democracy: Geopolitical competition in the International System', 78; see also Shah, 'The 'Unwilling' and 'Unable' Test in International Law: The Use of Force against Non-State Actors, 109.

[3] Henderson, 'The Bush Doctrine: From Theory to Practice', 3; see also Shah, 'Self-defence, Anticipatory Self-defence and Pre-emption', 95.

M. Z. Sabuj, *The Legitimacy of Use of Force in Public and Islamic International Law*,
https://doi.org/10.1007/978-3-030-77298-7_2

preventive use of force, and foreign intervention. This chapter addresses these legitimacy claims and explores the issues surrounding the legitimacy question with political and social analysis.

This chapter's overarching theme concerns the articulation of the legitimacy of use of force in Public international law and the responses to this by Muslim states and armed non-state actors. It begins with an outline of the meaning and significance of legitimacy. It explores the claims of legitimacy of anticipatory and preventive use of force, foreign intervention without authorization from the Security Council, and responses of the subjects of these claimed legitimate use of force, that is descriptive legitimacy deficit. It focuses on the current practices of states and regional organizations around the UN Collective Security system, and particularly on the legitimacy arguments made by the militarily powerful states under the auspices of Public international law on the use of force. This chapter concludes that although the legitimacy of anticipatory and preventive self-defence has claimed and seen to be a widespread practice of militarily powerful states, they have not overcome the descriptive legitimacy deficit.

2.2 Legitimacy: Meaning and Significance

According to *Black's Law Dictionary* 'legitimate' is that which is 'lawful, legal, recognized by law, or according to law'.[4] This definition provides the meaning of legitimacy in a theoretical way which is very simple, and for this reason, it does not provide a significant meaning. To develop a significant meaning, it is essential to explain rather than to define the term 'legitimacy'.

Legitimacy, as far as Public international law on the use of force is concerned, is not necessarily identical to legality. A use-of-force decision might not be legal if it exceeds the legal extent, but it may be legitimate given political considerations. For instance, a claim of legitimacy of use of force is made on the justification which may include political grounds such as self-preservation of states. As a result, the significant meaning of legitimacy as understood in this book is 'justification of authority' and its acceptance by those who are most affected by the use of force.

[4] Black's Law Dictionary.

Public international law on the use of force acts in the political environment, and it must consider the political realities too.[5] Political power often seeks 'legitimacy' for the justification and acceptance of their political authority.[6] However, this political power must be exercised according to the law. If exercise of political power cannot become law, it may continue to seek legitimacy until it becomes law. As a result, seeking and claiming legitimacy persistently by the exercise of political power often become the preliminary steps towards its addition to the legal framework. However, until it becomes an addition to the legal framework any exercise of political power must be legitimate. Therefore, the significance of the legitimacy of use of force in Public international law is that legitimacy must be queried in relation to every indication of political will and power in pursuit of the state's argument that their use of force is justified. In this way, legitimacy develops the law necessary to meet the needs of time and circumstances.

The relationship between legitimacy and legality is among the most significant in Public international law on the use of force. As one of the first steps towards an addition to the legal framework, use of force based on legitimacy sets out as a source of law that originates from the political exercise of power. In this setting, on the one hand, political authority seeks the legitimacy of use of force to stretch the current legal framework, and on the other hand, the legal framework seeks to exercise control over political authority. Until a political authority is added to and recognized by the legal framework, legitimacy cannot provide a platform for Public international law to serve that political interest under legal control. In these circumstances, legitimacy is still a contentious question as any use of force based on legitimacy may or may not become the law. If it becomes law the exercise of political power becomes under legal control. If it does not become law the contentious question of the legitimate use of force continues. The more political authorities exercise 'legitimacy' the more force it gains. The more force it gains the more it becomes closer to becoming the law. However, until it becomes the law it must keep justifying political authority by answering the legitimacy question, that is where does the legitimacy lie?[7] This is because every claim of legitimacy cannot

[5] Müllerson, 'Roundtable discussion following presentations' in Wolfrum R. and Roben V. (eds.), *Legitimacy in International Law*, 215.

[6] Ibid.

[7] For a discussion on 'the context of the legitimacy question' see 'introduction'.

adequately justify becoming the law and thereby questionable. Those claims of legitimacy which can neither justify recourse to force nor answer the legitimacy question or overcome the legitimacy deficits are illegitimate and must not become the law.[8] Therefore, answering the legitimacy question will identify those claims which are illegitimate.

2.3 Legitimacy of Anticipatory and Preventive Use of Force

The decision to use force by states and regional organizations such as the United States, United Kingdom, and NATO has made the claims of the legitimate use of force in Public international. These claims have offered justifications for extra-Charter use of force, namely national security, the exercise of the right of self-defence, and maintenance of international peace and security. However, these justifications are mainly political. They emphasize political considerations to pursue the legitimacy of use of force beyond that of pre-emptive self-defence.[9] They claim that pre-emptive self-defence in response to an imminent armed attack is insufficient to uphold the legitimate needs of self-defence of a state in the modern world.[10] This is because it is unreasonable for a state to wait until it has reasonable grounds for believing that an attack is imminent. The nature and extent of an attack can be so imminent that a victim state might not get the chance to respond to an imminent armed attack before it is destroyed and/or defeated.[11] In these situations, a victim state can legally exercise its right of self-defence to prevent neither the attack from occurring nor recourse to proportionate response to the attack, which could have been prevented by the use of anticipatory or preventive force in self-defence. As a result, powerful states which experience the threat of armed attack from foreign states and armed non-state actors claim that Public international law on the use of force as it currently stands does not guarantee self-preservation of states.[12] These states claim the legitimacy of

[8] O'Connell, 'Presumption of Peace: Illegal War, Human Rights, and Humanitarian Law', 526.

[9] Henderson, 'The Bush Doctrine: From Theory to Practice', 3.

[10] Ibid.

[11] Brunnée and Toope, *Legitimacy and Legality in International Law*, 292.

[12] Franck, Legitimacy in the International System, 712.

anticipatory and preventive use of force to respond to any threat of an 'armed attack' as opposed to an 'actual armed attack'.

In response to the claim made by states, the Restrictivists argue that recognizing the legitimacy of anticipatory and preventive use of force will result in a violation of the prohibition of the use of force as proscribed by article 2(4) of the UN Charter and unreasonable stretch of article 51 requirement of an actual 'armed attack'.[13] The unreasonableness lies in the fact that such a stretch would allow the states to use aggressive force under the banner of self-defence against their enemy states.[14] Furthermore, in this circumstance an enemy state, as discussed in Chap. 1, would likely use defensive force accusing the first state to have used force in aggression. An example is Israel's attack on Egypt in 1967 after the Egyptian government unilaterally ordered the withdrawal of the United Nations Emergency Force, which since 1956 served as a buffer between the two enemies and redeployed its forces to occupy the buffer zone in a threatening posture.[15] Such a situation would also result in the aggressive use of force by elite and militarily powerful states against their enemy states.

In the presence of controversy on the legitimacy of anticipatory and preventive use of force, the current state practices can be very useful to consider. After 9/11, there has not been any such situation where recourse to anticipatory or preventive force was legitimately necessary. Although there had been a few terrorist attacks that took place since 9/11, they were sporadic and did not have the 'intensity' to invoke anticipatory or preventive self-defence. Moreover, the recognition of the legitimacy of pre-emptive use of force and its common practices among states, as discussed in Chap. 1, are proven to be sufficient to respond to the challenges posed by a threat to national security and cross-border terrorism. As a result, in the current situation on security and threat of force, it does not seem necessary to stretch the right of self-defence beyond pre-emptive use of force in response to an imminent armed attack. The Restrictivists argue that this situation can be seen from the massive change in the US National Security Strategy in recent years. For instance, at once following the 9/11 terrorist attack the US National Security Strategy included the pre-emptive, anticipatory, and preventive self-defence, but the 2011 National

[13] Martineau, Concerning Violence, 98.

[14] Sofaer, On the Necessity of Pre-emption, 211.

[15] Franck, The Power of Legitimacy and the Legitimacy of Power, 104.

Security Strategy does not discuss the use of force except in pre-emption.[16]

Furthermore, recognition of the legitimacy of anticipatory and preventive use of force will be problematic since the decision to figure out 'if an "armed attack" will occur' will be left in the hands of states. The problem with this approach is that states may abuse this option against their opponents if there is no provision for scrutiny by an independent body.[17] For example, the decision of the USA-UK coalition force to attack Iraq in 2003 on their assessment of the threat of Weapons of Mass Destruction (WMS).[18] In these circumstances, the questions of who or which institution, which judge or jury, should decide whether the norm's requisites for anticipatory or preventive use of force have been asked.[19] In the absence of any scrutiny of the claims of legitimacy of such use of force with the added risk of abuse, they will continue to suffer from legitimacy deficits and eventually be illegitimate.

2.4 Foreign Intervention Without Authorization from the Security Council

Public international law on the use of force is constituted not only by its substantive rules but also by those institutional processes that implement the rules.[20] These institutional processes are concerned with the mechanisms by which power is conferred and exercised.[21] They prioritize the formal validity of power, focusing on secondary rules about the making, changing, and destruction of laws.[22] For example, the process to be

[16] National Security Council; see also Henderson, 'The 2010 United States National Security Strategy', 403.

[17] Orford, *International Authority and the Responsibility to Protect*, 40; see also Corten O., 'A Plea against the Abusive Invocation of Self-Defence as a Response to Terrorism', EJIL Talk!, (14 July 2016) cited in O'Connell M. E., 'Self-Defence, Pernicious Doctrines, Peremptory Norms' in O'Connell M. E., Tams C. J., and Tladi D. (eds), *Self-Defence against Non-state actors*, 174.

[18] Bush, Address before a Joint Session of the Congress on the State of the Union; see also (David Kay) Again Says Forbidden Arms Probably Didn't Exist; see also Borger, A Vice President Unbound, 34.

[19] Franck, The Power of Legitimacy and the Legitimacy of Power, 102.

[20] ibid; see also Brunnée and Toope, *Legitimacy and Legality in International Law*, 95.

[21] Friedman, *Law and Society*, 139.

[22] Thomas, The Uses and Abuses of Legitimacy in International Law, 750.

followed in the Security Council for authorization of use of force.[23] As a result, the legitimacy of a rule, or rule-making or rule-applying institutions, is a function of the perception of those in the community who are concerned that the rule, or the institution, has come into being endowed with legitimacy, which is following the right process.[24]

The decision to use force, at the international level, is entrusted to the Security Council, which is an international institution set up by the United Nations Charter to protect and promote international peace and security. The design and operation of an international institution like the Security Council are often dominated by more powerful states and used to serve their ends, thereby making it questionable to claim that recourse to force by those states is legitimate.[25] For instance, states and regional organizations often claim the legitimacy of foreign intervention without obtaining authorization from the Security Council. However, both Muslim states and armed non-state actors have challenged these claims of the legitimate use of force.[26] Examples include but are not limited to the invasion of Iraq in 2003[27] and Russia's actions in Ukraine in 2014.[28] Similarly, the use of force to end humanitarian crises had been claimed to be legitimate even when such force was used without authorization from the Security Council. For example, NATO's intervention in Kosovo to end humanitarian crises was claimed as legitimate, although not legal, as no authorization from the Security Council was obtained.[29]

However, mere authorization from the Security Council itself cannot be sufficient for the legitimacy of use of force. For example, in 2011 the Security Council authorized the peace enforcement operation to NATO in Libya.[30] There is evidence to suggest that NATO was involved in supplying arms and ammunition to the rebel forces to facilitate regime change

[23] For a discussion about the process followed by the Security Council see Chap. 1.

[24] Franck, Legitimacy in the International System, 711; for *contra* see Hyde, The Concept of Legitimacy, 379.

[25] Meyer and Sanklecha, 'Introduction' in Lukas Meyer L. (ed), *Legitimacy, Justice and International Law*, 4.

[26] For a discussion on these challenges see Chap. 1.

[27] Taft and Buckwald, Preemption, Iraq, and International Law, 557.

[28] Weller, 'Introduction: International Law and the Problem of War' in Weller M. (ed), *The Oxford Handbook of the Use of Force in International Law*, 25.

[29] Krisch, Unilateral Enforcement of the Collective Will, 81; see also Schroeder, The Kosovo Crisis, 179.

[30] Orford, NATO, Regionalism, and the Responsibility to Protect, 302.

and thus violated the mandate of the Security Council.[31] NATO's operation was permitted to provide humanitarian protection, but it ignored its restrictions, spurned hints of a negotiated ceasefire, and broke the arms embargo of the UN by supplying weaponry to the rebels.[32] Therefore, the Libya experience guided the international community on the notion that violation of the mandate of the Security Council is illegitimate.

The instances of the use of force, as stated above, were all (except the NATO intervention in Libya in 2011) beyond the ambit of the UN Charter. Among these uses of force, except the NATO intervention in Kosovo in 1998, all were questioned for their legitimacy deficits. However, the legitimacy of Kosovo intervention was successfully claimed by NATO based on its descriptive legitimacy, that is the people who were affected by the intervention perceived it as necessary and legitimate.[33] As a result, except for a very few such as the Kosovo intervention, the claims of the legitimate use of force have created controversial political legacies which are being challenged by descriptive legitimacy deficits.

2.5 Legitimacy Deficits in the Descriptive Sense

Legitimacy, in the descriptive sense, is based on the belief of the subjects of use of force that recourse to force is legitimate. This belief must be correct to profess such legitimacy which lies on the issue 'whether a norm or institutional arrangement on the use of force satisfies certain specified conditions for possessing legitimacy.'[34] Therefore, the focal point of the legitimacy of Public international law on the use of force is a 'belief' within an action, rule, actor, or system that such action, rule, actor, or system is legitimate.[35] In this regard, the inquiry includes the challenges posed to the use of force provisions of the UN Charter. The inquiry advances by scrutinizing the legitimacy of Public international law on the use of force which describes itself as universal, objective, and neutral.

[31] Hoerauf, The Status of the Libyan Rebels under the Laws of War, 93.

[32] Thakur, 'Reconfiguring the UN System of Collective Security' in Weller M. (ed), *The Oxford Handbook of the Use of Force*, 196.

[33] For an analysis of descriptive legitimacy see Sect. 2.5 (below).

[34] Meyer and Sanklecha, 'Introduction' in Meyer L. (ed), *Legitimacy, Justice and International Law*, 2.

[35] Hurd, *After Anarchy*, 7.

Legality, as opposed to legitimacy, is obtained when the legal requirements are complied with by an action, rule, actor, or system.[36] This is because, the formal fact of legal validity engenders an obligation to obey the law based on its legality, but not necessarily of its legitimacy.[37] Seen in this way, legitimacy does not make a normative commitment to any relationship of power; it treats legitimacy as a social fact, not a normative goal.[38] Therefore, legitimacy is specifically concerned with what forms of use of force people believe to be justified.[39] The beliefs generally emanate from their cultural, religious, and political values. For example, whereas the Western political values do not believe that the Security Council may retain its legitimacy when it struggles to confront the threat of force directed to the West, the Muslim states and most third world states believe that the Security Council may retain its legitimacy by effectively regulating the use of force as provided by the UN Charter, that is use of force, whether individual or collective, must be authorized by the Security Council.[40] As a result, an internal disconnection exists on the legitimacy of use of force between the subjects of Public and Islamic international law. This disconnection has posed challenges to Public international law for its self-description of being universal, objective, and neutral. This position of Public international law is questionable due to its lack of inclusive approach to another major legal system, namely Islamic international law that represents the religion of over 1.5 billion Muslims.[41]

The legitimacy of use of force in Public international law must recognize the cultural and religious diversity of its subjects. This is because the use of force must be understood and accepted as legitimate by those subjects who are affected by this.[42] The legitimacy of use of force cannot be secured by accommodating only the political legacies of few powerful states but it must also accommodate the legal and political legacies of the Muslim states that are often being victims of foreign intervention and

[36] Brunnée and Toope, *Legitimacy and Legality in International Law*, 53.

[37] Franck, *Fairness in International Law and Instructions*, 26; see also Thomas, The Uses and Abuses of Legitimacy in International Law, 729.

[38] Thomas, The Uses and Abuses of Legitimacy in International Law, 741.

[39] Ibid.

[40] Ibid., 746.

[41] http://www.oic-oci.org/oicv3/page/?p_id=52&p_ref=26&lan=en (accessed on 20th June 2020).

[42] Bennouna, *International Law: Between the Letter and Spirit*, 220.

external aggression.[43] On this basis, the use of force in Public international law obtains legitimacy when it is descriptive.[44] Therefore, legitimacy denotes the inclusion of perceptions of the subjects of Public international law not only about its binding nature but also about its general acceptability.[45] In this sense, the use of force is legitimate when the political and cultural or religious values of the subjects are represented in the law-making process, and the decision-making process is transparent, in particular when those affected have a chance to have their say.[46]

Current Public international law on the use of force is articulated in the United Nations Charter and the practices prevalent among states under the Charter system. An overview of the charter system and the state practices under this system suggest that Public international law on the use of force is disconnected from Islamic international law.[47] The disconnection lacks inclusiveness and rejects the potential connectedness with Muslim states and their laws. This disconnection is visible from the claims of the legitimacy of use of force during the Iraq War in 2003, intervention in Libya and Georgia in the second decade of this century, conflict in Syria, and the ongoing conflict in Yemen. These conflicts are clear examples where the states using force, whether Western or Muslim, have not considered Islamic international law to justify the use of force. Although these states are indeed members of the United Nations, they do not adhere to the same fundamental principles of inter-state policies. States maintain their international relations according to their principles, and such principles could vary according to the political, cultural, and religious beliefs of the subjects. If Public international law does not institutionalize Islamic international law as its source, the people of Muslim states may not consider the law and its institution as legitimate.[48]

[43] For a discussion on the legal-political legacies developed within Islamic international law see Chap. 5.

[44] Franck, *The Power of Legitimacy Among Nations*, 19; see also Simpson, *The Nature of International Law*, xxxi; Buchanan and Keohane, 'The Legitimacy of Global Governance Institutions' in Meyer (ed), *Legitimacy, Justice and International Law*, 38; Wolfrum, 'Legitimacy in International Law from a Legal Perspective' in Wolfrum and Röben (eds), *Legitimacy in International Law*, 6.

[45] Focarelli, *International Law as a Social Construct*, 245.

[46] Ibid.

[47] For an overview of the charter system see Chap. 1.

[48] For a discussion about the institutionalization of Islamic international law on the use of force see Chap. 5.

According to Francisco Suarez (1548–1617), 'only that precept is a law which is instituted in general for all the persons included within a given community.'[49] The shortcoming of Public international law on the use of force can be found in his view of the law, and even today such shortcoming can be seen. Public international law on the use of force, as it currently stands, does not exist for the belief of many of its subjects such as the Muslim states and armed non-state actors. As a result, the claim of the legitimacy of use of force made by Public international law for being objective, neutral, and universal lacks justification among the people of Muslim states and armed non-state actors functioning within those states. Public international law must overcome the legitimacy deficits. However, it cannot overcome the legitimacy deficits until the legitimacy of use of force in Islamic international law is viewed as part and parcel of Public international law. In other words, if Public international law does not recognize Islamic international law as its legitimate source, it may lose its legitimacy to the subjects in Muslim states and non-state actors. Therefore, Public international law must overcome this legitimacy deficit to be more universal, neutral, and objective. Overcoming this legitimacy deficit is also necessary to build trust and confidence in the system by those who are most affected by this, that is Muslim states and armed non-state actors.

2.6 Sovereignty of the Muslim States and the Legitimacy of Use of Force

Following the Second World War, Public international law recognized the sovereignty of the Muslim states subject to their responsibility as state parties to the international legal framework such as the UN Charter.[50] On this basis, state sovereignty can be of two types, namely internal and external sovereignty. Whereas internal sovereignty enables a state to be free from foreign intervention, external sovereignty denotes its recognition as a sovereign entity at the international level.[51] The former is the right of a state to use force in dealing with its internal affairs, and the latter is the right to be recognized as a sovereign entity for being a member of the international legal system that consists of other sovereign entities. Therefore, on

[49] Suarez, *A Treatise on Laws and God the Lawgiver*, 74.

[50] Fassbender, 'Sovereignty and Constitutionalism in International Law' in Walker N. (ed), *Sovereignty in Transition*, 115.

[51] Ibid.

the one hand, sovereignty works as a shield against foreign intervention and, on the other hand, it supplies a legitimate basis for such intervention by invitation from another state.[52] As a result, these two types of sovereignty are interrelated to each other as if these are two sides of the same coin.

The concept of sovereignty which was introduced by Jean Bodin to the political and legal lexicon appealed to national unity and allowed states to consolidate their power.[53] The antagonism between natural and positive law precepts to appropriate sovereignty has since then marked the legal architecture.[54] Moreover, the influence of Positive laws as man-made and emanating from the sovereign's will was gradually becoming unquestionable.[55] Eventually, in the process of consolidating state power sovereignty became a predominantly political notion that enabled the states to interact with each other regarding their external affairs, which is external sovereignty, without sacrificing interference in the internal affairs of states, which is internal sovereignty.

The membership of a state in the international system provides internal as well as external sovereignty. Such membership also gives rise to a correlated responsibility of every member state to respect the entitlement of other members. Articles 12, 16, 47, 48, and 50 of the International Law Commission's Restatement of the Law of State Responsibility provide for state responsibility of every state for committing or aiding to commit internationally wrongful acts, such as the use of force against another state, a group of states, or regional organization.[56] Besides, article 49 permits countermeasures by an injured state against another state that is responsible for the wrongful act to induce the latter to comply with its obligation.[57] These provisions have, in effect, provided for suspension or extinction of internal sovereignty for any state which is responsible for certain internationally wrongful acts. However, there is no provision in the Draft Articles on State Responsibility or elsewhere providing the extent to which internal sovereignty can be interfered with based on

[52] Vanhullebusch, *War and Law in the Islamic World*, 98, 120.

[53] Hinsley, *Sovereignty*, 27; see also Wildhaber, 'Sovereignty and International Law' in Macdonald R. St. J. and Johnston D. M. (eds), *The Structure and Process of International Law*, 425.

[54] Tsagourias, *Jurisprudence of International Law*, 25.

[55] Hobbes, *Leviathan*, 121.

[56] Responsibility of States for Internationally Wrongful Acts, art 48.

[57] Ibid., art 50.

suspension or extinction. In the absence of such provision, it is necessary to articulate the extent to which interference with internal sovereignty is legitimately permissible.

Article 2(7) of the United Nations Charter does indeed guarantee states' freedom of choice as a guard against dictatorial interference by the UN and any of its organization.[58] However, since the charter's primary objective is the prevention of war, freedom of choice is a welcome but far from exclusive ordering principle.[59] Therefore, an international organization like the UN is entitled to take collective measures and as such intervene in the internal sovereignty of a state in certain circumstances. This is because states are not anthropomorphic, enjoying an autonomous moral standing, but are composed of individual human beings.[60] However, the question is 'to what extent such sovereignty can be interfered?' State sovereignty has been recognized by article 2(7) of the UN Charter. It provides that:

> Nothing contained in the present Charter shall authorize the United Nations to intervene in matters which are essentially within the domestic jurisdiction of any state or shall require the Members to submit such matters to settlement under the present Charter; but this principle shall not prejudice the application of enforcement measures under Chapter VII.

Despite the prohibition of intervention in the internal or domestic affairs of states, there have been circumstances where the UN forces intervened. For example, in Congo, Yemen, Iraq, former Yugoslavia, Somalia, Haiti, and Sierra Leone.[61] From a practical perspective, such interventions were claimed as legitimate based on an invitation from the governments of those states.[62] However, the claims of legitimate intervention by invitation are not authorized by the Charter.[63] This is because the only circumstance that would trigger forceful intervention into the sovereignty of a state is

[58] UN Charter, art 2(7).

[59] Ibid.; see also Stürchler, *The Threat of Force in International Law*, 61.

[60] Lauterpacht, The Grotian Tradition in International Law, 1.

[61] See S. Res. 232 (1966) of 16 December 1966 (Rhodesia); S. Res 418 of 4 November 1977 (South Africa); S/RES/940 (1994) of 31 July 1994; S/RES/1160 (1998) of 31 March 1998; S/RES/1199 (1998) of 23 September 1998; S/RES/1203 (1998) of 24 October 1998; S/RES/1244 (1999) of 10 June 1999.

[62] See Chap. 1.

[63] Franck, *Recourse to Force*, 41.

on the ground of 'breach of international peace and security'.[64] Moreover, if state legitimacy is viewed in contractual terminology as protecting the basic human rights to liberty and life of its citizens, any aberration from this course may invite intervention because sovereignty is overridden through de-legitimation.[65] In other words, the ultimate justification of the existence of a state is the protection and enforcement of the natural rights of the citizens; otherwise, it forfeits not only its domestic legitimacy but its international legitimacy.[66]

The threshold for triggering the use of force on the ground of 'breach of international peace and security' has been gradually lowered in the practice of the UN's principal organs.[67] In the *Tadic* appeal, the International Criminal Tribunal of former Yugoslavia (ICTY), referring to evidence that 'the practice of the Security Council is rich with cases of civil war or internal strife which is classified as a 'threat to peace' and dealt with under Chapter VII' concluded, 'that the 'threat to peace' of article 39 may include, as one of its species, internal armed conflicts.'[68] On this basis, in 1999, the then UN Secretary-General Kofi Annan invited the states to redefine the parameters of sovereignty from the perspectives of globalization and international co-operation.[69] Also, in some instances, the United States and the United Kingdom as well as regional organizations such as NATO have intervened in the domestic affairs of different states.[70] This course of action has given rise to a necessity to revisit the concept of sovereignty in the modern world.

'Peace' within a territory is often left within the sovereign territory of a state where a state government or ruler handles the maintenance of peace. However, what if the government or ruler is not legitimate due to being a usurper or tyrant? It is not legitimate for the people to be ruled by a tyrant or a ruler who came into power by illegal means, for instance by corruption rather than democratic or constitutional means. There may be peace in that territory as the new government or ruler might have been able to

[64] UN Charter, art 39.

[65] Montague, Two Concepts of Rights, 160; see also Walzer, 'The Theory of Aggression' in Luper-Foy S. (ed), *Problems of International Justice*, 151.

[66] Tesón, *Humanitarian Intervention*, 15.

[67] Franck, *Recourse to Force*, 41.

[68] *Prosecutor v. Tadic*, para. 30.

[69] Report of the Secretary-General on the Work of the Organisation, G.A.O.R; see also Orford, *International Authority and the Responsibility to Protect*, 33.

[70] Roberts, 'The Use of Force' in David Malone (ed), *The UN Security Council*, 136.

extinguish all rivalry movements by use of force, but what about the status of the government or ruler and the means they are using to maintain such peace within the territory? This question gives rise to an inquiry into whether such government or ruler and their use of force are legitimate. The answer to this inquiry reflects on the view of Hans Kelsen, who stated that 'the overwhelming interest that those in power, as well as those craving for power, have in a theory is pleasing to their wishes, which is in a political ideology.'[71] This political ideology can be successfully implemented under the shield of sovereignty, and hence it suffers from legitimacy deficit as well as injustice.[72]

Justice often requires the restoration and establishment of a new government or ruler, and it may result in the breach of peace, at least in the short term. Although the instances of international armed conflict are indeed decreasing, it is also true that the instances of internal armed conflict are rising.[73] Moreover, the complexity of internal armed conflict and its frequent occurrence has given rise to not only breach of peace, either in the short or in the long term, but also long-term injustice. It is understandable if the UN Charter promotes negative peace at the expense of short-term injustice,[74] but it is not legitimate to maintain such peace at the expense of long-term injustice. This is because long-term injustice can lead to a long-term breach of peace, which is positive peace.[75] For example, the interventions in Syria and Libya have caused the recurrence of breach of peace situations as well as a long-term injustice. In these circumstances, it is necessary to find 'whether peace should be preferred over justice?' In other words, is peace legitimate, or even possible, without justice?

These questions lead the way to the most important as well as the controversial condition of peace as designed in the Charter system, which is under sovereignty. The concept of sovereignty emerged to stabilize and incarnate a political order, national or international, against the entanglements of personal predilections and individual moralities.[76] The extrapolated international rules, in particular the rule on the non-use of force,

[71] Kelsen, *General Theory of Law and State*, xvii.
[72] Koskenniemi, The Future of Statehood, 397.
[73] Tonca, *Foreign Armed Intervention in Internal Conflict*, 147.
[74] Tsagourias, *Jurisprudence of International Law*, 40.
[75] Glennon, The New Interventionism, 2.
[76] Tsagourias, *Jurisprudence of International Law*, 31.

reflect this purpose.[77] International law on the use of force is designed primarily to promote peace at the international level by leaving the states to control ideological differences within the territory under their sovereign power so that these ideological differences do not transform into a breach of the peace at the international level.[78] An international organization, like the Security Council, which is responsible for a system of collective security can leave any state alone to sacrifice the lives of its subjects if doing so protects peace and security at the international level. In the words of Koskenniemi:

> Statehood functions as precisely that decision-process which tackles the problems of multiplicity of ideas and interpretative controversy regarding their fulfilment. Its very formality intends to operate as a safeguard so that these different (theological) ideals are not transformed into a globally enforced tyranny.[79]

The existence of statehood under the shield of sovereignty can be a cause for injustice in another legal system than Public international law. For instance, the injustice of this nature is recognized in Islamic international law.[80] It begins at the state level and may escalate at the inter-state level on a legitimate basis. For example, rebellion against any tyrant and despotic government or ruler may give rise to internal armed conflict and eventually result in international armed conflict by the transformation of such rebellion into the right of self-defence against a foreign state that colluded with the ruler or government.[81] In these circumstances, such extraterritorial defensive use of force (actual or pre-emptive) by non-state actors like armed rebels is claimed to be legitimate in Islamic law. This claim gains more strength from the fact that rulers or state authorities are in a better position under Public international law as it enables them to exercise their sovereign power to invite another state to suppress the

[77] Ibid.

[78] *The Corfu Channel Case*, ICJ Rep. (1949) 4, 35.

[79] Koskenniemi, 'Theory: Implications for the Practitioner' in Allott, Carty, Koskenniemi, and Warbick (eds), *Theory and International Law*, 42.

[80] This issue has been discussed in Chaps. 3 and 4.

[81] Collusion with foreign powers and the claim of the legitimate use of force by non-state actors in Muslim majority states has been discussed in Chaps. 3, 4, and 5.

rebellion.[82] The unequal position between non-state actors and rulers in Public international law shows clear discrimination. Although Public international law recognizes this discrimination based on the internal sovereign power of state authorities, it is a result of the political management that exists at the international level where states themselves do not entertain sovereign equality.[83] In these circumstances, the question 'whether a use of force is legitimate in Public international law' is incrementally being complemented by the question 'whether such force is being used in conformity with Islamic international law.'

Both states and regional organizations are authorized to recourse to force by the UN Charter. However, except the defensive use of force under article 51 of the UN Charter, extraterritorial use of force must be authorized by the Security Council.[84] It is questionable if the Security Council, as an international institution, has the necessary legitimacy to make decisions concerning the use of force.[85] The legitimacy of an international institution like the Security Council derives from the procedures that it follows in making decisions.[86] The design and operation of the Security Council are often dominated and managed by more powerful states and used to serve their ends, thereby resulting in legitimacy deficits and making it difficult to claim that the institution is legitimate.[87] For example, the domination of the permanent members at the Security Council by exercise or threat to exercise of their veto power.

The UN Charter has recognized the principle of sovereign equality of its members.[88] This principle has been implemented by the rule that each member state of the General Assembly shall have one vote.[89] However,

[82] For a discussion on the unequal position of rebels and rulers in Public international law see Chap. 1.

[83] Henderson, 'The Arab Spring and the Notion of External State Sovereignty in International law', 175.

[84] For a discussion about the role of the Security Council in the decision-making process about inter-state use of force see Chap. 1.

[85] Taubman, Towards a Theory of Democratic Compliance, 161.

[86] Besson, 'Institutional Global demoi-cracy' in Meyer L. (ed), *Legitimacy, Justice and International Law*, 58; see also Brunnée J. and Toope S., *Legitimacy and Legality in International Law*, 95.

[87] Meyer and Sanklecha, 'Introduction' in Meyer (ed), *Legitimacy, Justice and International Law*, 4.

[88] UN Charter, art 2 (1); see also Henderson, 'The Arab Spring and the Notion of External State Sovereignty in International Law', 175.

[89] UN Charter, art 18.

this principle has not been so implemented in the decision-making process at the Security Council, where major decisions concerning the use of force are being taken.[90] Most substantive decisions of the Security Council require not only the support of a majority of nine members but the concurring votes of the permanent members.[91] This is known as the 'veto' system which has apparently disregarded the principle of sovereign equality and thereby undermined consistency in the decision-making process at the Security Council.[92] As a result, the decision-making process at the Security Council concerning the use of force lacks legitimacy.

The legitimacy of the 'veto' system is questionable due to unequal sovereign power among the member states at the Security Council. But the legitimacy of this system can be claimed as valid if it can make a case for such power to be rationally coherent.[93] Such case of coherence has been made on the ground that the permanent members should have a greater say in the decision-making process at the Security Council because they bear most of the costs of the organization and are expected to assume the military as well as fiscal responsibilities for carrying out the Charter's mandate.[94] Moreover, the power-five (permanent) member states could not be compelled in reality to any decision against their will.[95] However, the case of coherence could be a valid claim of the past, and it is not persuasive in the modern world. This is because most peacekeeping and peace enforcement measures recently taken by the UN are being supported by military and fiscal support from non-permanent members like northern Europe and third world countries.[96] As a result, the permanent members no longer solely discharge the functions of the Security Council in the maintenance of international peace and security. The emerging powers in the world community like Germany, Japan, India, Brazil, and Nigeria now have a particularly good claim of being preferred states on economic, military, geographic, and demographic grounds.[97] This is a very common

[90] See Chap. 1.

[91] UN Charter, art 27.

[92] Henderson C., 'The Arab Spring and the Notion of External State Sovereignty in International Law' (2014) 35 Liverpool Law Review 175.

[93] Franck, *The Power of Legitimacy Among nations*, 176.

[94] Ibid.

[95] Ibid.

[96] Coicaud, 'The Evolution of International Order' in Charlesworth H. and Coicaud J-M. (eds), *Fault Lines of International Legitimacy*, 107.

[97] Franck, *The Power of Legitimacy Among nations*, 177.

scenario for an international institution like the Security Council, where the position of powerful states changes very often in line with their political positions at the international level. Therefore, the legitimacy of the Security Council heavily depends on the implementation of sovereign equality of states in the decision-making process.

It appears that the permanent members have focused on strengthening the military ability of their national or regional force rather than that of the United Nations.[98] Also, the way that the permanent members have exercised the veto power so far does not reflect what was agreed during the drafting negotiations. The permanent members agreed to exercise the veto only in situations having the most serious impact on their basic interests.[99] They also agreed that when the Security Council was considering measures for peaceful settlement of disputes, they would abstain.[100] But the veto power has been used at the convenience of the permanent members as opposed to what was agreed between them.[101] For instance, the US did not abstain from vetoing a 1986 resolution calling on it to execute the International Court of Justice (ICJ) judgement on a case brought by Nicaragua.[102] Therefore, the case of coherence concerning the exercise of the veto power by permanent members is not persuasive in the modern world. Moreover, it has been argued that the nature of the Security Council could be defended on impartial utilitarian-type grounds as otherwise it would be paralyzed with a large membership or that the veto promotes stability and peace.[103] This justification is based on the benefits that such a composition of the Security Council would generate (in theory) for all countries, namely the preservation of international peace and security. For instance, peace, stability, and collective security are promoted when states with power stand behind a resolution of the Security Council and weakened without their endorsement.[104] However, if this justification is

[98] Coicaud, 'The Evolution of International Order' in Charlesworth H. and Coicaud J-M. (eds), *Fault Lines of International Legitimacy*, 105.

[99] 'Basic Documents of the United Nations' (1982) 45–49.

[100] Ibid.

[101] United States Mission to the United Nations, 'List of Vetoes Cast in Public Meetings of the Security Council (unpub. Mimeo)' cited in Franck, *The Power of Legitimacy Among nations*, 279.

[102] 41 U.N. Security Council (2704th mtg.).

[103] Ratner, 'Do International Institutions Play Favourites?' in Meyer (ed), *Legitimacy, Justice and International Law*, 144.

[104] Ibid.

examined from a non-ideal institutional principle (practical perspective) aiming to create a fair political framework, the authority of the Security Council ought to aim at legitimacy. The dominance and political management of powerful states at the Security Council show the arbitrary exercise of the veto power by the permanent members which lack legitimacy. As a result, the Muslim states and armed non-state actors perceive the decision-making process at the Security Council as illegitimate. As these states and non-state actors have been the subjects of the most use of force in the twenty-first century, any use of force must be legitimate in their belief lest Public international law loses its application and acceptance in the Muslim world.

2.7 Conclusion

Public international law on the use of force as enshrined in the United Nations Charter is not instituted in general for all people in the world. This chapter has shown how powerful states claim the legitimacy of use of force to pursue their national and geopolitical interests. They claim the legitimacy of extra-Charter use of force in the form of anticipatory and preventive self-defence. Moreover, they have a greater stake in the decision-making process at the Security Council. As a result, Public international law on the use of force is suffering from legitimacy deficits as understood in the descriptive sense where the people, who are most affected by such use of force, do not consider it to be legitimate. For instance, although most armed conflicts in the twenty-first century have involved one or more Muslim states, Public international law has not examined the legitimacy of those conflicts in Islamic international law. This position shows the manifestation of relegating Islamic international law by the elite and powerful states in the formation and development of Public international law on the use of force. This is a substantial shortcoming for Public international law in overcoming its legitimacy deficits. It is expedient for Public international law to overcome the legitimacy deficits or become redundant in the Muslim World.

The self-description of Public international law as universal, objective, and neutral is untenable for its reluctance to include the political, cultural, and religious values of other major legal systems. This claim puts Public international law under scrutiny, where it senses its legitimacy from its purported universality. To pass this scrutiny Public international law must show that it is no longer relegating Islamic law and following a false sense of legitimacy. It must recognize the legitimacy of use of force as formed by the legal-political legacies of Islamic international law. In the recognition process, Public international law must play the key role as it is the genus that can recognize Islamic international law as its species. Once it adopts Islamic international law as a legitimate source, Public international law will become legitimate among the subjects of Muslim states. In this way, it can make a strong claim for its objective, neutral, and universal application in the Muslim world.

References

U.N. Security Council (2704th mtg.), U.N. Doc. S/PV. 2704 (prov. Ed. 1986), reprinted in 25 Int'l Legal Mat. 1353, 1363 (1986).

Abi-Saab G. M., 'The Newly Independent States and the Rules of International Law: An Outline' (1962) 8 Howard Law Journal 95.

Alexandrowicz C. H., *An Introduction to the History of the Law of Nations in the East Indies* (Oxford: Clarendon Press, 1967).

Allott P., Carty T., Koskenniemi M., and Warbick C. (eds), *Theory and International Law: An Introduction* (The British Institute of International and Comparative Law, 1991).

Anand R. P., 'Role of the "New" Asian-African Countries in The Present International Legal Order' (1962) 56 American Journal of International Law 383.

Bennouna M., *International Law: Between the Letter and Spirit* (Brill, 2019).

Berman N., *Passion and Ambivalence: Colonialism, Nationalism, and International Law* (Martinus Nijhoff, 2012).

Black's Law Dictionary (Seventh edn, West Publishing Co, 1999).

Borger G., A Vice President Unbound, U.S. News & World Rep., June 28, 2004, 34.

Brunnée J. and Toope S., *Legitimacy and Legality in International Law* (Cambridge University Press, 2010).

Bull H. and Watson A. (eds), *The Expansion of International Society* (New York: Oxford University Press, 1984).

Bush G. W., Address before a Joint Session of the Congress on the State of the Union (Jan. 28, 2003) 39 Weekly Comp. Press. Doc. 109 (Feb. 3, 2003).

Charlesworth H. and Coicaud J-M. (eds), *Fault Lines of International Legitimacy* (Cambridge University Press, 2010).

Elias T., *Africa and the Development of International Law* (Leiden: A.W. Sijthoff, 1972).

Ex-Inspector (David Kay) Again Says Forbidden Arms Probably Didn't Exist, Wash. Post, Jan. 29, 2004, A1.

Fain H., *Normative Politics and the Community of Nations* (Philadelphia: Temple University Press, 1987).

Fatouros A. A., 'International Law and the Third World' (1964) 50 Virginia Law Review 783.
Focarelli C., *International Law as a Social Construct* (Oxford University Press, 2012).
Franck T., *The Power of Legitimacy Among Nations* (Oxford University Press, 1990).
———, *Recourse to Force: State Action Against Threats and Armed Attacks* (Cambridge University Press, 2002a).
———, *Fairness in International Law and Institutions* (Oxford University Press, 2002b).
———, 'The Power of Legitimacy and the Legitimacy of Power: International Law in an Age of Power Disequilibrium' (2006) 100 America Journal of International Law 88.
———, 'Legitimacy in the International System' (1988) 82 American Journal of International Law 712.
Friedman L., *Law and Society—An Introduction* (Prentice Hall, 1977).
Furedi F., *The New Ideology of Imperialism: Renewing the Moral Imperative* (London: Pluto Press, 1994).
Glennon M.J., 'The New Interventionism: The Search for a Just International Law' (1999) 78 Foreign Affairs 2.
Guha R. (ed), *A Subaltern Studies Reader, 1986–1995* (University of Minnesota Press, 1997).
Henderson C., 'The Arab Spring and the Notion of External State Sovereignty in International Law' (2014) 35 Liverpool Law Review 175.
———, 'The Bush Doctrine: From Theory to Practice' (2004) 9(1) Journal of Conflict and Security Law 3.
———, 'The 2010 United States National Security Strategy and the Obama Doctrine of Necessary Force' (2010) 15 (3) Journal of Conflict & Security Law 403.
Hinsley F. H., *Sovereignty* (Cambridge University Press, 1986).
Hobbes T., *Leviathan*, R. Tuck (ed) (Cambridge University Press, 1991).
Hoerauf D., 'The Status of the Libyan Rebels under the Laws of War: A Litmus Test for the Lawfulness of NATO's Libyan Engagement under UN Resolution 1973' (2012) 6 Phoenix Law Review 93.
Hurd I., *After Anarchy: Legitimacy and Power in the United Nations Security Council* (Princeton University Press, 2007).
Hyde A., 'The Concept of Legitimacy in the Sociology of Law' (1983) Wisconsin Law Review 379.
Jennings R. and Watts A. (eds), *Oppenheim's International Law*, vol 1, peace (Longman: London 1992).
Keene E., *Beyond the Anarchical Society: Grotius, Colonialism and Order in World Politics* (Cambridge University Press, 2002).

Kelsen H., *General Theory of Law and State* (A. Wedberg tr, Harvard University Press, 1949).

Kennedy D., 'International Law and the Nineteenth Century: History of an Illusion' (1997) 12 Quinnipiac Law Review 99.

Koskenniemi M., Rech W. and Fonesca M. J. (eds), *International Law and Empire* (Oxford University Press, 2017).

Koskenniemi M., 'The Future of Statehood' (1991) 32 Harvard ILJ 397.

Krisch N., 'Unilateral Enforcement of the Collective Will: Kosovo, Iraq, and the Security Council' (1999) 59 Max Planck Yearbook of United Nations Law 81.

Lauterpacht H. and Lauterpacht E. (eds), *International Law*, vol. 3 (Cambridge University Press, 1970).

Lauterpacht H., 'The Grotian Tradition in International Law' (1946) 23 BYBIL 1.

Luper-Foy S. (ed), *Problems of International Justice* (Boulder, Westview Press, 1988).

Macdonald R. (ed), *Essays in Honour of Wang Tieya* (Dordrecht: Martinus Nijhoff, 1994).

Macdonald R. St. J., and Johnston D. M. (eds), *The Structure and Process of International Law: Essays in Legal Philosophy, Doctrine and Theory* (Martinus Nijhoff, 1983).

Malone D. (ed), *The UN Security Council: From the Cold War to the 21st Century* (Lynne Rienner Publishers, 2004) 136.

Markowitz, Jonathan N. and Fariss C. J., Power, Proximity and Democracy: Geopolitical competition in the International System (2018) 55 Journal of Peace Research 78.

Martineau A-C., 'Concerning Violence: A Post-Colonial Reading of the Debate on the Use of Force' (2016) 29 Leiden Journal of International Law 95.

Meyer L. (ed), *Legitimacy, Justice and Public International Law* (Cambridge University Press, 2009).

Mickelson K., 'Rhetoric and Rage: Third World Voices in International Legal Discourse' (1998) 16 Wisconsin International Law Journal 353.

Montague P., 'Two Concepts of Rights' (1980) 9 Philosophy and Public Affairs 160.

National Security Council, the National Security Strategy of the United States of America (2011) https://www.whitehouse.gov/sites/default/files/microsites/2011-strategy-combat-transnational-organized-crime.pdf accessed 25 October 2020.

O'Connell M. E., Tams C. J., and Tladi D. (eds), *Self-Defence against Non-state actors* (Cambridge University Press, 2019).

O'Connell M. E., 'Presumption of Peace: Illegal War, Human Rights, and Humanitarian Law' in Sadat L. N. (ed), *Seeking Accountability for the Use of Force* (Cambridge University Press, 2018).

Orford A., *International Authority and Responsibility to Protect* (Cambridge University Press, 2011).
Orford A., 'NATO, Regionalism, and the Responsibility to Protect in Shapiro I. and Tooze A. (eds), *Charter of the North Atlantic Treaty Organisation together with Scholarly Commentaries and Essential Historical Documents* (Yale University Press, 2018).
Pahuja S., *Decolonising International Law* (Cambridge University Press, 2011).
Report of the Secretary-General on the Work of the Organisation, G.A.O.R., 54th Sess., 4th Plen. Meeting, A/54/1, 20 September 1999.
Responsibility of States for Internationally Wrongful Acts, 31 May 2001, International Law Commission.
Schroeder E., 'The Kosovo Crisis: Humanitarian Imperative versus International Law' (2004) 28 Fletcher Forum of World Affairs 179.
Shah N. A., 'Self-defence, Anticipatory Self-defence and Pre-emption: International Law's Response to Terrorism' (2007) 12 (7) Journal of Conflict & Security Law 95.
———, 'The 'Unwilling' and 'Unable' Test in International Law: The Use of Force against Non-State Actors in Pakistan and Afghanistan' (2020) 4 Asian Yearbook of Human Rights and Humanitarian Law 109.
Simpson G., *The Nature of International Law* (Dartmouth: Ashgate, 2001).
Sofaer A.D., 'On the Necessity of Pre-emption' (2003) 14 Eur. J. Int'l L. 209.
Stürchler N., *The Threat of Force in International Law* (Cambridge University Press, 2007).
Suarez F., *A Treatise on Laws and God the Lawgiver* (Bk. I, 2 Suarez, Classics of International Law, 1944).
Taft W. H. and Buckwald T. F., 'Preemption, Iraq, and International Law' (2003) 93 American Journal of International Law 557.
Taubman J., 'Towards a Theory of Democratic Compliance: Security Council Legitimacy and Effectiveness after Iraq' (2004) 37 New York University Journal of International Law and Politics 161.
Tesón F. R., *Humanitarian Intervention: An Inquiry into Law and Morality* (2nd edn, Dobbs Ferry Transnational Publication, 1997).
Thomas C., 'The Uses and Abuses of Legitimacy in International Law' (2014) 34 Oxford Journal of Legal Studies 729.
Antonio Tonca, *Foreign Armed Intervention in Internal Conflict* (Martinus Nijhoff, 1993).
Tsagourias N. T., *Jurisprudence of International Law: The Humanitarian Dimension* (Manchester University Press, 2000).
Vanhullebusch M., *War and Law in the Islamic World* (Brill 2015).
Verzijl J. H.W., *International Law in Historical Perspective*, vol 10 (Leyden: A.W. Sijthoff, 1968).
Walker N. (ed), *Sovereignty in Transition* (Hart Publishing, 2003).

Weller M. (ed), *The Oxford Handbook of the Use of Force in International Law* (Oxford University Press, 2015).

Westlake J., *Chapters on the Principles of International Law* (Cambridge University Press, 1894).

Wheaton H., *History of the Law of Nations in Europe and America from the Earliest Times to the Treaty of Washington* (Gould, Banks & Co, 1845).

Wolfrum R. and Roben V. (eds.), *Legitimacy in International Law* (Springer: Heidelberg, 2010).

Young J. C., *Postcolonialism: An Historical Introduction* (Oxford: Blackwell, 2001).

CHAPTER 3

Use of Force in Islamic International Law

3.1 Introduction

The origin of Islamic international law can be traced back since Prophet Muhammad migrated to Medina in 622 CE. Since then, it had been developing in the primary sources such as the Qur'an and Sunna (narrations of the words and actions of Prophet Muhammad). According to the guidance of primary sources, Islamic international law continued to develop with secondary sources such as Ijma (consensus), Qiyas (analogy), and *Siyar*.[1] It has been developing in the modern day by Islamic jurisprudence underpinned by the method of Ijtihad (exertion of intellectual reasoning) and juristic interpretation (*Fiqh*).[2] A combination of the primary and secondary sources, *Siyar*, and Islamic jurisprudence propped up the Shari'a as a living mechanism that provided Islamic solutions to new issues and circumstances surrounding the use of force in Islamic international law.[3]

This chapter gives a historical, legal, and political account of the development of Islamic international law on the use of force. It defines and interprets the fundamental principles of use of force in Islamic international law and analyses the significance of these principles, such as jihad, in

[1] For a discussion on Ijma, Qiyas, and *Siyar* see below; see also Chap. 5.
[2] An-Na'im, *Islam and the Secular State*, 12.
[3] Ibid., 3.

M. Z. Sabuj, *The Legitimacy of Use of Force in Public and Islamic International Law*,
https://doi.org/10.1007/978-3-030-77298-7_3

scrutinizing the legal and political authorities to use force in Muslim states. This chapter also examines the nature and extent of the use of force in the practices and ideologies of armed non-state actors that are functioning in Muslim states. Finally, this chapter evaluates the use of force provisions in Islamic international law followed by a critical analysis of the legal and political position of these provisions in the core values of Islamic international law such as the Qur'an and the Sunna, *Siyar*, the juristic opinions of different schools of thought (*Madhhab, pl. Madhahib*), and the treaties concluded between Muslim and non-Muslim territories.

3.2 What Is Islamic International Law?

The use of force in Islamic international law may be studied from the viewpoints of Islamic jurisprudence and Muslim states' practice.[4] Whereas Islamic jurisprudence has developed surrounding the main sources of the religion such as the Qur'an, Sunna, Ijma, and Qiyas as well as the concomitant juristic opinions of the different schools of thought (*Madhhab*), the foundation of Islamic international law was built on *Siyar*, which contains orthodox practices of the early Caliphs and other Muslim rulers; arbitral awards, treaties, pacts, and other conventions; official instructions for commanders, admirals, ambassadors, and other state officials; and internal legislations for conduct regarding foreigners and foreign relations, customs, and usages.[5]

Siyar has made a significant contribution to Islamic international law.[6] It has introduced Islamic international law under the Arabic word '*sirah*' (plural *Siyar*).[7] *Sirah* is a technical term in the Islamic sciences meaning the biography of the Prophet, while its plural form *Siyar* refers to legal matters.[8] The Qur'an and Sunna provided the framework of the relationship between Muslims and non-Muslims. However, they never specifically provided for provisions of Islamic international law. Therefore, Islamic international law developed through the practices of rulers beginning from the Prophet himself up until the current world. The development

[4] Mahmoudi, The Islamic Perception of the Use of Force in the Contemporary World, 13.

[5] Hamidullah, *Muslim Conduct of State*, 18.

[6] Khadduri, *The Islamic Law of Nations*, 38; See also Bsoul, *International Treaties (Mu'ahadat) in Islam*, 1.

[7] Badar, Jus in bello under Islamic International Law, 593.

[8] Ibid.

began since the Prophet migrated to Medina in 622 CE and formed an Islamic community. The later conquest of Mecca followed by the astonishing conquests by the Prophet and his rightly guided Caliphs developed the major practices of Islamic international law.[9] Since the death of Prophet Muhammad, Islamic international law has evolved through the work of jurists as a response to the needs created by the progress of the changing Islamic society.[10] *Siyar* is the sum total of the rules and practices of Islam's intercourse with other people.[11] Therefore, *Siyar* is an integral part of Islamic international law that built law, custom, and treaty obligations which Muslim states observed in their dealings with each other.[12]

The practices of these Muslim states had been the subject of an intensive analysis of jurists in the second century of Islam (eighth century CE) when juristic development of Islamic international law took place. The exegetical works of these jurists resulted in different schools (*Madhahib*) based on different methods of interpretation adopted by these schools.[13] However, the most significant in Islamic international law-related matters came from the Sunni branch. The first and major classical work came from a Hanafi jurist of the Sunni branch, Al-Shaybani, whose remarkable treatise *al-Siyar al-Kabir* (the Major *Siyar*) serves as a standard work of reference to date.[14] In addition, 'Abd al-Rahman al-Awza'i had also contributed to *Siyar* by writing a treatise on this subject, but his work is publicly unavailable and hence has failed to reach modern jurists.[15] However, his doctrines were primarily based on the Sunna of the Prophet as well as the practice of Muslims of his time including official orders, which were preserved in the works of Abu Yusuf and Al-Shaf'i.[16]

Like Roman Law, Islamic international law used to be a 'jurist law', in the sense that it was neither a product of legislative authority nor a case law, but a creation of the classical jurists, who elaborated on the sacred text

[9] 'Rightly guided caliphs' are the first four Caliphs of Islam such as Abu Bakr, Umar, Uthman, and Ali.

[10] Mahamassani, The Principles of International Law in the Light of Islamic Doctrine, 205.

[11] Khadduri, *War and Peace in the Law of Islam*, 47; see also Vanhullebusch, *War and the Law in Islamic World*, 21.

[12] Hamidullah, *Muslim Conduct of State*, 3.

[13] Sharastani, *Muslim Sects and Divisions*, 10.

[14] Al-Ghunaimi, *The Muslim Conception of International Law and the Western Approach*, 33–35.

[15] Khadduri, *The Islamic Law of Nations*, 24.

[16] Schacht, *Origins of Muhammadan Jurisprudence*, 34.

such as the Qur'an and Sunna.[17] Therefore, Islamic international law began its foundation surrounding the principles of Shari'a. In other words, its development has depended on its compliance with the Shari'a, which is primarily based on the text.[18] While the Western notion of international law rests on a post-Westphalian premise of territory-based nation-states who, albeit controversially, enjoy full sovereign rights and equality of status,[19] the 'Islamic Law of Nations' is a legal system based on Shari'a that is intended to apply universally to all people in every time and place.[20] Whereas Qur'an is the unique and authentic source of Shari'a, the authenticity of Sunna depends on the authenticity of the chain of transmission (*isnād*).[21] Therefore, all the Sunna are not authentic, and there are disagreements among the jurists about authenticity of transmission, and each jurist cites only what she or he considers to be authentic.[22] However, the chain of transmission provides a link between the source of a Sunna and its trustworthiness. The general principle is that the more remote a chain, the more unauthentic it is. As a result, the chain of transmission is the key to the authenticity of any Sunna. Where the primary source of Islamic international law cannot provide specific guidelines on the use of force, the scope of the law can recourse to Islamic jurisprudence (*Fiqh*).[23] However, the process of interpretation (Ijtihad) requires more than simply citing the texts. It requires exertion of intellectual reasoning in seeking and arriving at rules from the various sources of law which are opposite to mere imitation.[24] It requires not to follow the opinions of others without understanding or scrutiny and not to accept the rulings of others when such rulings are uncoupled with a conclusive argument.[25] Moreover, it involves

[17] Hasan, The Sources of Islamic Law, 65.

[18] Vanhullebusch, *War and the Law in Islamic World*, 18.

[19] 'Equality of status' of sovereign states is meant herein a theoretical sense without taking into account the sovereign inequality in the decision-making process at the Security Council. For a discussion on this issue see Chap. 2.

[20] Ali, 'Resurrecting Siyar through Fatwas?' in Bassiouni and Guellali (eds.), *Jihad and its Challenges to International and Domestic Law*, 116.

[21] al-Tabari, *AL-Tabari's Book of Jihad*, 36; See also El Fadl, *Reasoning with God*, xxxv; Schacht, *An Introduction to Islamic Law*, 47.

[22] Kamali, *Principles of Islamic Jurisprudence*, 57; see also Khadduri, *Al-Shafi's Risala*, 279.

[23] Fyzee, *Outlines of Muhammadan Law*, 10; see also Kamali, *Principles of Islamic Jurisprudence*, 12; Khadduri, *Al-Shafi's Risala*, 21.

[24] Vanhullebusch, *War and the Law in Islamic World*, 122.

[25] al-Ghazzāli, *Al-Mustafa min 'Ilm al-Usūl*, 132 cited in Mahmassani S., *Falsafat al-Tashri Fi al-Islam*, 89.

a search for a fit between the history and present circumstance, or between the approved texts and new contexts.[26] This process of interpretation has made Islamic international law a living mechanism, where the nature of the finding changes with the change of circumstances but always under the scrutiny of Shari'a. In the words of Joseph Schacht:

> ... the interpretation of a religious ideal not by legislators but by scholars, and the recognized handbooks of the several schools are not 'codes' in the Western meaning of the term. Islamic law is a 'jurists' law' par excellence: Islamic jurisprudence did not grow out of an existing law, it itself created it.[27]

The process of interpretation, as a popular method of Islamic jurisprudence, has extended the sphere of Shari'a following the deaths of the Prophet, his rightly guided Caliphs, and companions. Muslim scholars adopted the method of Ijtihad to interpret the principles of Shari'a and to provide Islamic solutions to new issues and circumstances. Islamic international law has evolved from these intellectual efforts for more than fourteen centuries and is not entirely devoid of influences from other legal systems and the experiences of other cultures with which the Islamic *ummah* (community) has been in contact.[28] Even when part of the religion is believed to be of divine origin, some people still offer their understanding of such divine material and attempt to infer the divine intention that lies behind it.[29] As a result, the dividing line between what is provided in the Shari'a and what is interpreted by a scholar about the meaning of Shari'a often becomes blurred. In the tenth century CE, the Sunni scholars became concerned with the influx of various new knowledge systems and their respective methods that came from other civilizations.[30] However, such influx was the result of the expansion of Islam into Europe, Persia, Greece, Byzantine, and India. In order to save the Shari'a from diverse interpretation, the then Sunni scholars[31] declared closure of Ijtihad by the end of the tenth century CE.[32]

[26] Kelsay, *Arguing the Just War in Islam*, 125.

[27] Schacht, '"Fikh," Encyclopaedia of Islam' cited in Al-Dawoody, *The Islamic Law of War*, 73.

[28] Bassiouni, *The Sharia and Islamic Criminal Justice*, 13.

[29] Al-Dawoody, *The Islamic Law of War*, 1.

[30] Bassiouni, *The Sharia and Islamic Criminal Justice*, 8.

[31] 'Ibn Taymiyya' was one of the influential Sunni scholars who supported the closure of *Ijtihad*.

[32] Bassiouni, *The Sharia and Islamic Criminal Justice*, 8.

The call to the 'closure of Ijtihad' had posed an enormous challenge to the Muslim jurists in the Modern period because this adversely affected their potential contribution to Islamic jurisprudence. Following the conclusion of the Abbasid period by the invasion from Mongol in tenth century CE and Seljuk in the twelfth century CE, the option of Ijtihad was practically closed.[33] Since then there were many refinements and additions to the legacy of that period.[34] However, the closing of Ijtihad brought about a stultification of theology with a regressive tendency that reversed the progressive tradition that existed between the ninth and twelfth centuries CE.[35] The closure could not prevent the Shari'a from the influx of other cultural and religious principles and practices into Islam.[36] Moreover, the closure had stimulated the uncontrolled innovation of Shari'a principles by both qualified and unqualified scholars. As a result, both methodologically strong and weak jurisprudence of Islamic law were developing, and this situation gave rise to the challenging task of identifying good laws from the bad ones. Those Muslim legal scholars who undertook these challenges realized that the challenging task would involve not only juristic expertise but also political authority.[37] The juristic expertise was applied by the judges who were under a duty to adjudicate legal matters to meet the socio-political conditions of their times.[38] These judges discharged their duty by advocating a method known as 'pragmatic eclecticism'.[39] This was designed by the judiciary, as the state's representative, as an overarching method granting the judges a discretionary power to use both Ijtihad and doctrinal eclecticism to adjudicate legal matters.[40] Exercise of this discretionary power and the resulted adjudication took into account inter-state matters and were sanctioned by the state through its judicial bureaucracy.[41] As a result, Islamic law was developed further by judicial

[33] Rabb, '"We the Jurists", 527.

[34] Bassiouni, *The Sharia and Islamic Criminal Justice*, 26.

[35] Ibid., 28.

[36] Esposito, *Islam*, 13; see also Moaddel, The Study of Islamic Culture and Politics, 359.

[37] al-Ghunaimi, *The Muslim Conception of International Law*, 116.

[38] Sachedina, 'The Development of Jihad in Islamic Revelation and History', in Johnson and Kelsay (eds), *Cross, Crescent, and Sword*, 35.

[39] For an analysis on the operation of 'Islamic pragmatism' in judicial adjudication see Chap. 5.

[40] Ibrahim, *Pragmatism in Islamic Law*, 2.

[41] Ibid.

adjudication of issues concerning internal and extraterritorial use of force. This development has paved the way for Islamic international law on the use of force to mingle with bureaucracy and political Islam.[42]

3.3 Islamic International Law on the Use of Force

Islamic international law on the use of force has been formulated through the stages of fighting that the first Muslims had undertaken under the leadership of Prophet Muhammad. There were two stages on which the Qur'an provided for the use of force. These stages had been developed through the historical and political situations that the Prophet had to undertake to protect the faith from aggression during its infancy.[43]

First Stage The first set of Qur'anic verses that permitted the use of force is against unbelievers who had oppressed the Muslims at the very early stage of the birth of Islam as a religion.[44] These Qur'anic verses proclaim that: Permission to fight is given to those against whom war is waged because they have been wronged. Most certainly, God has the power to grant them victory. Those are the ones who have been driven from their homelands against all right for no other reason than their saying, "Our Lord is God!" Were it not that God repels some people through others, monasteries, churches, synagogues, and mosques—in all of which God's name is abundantly extolled—would surely have been destroyed. God will most certainly succour him who succours God's cause. God is certainly Most Powerful, Almighty.[45]

These verses discuss and justify permission to use force due to the injustices that Muslims faced during the early days of Islam and that they were expelled from their homes and forced to emigrate.[46] These verses provide for the imperative of meeting force with equal force to prevent defeat and

[42] Vanhullebusch, *War and the Law in Islamic World*, 128. For a discussion about 'the connection between the legal and political elements in Islamic international law which was contested by the Muslim nation-states and armed non-state actors in the 19th and 20th century' see Chap. 4.

[43] Rahman, *Encyclopedia of Seerah*, 79.

[44] Ishaq, *The Life of Muhammad*, 212.

[45] Al-Qur'an 22:39-40, Abu Yusuf translation.

[46] Al-Dawoody, *The Islamic Law of War*, 59.

discourage future aggression.[47] However, the Classical exegetes differ on whether chapter 2:190 was the first to be revealed about fighting (*qital*).[48] It may be appropriate to consider that, as chapter 22:39 (which was revealed in Medina, where the Prophet migrated to avoid persecution from the Meccan polytheists) preceded chapter 2:190 (which was also revealed in Medina to authorize the use of defensive force to protect the people who became Muslims by responding to the call of Prophet Muhammad), the former constitutes permission to engage in fighting that was prohibited *ab initio*, whereas the latter ordains fighting for self-defence.[49] However, at that stage fighting was allowed to fend off aggression, and this has been exemplified in verses 2:190, 194; 4:91; 9:36; and 22:39 of the Qur'an.[50]

Second Stage This stage is marked by the verses that directly ordered Muslims to fight those who fight them.[51] This is a continuation of the defensive force that was allowed at the first stage. At the second stage, recourse to pre-emptive force was permitted for Muslims according to verse 4:75.[52] It commands that: Would not you fight in the way of Allah for *al-mustadafin* (the oppressed socially weak Muslims) from men, women, and children who pray: Our Lord! Take us from this city of the oppressive people and appoint for us from Your side a guardian and appoint us from Your side a protector. Those who have believed fight in the way of Allah and those who disbelieve fight in the way of Satan, so fight the allies of Satan; surely the plot of Satan is weak.[53]

After the Prophet had migrated to Medina a few Muslims remained in Mecca although they could not practise their religion, and some Meccans wished to become Muslims but would not convert out of fear of their fellow tribesmen.[54] In both cases, these difficulties were due to the weakness

[47] Hayward, 'Warfare in the Qur'an' in Muhammad P. G., Kalin I. and Hashim Kamali M. H. (eds), *War and Peace in Islam*, 46.

[48] Vanhullebusch, *War and the Law in Islamic World*, 141.

[49] Amin, *Reclaiming Jihad*, 88.

[50] Haykal, *'al-Jihad'* cited in Amin E. M. A., *Reclaiming Jihad*, 89.

[51] Al Baqarrah 2:191 and 194, and At Tawbah 9:36; see also al-Jawziyya, *Zad al-Ma'ad fi Hady Khayr al-'Ibad*, 45.

[52] Haykal, *'al-Jihad'* cited in Amin E. M. A., *Reclaiming Jihad*, 89.

[53] Al-Qur'an 4:75-76, Abu Yusuf translation.

[54] Kathir, *Tafsir al-Qur'an al-'Azim*, 698.

of these people *vis-à-vis* the polytheistic members of their own clans who sought to oppress them with threats and even torture.[55] Therefore, verse 4:75 was revealed to call the Muslims of Medina to use force: (a) to free their brethren who were left behind in Mecca from religious oppression and (b) to give those Meccans who desired to convert the ability to do so without fear of reprisals from the enemies of Islam.[56]

3.3.1 The Origin and Development of Islamic International Law on the Use of Force

The history of Islam suggests that Prophet Muhammad was not permitted to use force, even for self-defence, until all the other alternatives were extinguished.[57] The Prophet and his companions remained in Mecca for thirteen years, where they were advocating the faith in the face of brutal persecution and injustice.[58] Throughout this period, they were instructed by God (Allah) to refrain from using force against their persecutors.[59] Only after the Prophet migrated to Medina, at the beginning of the fourteenth year of his message, permission to fight against oppression was given.[60] Therefore, the Qur'anic reference to the defensive force can be found in Medinan verses.[61]

The Qur'anic permission to use force in self-defence was seen to have been extended in the practices of Prophet Muhammad and his rightly guided caliphs.[62] The history of the origin of use of force in Islam suggests that defensive force had been used in the infancy of Islam when aggression was incumbent but had not materialized.[63] For example, defensive force had been used against the Byzantines in the Battle of Mu'tah, against the Jews in the Battle of Khaybar, where the Muslims mounted a surprise attack, and against the Quraysh when the Prophet triumphed back to

[55] Vanhullebusch, 'Islamic Law and the Responsibility to Protect', 191.

[56] Dakake, 'The Myth of Militant Islam' in Muhammad, Kalin and Kamali (eds), *War and Peace in Islam*, 128.

[57] Ali, *A Critical Examination of the Life and Teachings of Mohammed*, 76.

[58] Salahi, *Muhammad*, 214.

[59] Ibid.

[60] Haykal, *The Life of Muhammad*, 256; see also Zawati, *Is Jihad a Just War?*, 29.

[61] Al-Qur'an 8:39, Abu Yusuf translation; for other Medinan verses see Bassiouni, Evolving Approaches to Jihad, 119.

[62] An-Na'im, *Toward an Islamic reformation*, 142.

[63] Ibid.

Mecca.[64] These defensive forces had been used to protect the faith from aggression from groups and tribes all around the Muslims. Such use of force was necessary to protect the faith during its infancy. As soon as the faith had been re-established in Mecca after the Prophet's return, force was used before suffering an attack only when it was necessary.[65] The Prophet's Sunna that supports this position is that 'now we campaign against them but are not campaigned against by them—we are going to them.'[66] Moreover, the practice of recourse to use of force in response to an imminent attack had continued when an enemy had the intention to cause harm or had been planning to cause harm, or conspiring with others who were already causing harm.[67] For example, the defensive force had been used against those tribes and groups which had broken treaty provisions with the Muslims such as Banu Mustaliq, Banu Khaybar, and Banu Ghatafan when they conspired to assassinate the Prophet, and against the Byzantines following the killing of the Prophet's envoy by the then Byzantine leader.[68] Furthermore, the use of force upon the enemy's breaking of their peace treaties with Muslims had been authorized in the Qur'an.[69] However, before using force Islamic international law requires Muslim rulers to have clear evidence of treachery.[70] Therefore, it is obligatory on the part of a Muslim head of government or their representative to apprise the enemy beforehand about the former's official withdrawal from the pacts and treaties.[71] Any recourse to force without this previous notice is unlawful. As a result, Islamic international law does not authorize the use of force before an attack based on mere intelligence information or suspicion unless there is clear evidence to support the information or suspicion. Moreover, any use of force that results from a breach of a treaty must precede by official notification of withdrawal from the treaty by the victim state unless such notification would be prejudicial to the exercise of the right of self-defence.

[64] Yusuf, Transitional Justice in the Middle East and North Africa, 145.

[65] An-Na'im, *Toward an Islamic reformation*, 158.

[66] Kathir, *Tafsir al-Qur'an al-'Azim*, 103.

[67] Allam, *The Ideological Battle*,175; see also Dagli, 'Jihad and Islamic Law of War' in Muhammad, Kalin and Kamali (eds), *War and Peace in Islam*, 70.

[68] Glubb, *A Short History of the Arab Peoples*, 46.

[69] Al-Qur'an 9:12, Abu Yusuf translation.

[70] Shah, The Use of Force under Islamic Law, 343.

[71] Ibid.

The development of Islamic international law on the use of force continued in the medieval imperial world order of which Muslim territories were a part. The expansion of Muslim territorial borders due to conquests (*fath*) provided economic, political, and demographic stability to the Muslims.[72] As a result, a distinction of the world into *Dar al-Islam* (abode of Islam) and *Dar al-harb* (abode of war) was created.[73] This distinction shows the reality, brutal and unavoidable, that the world was not always governed by the universal treaties of today.[74] The terms *Dar al-Islam* and *Dar al-harb* are not from the Qur'an, Sunna, or the teachings of the Prophet but grew out of the work of jurists.[75] The invention of these terms was based on *ad hoc* juristic interpretations of particular verses 9:5 and 9:29, and largely in deference to realpolitik in the Abbasid period.[76] It seems that this dichotomous classification is a product of the exertion of intellectual reasoning (Ijtihad) in understanding the law that is mainly based on the attitude of Muslim states towards their enemies and friends during the second Islamic century.[77]

The Muslim conquests in the medieval imperial world order expanded to include the northern regions until the eleventh and twelfth centuries CE when the Muslim states were confronted with political realities other than unabated conquest and resounding victories.[78] As a result, the terms *Dar al-ʿAhd* ('Abode of the treaty') and *Dar al-Sulh* ('Abode of Reconciliation') emerged regarding the existence and conclusion of treaties between the Muslim and non-Muslim territories.[79] However, this change in tone and emphasis was not a complete novel phenomenon as the concept *Dar al-Sulh* can be traced back to the treaty that the Prophet had signed with the Christian population of Najran when he was in Medina.[80] This division had played a key role in Islamic international law in facilitating the rulers to identify what rules of law applied to that part of

[72] Hitti, *History of the Arabs*, 145.

[73] Vanhullebusch, 'Islamic Law and the Responsibility to Protect', 26.

[74] Dagli, 'Jihad and Islamic Law of War' in Muhammad, Kalin and Kamali (eds), *War and Peace in Islam*, 72.

[75] Ibid.

[76] Afsaruddin, Views of Jihad throughout History, 167.

[77] Al-Shaybani, *The Islamic Law of Nations*, 194.

[78] Hitti, *History of the Arabs*, 145.

[79] Kalin, 'Islam and Peace' in Muhammad, Kalin and Kamali (eds), *War and Peace in Islam*, 235.

[80] Ibid.

the world, namely concerning self-defence, prohibition, and restriction on exports, imports, and migration (Fig. 3.1).[81]

Because of repeated denial of elaboration of the Islamic Empire by the Christian crusaders, Tartars, and Mongolian invaders, the European power emerged in the Classical Age, and this had resulted in the remaining *Dar al-Islam* becoming under the rule of the Ottoman Empire up to the twentieth century.[82] Following the decline of territorial expansion of *Dar al-Islam* and the growing influence of foreign power in the territories under Muslim rulers, it became impracticable to expand the territory further. Therefore, the focus of Muslim leaders was to liberate the territory from foreign intervention. As a result, the bipolar division between *Dar al-harb* and *Dar al-Islam* became obsolete with the collapse of the Turkish Ottoman Empire in 1922.[83] In this period the legitimacy of use of force was restricted to 'defensive force only'.[84] Following the decolonization

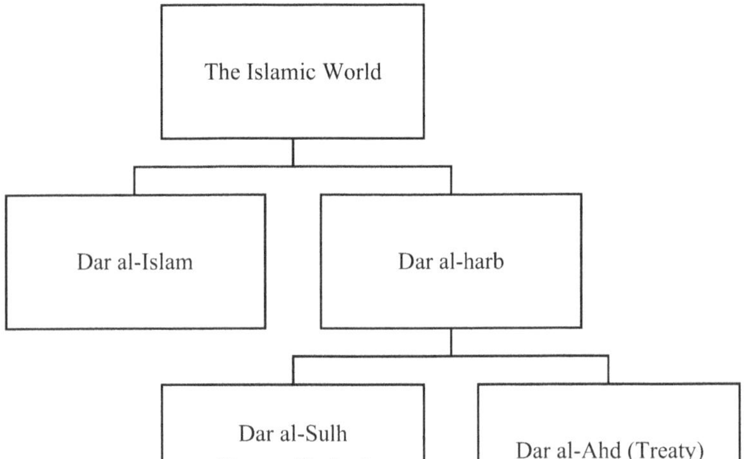

Fig. 3.1 Divisions of the world in Islamic international law

[81] Calasso, 'Introduction' in Calasso and Lancioni (eds), *Dar al-Islam/Dar al-harb*, 11.
[82] Kissling, *The Muslim World*, 3.
[83] Calasso, 'Introduction' in Calasso and Lancioni (eds), *Dar al-Islam/Dar al-harb*, 14.
[84] Ibid.

and resulting emergence of nation-states in Muslim territories, the bipolar division became a profane matter in Islamic international law.[85] However, in the modern world, this bipolar division is still relevant to show the sovereign nature of Muslim states that should be free and independent from illegitimate foreign intervention.

3.3.2 *Islamic Law on the Use of Force Against Oppressive Regimes*

Muslim states are responsible to eliminate any foreign power that prevents their people from knowing any doctrine except that dictated to them and to liberate the people that they may freely choose the creeds they want.[86] Recourse to force for this purpose is permissible under the principle of self-defence. For instance, with citations from al-Ghazali (d. 1111), al-Sulami stipulated that 'if a town in, say, Syria is attacked by the Franks and cannot defend itself, all the other (Muslim) cities of the region are obligated to come to its aid.'[87] As a result, the use of force in Islamic international law stipulates a responsibility on the Muslim states to protect each other from foreign aggression. This is like a provision for collective security among the Muslim states. However, intervention by a Muslim state to aid in defending another Muslim state from foreign aggression requires an invitation from the latter's ruler who may invite the former after consulting with the public (*Shura*).[88] This is because only a Muslim ruler can use extraterritorial force if another Muslim ruler seeks aid.[89]

Moreover, a Muslim state can use force against another Muslim state under Islamic international law, where the ruler of the second state persecutes the people.[90] In other words, unless there is a valid peace treaty between two Muslim states Islamic international law permits intervention in one Muslim state by another to protect the persecuted Muslims. However, the threshold for using force in the defence of oppressed and weak Muslims is that the oppression suffered must be so severe as to

[85] Nafi, Fatwa and war, 78.

[86] Kurdi, *The Islamic State*, 107.

[87] Ibid.

[88] The requirement of public consultation is provided in the Qur'an. See Al-Qur'an 3:159, Abu Yusuf translation.

[89] Bukhari, *Sahih al-Bukhari*, hadith no. 2957.

[90] Al-Dawoody, *The Islamic Law of War*, 59.

compel Muslims to leave their homes, for instance, genocide or torture.[91] The Qur'an commands to the use of force to liberate Muslims from persecution (*fitna*). It commands that:

> But if they [Muslims who have not come into exile] seek your aid in religion, it is your duty to help them, except against a people with whom you have a treaty of mutual alliance. And Allah sees all that you do.[92]

This Qur'anic command has been confirmed by the Shi'a Muslims too. They have recognized the legality of inviting neighbouring Muslim states for help where enemy forces raise the spectre of an emergency.[93] Ayatullah Murtaza Mutahhari (d. 1979) argued that at least in some cases, fighting in defence of the oppressed citizens of another country may be classified as an imposed war and seen as even greater or higher duty than defence of one's homeland.[94] Moreover, intervention by invitation has also taken a place in article 3 of the Constitution of the Islamic Republic of Iran, which provides that:

> fostering virtue in citizens is one of the goals of the Islamic state, and that the foreign policy of the republic is devoted to the defence of Islamic values, first in the sense of maintaining its boundaries, and second in the sense of a readiness to intervene in cases in which Islamic interests are at stake—for example, in the struggle against tyranny.[95]

The Qur'anic provision, Sunna of the Prophet, and practice of the Muslim states suggest that extraterritorial use of force against an oppressive regime to protect the persecuted Muslims is allowed in Islamic international law. As a result, every Muslim state has a duty (by implication) to defend Islam and oppressed Muslims who live inside ISIS-occupied territories.[96] However, if there is a valid treaty between two Muslim states, the law requires the intervening state to issue a formal notice of termination

[91] Shah, The Use of Force under Islamic Law, 343.
[92] Al-Qur'an 8:72, Abu Yusuf translation.
[93] Kelsay, *Arguing the Just War in Islam*, 124.
[94] Mutahhari, 'Jihad' cited in Kelsay, *Arguing the Just War in Islam*, 244.
[95] Kelsay, *Arguing the Just War in Islam*, 218.
[96] Van Engeland, 'Statehood, Proto States and International Law', 75.

of the peace treaty before using force to rescue the persecuted Muslims. Intervention to a non-Muslim state is regulated by the Islamic law of treaties, which is a branch of Islamic international law.

3.3.3 *The Role of Treaties in Islamic International Law on the Use of Force*

The treaties concluded by Prophet Muhammad and four rightly guided Caliphs are the foundations of Islamic international law.[97] The Prophet himself emphasized the binding nature of every treaty concluded by Muslims.[98] One of his Sunna confirms him saying that 'the Muslims are bound by their obligations, except an obligation that renders the lawful unlawful, and the unlawful lawful.'[99] The binding nature of treaties has also been reiterated in the following chapters of the Qur'an:

> And fulfil (every) engagement, for (every) engagement will be enquired into (on the Day of Reckoning).[100]
>
> Fulfil the contracts you have made ... such are the people of truth who fear Allah.[101]
>
> ... it is righteousness ... to fulfil the contracts which you have made ... Such are the people of truth, the Allah-fearing.[102]

A treaty is valid and takes precedence over all other laws and regulations as long as it is not inconsistent with the Shari'a.[103] However, any inconsistency shall be considered in the light of values, goals, and purposes involved and ascertained through the application of the Shari'a.[104] For example, in the Treaty of *Hudaibiyya*, the Prophet entered into a peace agreement with the Quraysh, whereby the Muslims were barred from going to pilgrimage (*hajj*) in Mecca even though the Shari'a specifically requires all able Muslims to go to

[97] Bsoul, *International Treaties (Mu'ahadat) in Islam*, x.
[98] Hisham, *Sirat al-Nabi*, 25.
[99] Bassiouni, *The Sharia and Islamic Criminal Justice*, 154.
[100] Al-Qur'an 17:34, Abu Yusuf translation.
[101] Al-Qur'an 5:1, Abu Yusuf translation.
[102] Al-Qur'an 2:177, Abu Yusuf translation.
[103] Bsoul, *International Treaties (Mu'ahadat) in Islam*, 115.
[104] Bassiouni, *The Sharia and Islamic Criminal Justice*, 154.

pilgrimage as it is one of the five pillars of Islam.[105] This requirement came from a chapter of the Qur'an, which was revealed to the Prophet long before concluding this treaty.[106] However, the Prophet agreed to suspend the pilgrimage to avoid bloodsheds and the aggression that Quraysh held towards Muslims. This example of the Prophet's action suggests that it is permissible to enter into an agreement against the proscriptions of Shari'a in exceptional circumstances where such agreement would bring greater good for the *ummah* (Muslim community) such as saving the community from imminent loss of lives.[107]

Historically, Islamic law encouraged entry into peace treaties with the abode of war (*Dar al-harb*) to maintain peace.[108] As long as the non-Muslims did not break the terms under the treaties they were in peace with the Muslims.[109] The Qur'an provides:

> But if they break their oaths after [making] their pact and assail your religion, then fight the leaders of unbelief—verily they have no [binding] oaths so that they might desist.[110]

Therefore, Islamic international law authorizes the use of force where a peace treaty is broken by an aggressor.[111] Muslim states are not allowed to use force on the sole ground that another state's ruler and people are non-Muslims.[112] Sustainable peace must exist between Islamic and non-Islamic states as long as no pacts are broken, *da'wah* (call to Islamic faith) is not attacked, and no obstacles are placed in the path of religion.[113] The use of

[105] The full text of the treaty can be found in Hamidullah, *Muslim Conduct of State*, 266–268.

[106] For a discussion about when pilgrimage was made obligatory to all Muslims, see Chap. 4.

[107] Hamidullah, *Muslim Conduct of State*, 5; see also al-Tabari, *AL-Tabari's Book of Jihad*, 80; Bsoul, *International Treaties (Mu'ahadat) in Islam*, 109; Vanhullebusch, 'Islamic Law and the Responsibility to Protect', 191.

[108] Bsoul, *International Treaties (Mu'ahadat) in Islam*, ix.

[109] Ibid., 133.

[110] Al-Qur'an 9:12, Abu Yusuf translation.

[111] Bsoul, *International Treaties (Mu'ahadat) in Islam*, 127.

[112] Ibid., 172.

[113] al-Ghunaimi, *The Muslim Conception of International Law*, 183; see also Bassiouni, Evolving Approaches to Jihad, 119; Shaltut, 'The Qur'an and Combat' in Muhammad, Kalin and Kamali (eds), *War and Peace in Islam*, 13.

force is not justified to impose Islam as a religion on unbelievers or to support a particular social regime but to repulse aggression only.[114]

Islamic international law on the use of force and its approach to treaty obligations may be drawn on to uphold the notion of peaceful and amicable relations between the members of the United Nations, which include Muslim and non-Muslim nations.[115] Muslim nations' propensity for territorial plurality and peaceable conduct has been borne out by their institution of regular treaty relations with non-Muslim states with which Islamic polities have in practice rejected to have been in an unmitigated state of hostilities on account of religious differences.[116] In this context, entering into bilateral and multilateral treaties can be one of the effective ways to accommodate conflicting legal systems at the international level to agree on the conduct of use of force.[117] On this footing, extraterritorial use of force in the modern world is regulated by the United Nations Charter, which every Muslim state has signed and ratified as an international treaty. According to this treaty obligation, Muslim states must follow the provisions of the Charter. If a term of the charter is broken by any state, Islamic international law provides for two options, namely (a) follow what the charter has provided where there is a breach or (b) withdraw from the peace treaty. Whereas option (a) enables a victim state to use defensive force to repulse the aggression, option (b) is likely to result in a threat to international peace and security for which the primary responsibility lies on the UN. In these circumstances, the legitimate response by a Muslim state to a breach of the UN Charter is to follow the provisions of the Charter, customary international law, judicial decisions of the International Court of Justice (ICJ), and resolutions of international institutions such as the Security Council.[118]

[114] Al-Buti, *Jihad in Islam*, 233; see also Abu Zahra, *Concept of War in Islam*, 18; Al-Dawoody, *The Islamic Law of War*, 40.

[115] Bakircioglu, *Islam and Warfare*, 173.

[116] Ibid., 182.

[117] Bsoul, *International Treaties (Muʿahadat) in Islam*, 111.

[118] For a discussion about the use of force in the UN Charter and other international institutions, see Chap. 1.

3.3.4 *Fundamental Principles of Islamic International Law on the Use of Force*

Islamic perception of the use of force may be studied from the viewpoints of both Muslim States' practice and Islamic jurisprudence.[119] Unlike Public international law, Islamic international law does not prohibit the use of force in general terms. It prohibits aggressive use of force but allows defensive force in certain circumstances. The Qur'an outlined these circumstances such as fending off aggression, protecting the call to the faith *(da'wah)*, and safeguarding freedom of religion.[120]

Islamic international law allows the use of force for fending off aggression and safeguarding freedom of religion for defensive purposes.[121] However, the use of force for protecting *da'wah* has been a point of controversy. The controversy lies in the extent of the use of force that is allowed by Islamic international law for this purpose. Some scholars (especially the fundamentalists)[122] have argued for the legitimacy of extensive use of force for calling to Islam, which includes aggressive force to conquer land and expand it under Islamic rule. On the contrary, modern scholars have confined legitimate use of force to peaceful calling to Islam and denied aggression. They have argued that aggressive use of force for *da'wah* is unjust and likely to bring hatred to the religion which the Qur'an forbids.[123] The Qur'an provided that 'Let not your hatred of a people cause you to be unjust. You must do justice.'[124]

Therefore, the use of aggressive force for spreading Islam is not supported by the Qur'anic provisions, and the extent to which call to Islam is allowed is limited to peaceful means only. Even when freedom of religion and call to the *da'wah* are denied, use of force is not allowed when doing so would result in unjust killing. The Qur'an proclaims that 'whosoever kills a human being for other than manslaughter or corruption in the earth, it shall be if he had killed all humanity.'[125] In such circumstances, only peaceful measures to protest such denial of freedom of religion and

[119] Mahmoudi, The Islamic Perception of the Use of Force in the Contemporary World, 13.

[120] Shaltut, *Jihad in Mediaeval and Modern Islam*, 55.

[121] Bennoune, 'As-salama 'alaykum? Humanitarian Law in Islamic Jurisprudence', 622; see also Allam, *The Ideological Battle*, 175.

[122] The term 'fundamentalists' is a contested term as it is derogatorily known in the West but not in the Muslim world.

[123] Al-Buti, *Jihad in Islam*, 233; see also Abu Zahra, *Concept of War in Islam*, 18.

[124] Al-Qur'an 5:8, Abu Yusuf translation.

[125] Al-Qur'an 5:32, Abu Yusuf translation.

call to the *da'wah* are permitted, which is recognized in Islamic jurisprudence as 'jihad by the tongue against a tyrant'.[126] However, if peaceful co-existence between Muslim and non-Muslim states becomes impossible to maintain by peaceful means, defensive force is permitted as a last resort to repel aggression and persecution.[127] Mahmud Shaltut (d. 1963), the then rector of al-Azhar University, opined that only defensive wars were permissible in response to aggression.[128] In support of this view, Shaltut relied on the history of Islam on the circumstances under which the Battle of Badr (624 CE) was fought. For instance, shortly before the start of the battle Prophet Muhammad sent a message to the Quraysh telling them that they had no reason to fight him and his companions, and therefore a peace arrangement should be easily agreed upon.[129] Although very few of the Quraysh leaders accepted the logic that a battle was unnecessary and tried to persuade their people to abandon the war, the hardliners were determined to go on the warpath and were soon able to drag everyone into the battle that was fought by the Prophet and his companions to defend themselves from the aggression of the Quraysh.[130]

The legitimacy of defensive force to fend off aggression must continue, according to the Qur'anic provision, until the aggression and the resulting persecution (*fitna*) end.[131] However, there are controversies about the meaning of *fitna* as provided in chapter 8:39 of the Qur'an. On the one hand, if it means unbelief in God (as interpreted by the Classical exegetes) this verse would require the Muslims to fight unbelievers until unbelief is eradicated, that is to wage a complete war against non-Muslims.[132] On the other hand, if it is interpreted to mean the persecution of Muslims until they recant (as interpreted by Modern exegetes), Muslims are required to fight their persecutors until they enjoy complete freedom of worshipping God without fear or the need to hide their belief.[133] Whereas the former interpretation upholds an offensive war the latter suggests a defensive war.

[126] Kamali, *Principles of Islamic Jurisprudence*, 279; see also Bennoune, 'As-salama 'alaykum? Humanitarian Law in Islamic Jurisprudence', 622.

[127] Ali, *A Critical Examination of the Life and Teachings of Mohammed*, 76.

[128] Shaltut, 'Koran and Fighting' cited in Afsaruddin, Views of Jihad throughout History, 169.

[129] Zebiri, *Mahmud Shaltut and Islamic Modernism*, 45.

[130] Ibid.

[131] Al-Qur'an 8:39, Abu Yusuf translation.

[132] Al-Dawoody, *The Islamic Law of War*, 62.

[133] Ibid.

As a result, the Islamic *casus belli* is the prevention of aggression and religious persecution, and so fighting must cease once religious freedom is secured, and the mission to preach Islam is protected.[134] This suggests that the preferred interpretation of *fitna* is 'persecution' rather than 'unbelief'. Rashid Ridā quotes Mohammad 'Abduh (a modern exegete) as saying that interpreting persecution in this verse to mean 'unbelief' takes the interpretation of the verse out of context.[135] The Classical Muslim jurists, who interpreted *fitna* as unbelief, formulated Islamic international law in a world 'where war was the natural state'.[136] However, since the shift of the natural state of war to peaceful co-existence of nation-states, modern Muslim jurists have been discussing the use of force through the lens of jihad.[137] The following section discusses the meaning and significance of jihad from the perspective of Islamic international law.

3.4 Jihad: Meaning and Significance

Islamic legal discourse discusses the use of force with reference to the term 'jihad'.[138] Many Muslim and non-Muslim scholars have interpreted jihad as the main provision of use of force in Islamic law.[139] As a result, the place of 'jihad' is at the focal point of analysis in Islamic law on the use of force. Being at the focal point of analysis 'jihad' has been a subject of extensive use and abuse. In the Classical period, the laws of jihad assumed that the default position between states was a state of war.[140] This was widely understood to mean that Muslims must consider themselves bound to wage war on all non-Muslim lands until they become part of *Dar al-Islam*. The relationship between Muslims and non-Muslims in this period was very hostile.[141] A state of war between the Muslims and, in Qur'anic terms, the idolaters/unbelievers/polytheists of Mecca was the norm until 628 CE

[134] Shaltut, 'Al-Islam wa al-Alaqat al-Dawliyyah' cited in Al-Dawoody, *The Islamic Law of War*, 68.

[135] Al-Rida, 'Tafsir al-Qur'an al-Hakim' cited in Amin, *Reclaiming Jihad*, 91.

[136] Esposito, *Unholy War*, 29.

[137] Mahmoudi, The Islamic Perception of the Use of Force in the Contemporary, 2.

[138] Van Engeland, 'When Two Visions of a Just World Clash', 156.

[139] al-Tabari, *AL-Tabari's Book of Jihad*; Al-Buti, *Jihad in Islam*; see also Firestone, *Jihad*; Bonney, *Jihad*.

[140] Al-Buti, *Jihad in Islam*, 59; see also Shaltut, *Jihad in Mediaeval and Modern Islam*, 44; al-Tabari, *AL-Tabari's Book of Jihad*, 1.

[141] Afsaruddin, *Jihad and Martyrdom in Islamic Thought and History*, 6; see also Amin, *Reclaiming Jihad*, 7.

when the treaty of al-Hudaybiyya was concluded.[142] The reasons for this enmity were hostility, persecution, and aggression.[143] On the contrary, the modernists' view of 'jihad' is to use force in the defence of aggression and persecution of Muslims.[144] However, recourse to the defensive force is allowed as a last resort, that is after extinguishing all other options to end aggression and persecution.[145] The modernists also do not support armed jihad to expand the territory of Muslim states and to facilitate forced conversion to Islam.[146]

3.4.1 *Meaning of Jihad*

Jihad is derived from the root word '*jahada*' (pl. *yujahiduna*), which means to strive or to exert effort.[147] The Qur'an refers to these two meanings in chapters 9:79 and 24:53.[148] Due to the limited scope to its meaning 'jihad' is commonly associated with Islamic violence by many Muslim and non-Muslim scholars.[149] Whereas the Classical meaning of jihad is limited to 'armed struggle', its meaning in modern context goes far beyond such limited scope.[150]

Understood in its comprehensive sense, jihad is an inherent aspect of the human condition in facing imperfections of this world.[151] Prophet Muhammad said that 'the *mujahid* (a person performing jihad) is the one who wages a struggle against himself.'[152] In the Qur'anic usage military activity is consistently identified by terms other than jihad (e.g., *qital*).[153]

[142] Al-Dawoody, *The Islamic Law of War*, 48.

[143] Ibid.

[144] Copinger-Symes, Is Osama bin Laden's Fatwa Urging Jihad Against Americans, 44.

[145] Asad, 'Islamic Humanitarian Law' cited in Bassiouni, *The Sharia and Islamic Criminal Justice*, 166; see also Bennoune, 'As-salama 'alaykum? Humanitarian Law in Islamic Jurisprudence', 622.

[146] Copinger-Symes, Is Osama bin Laden's Fatwa Urging Jihad Against Americans, 44; see also Van Engeland, 'Islam as Religion of Peace', 243.

[147] al-Tabari, *AL-Tabari's Book of Jihad*, 1; see also Bassiouni, Evolving Approaches to Jihad, 119; Bowering (ed), *The Princeton Encyclopedia of Islamic Political Thought*, 273; Thomas, *Dictionary of Islam*, 243; Netton, *A Popular Dictionary of Islam*, 136.

[148] Al-Asfahani, 'Mufradat Alfaz' cited in Amin, *Reclaiming Jihad: A Qur'anic Critique of Terrorism*, 79.

[149] Bassiouni, *The Sharia and Islamic Criminal Justice*, 198.

[150] Amin, *Reclaiming Jihad*, 80.

[151] Khadduri, *War and Peace in the Law of Islam*, 56.

[152] al-Rahman 'Utham A. (ed), *Tuhfat al-Ahwazi bi-Sharh Jami' al-Tirmidhi*, 1671.

[153] Shah, *Islamic Law and the Law of Armed Conflict*, 31.

The place of jihad is reserved for the overall religious struggle whether in the form of personal purification or in the form of collective effort to establish an Islamic social order.[154] Therefore, the significance of jihad includes both forceful and non-forceful struggles.

The literal meaning of the word jihad is effort or struggle, and the greater jihad as defined by the Prophet is the *jihad al-nafs*, the struggle against the soul.[155] The priority thus accorded to inward and spiritual effort over all outward endeavours must never be lost sight of in any examination of jihad.[156] Therefore, jihad should be 'for Allah's sake' (*fi sabilillah*) even when it is related to fighting (*qital*).[157] The Qur'anic term *'fi sabilillah'* is not as widely attached to military jihad as often depicted by few modern non-Muslim researchers, such as Randall and Firestone,[158] who attempt to interpret jihad and *'jihad fi sabilillah'* in the same way.[159] It carries both military and non-military meanings, and it generally refers how a believer chooses to live to please Allah.[160] For example, spending in the cause of Allah and emigrating for fear of persecution. Therefore, jihad does not always denote fighting in the Qur'an. Therefore, every *qital* (fighting) is jihad but every jihad is not *qital*.[161]

The Qur'an makes several references to jihad, some of which have the distinct meaning of war-like activities in defence of the religion.[162] Nevertheless, the spiritual aspect of jihad was prevalent, predominant, and particularly practised by the early Meccan Muslims between 611 and 632 CE, the period when the Qur'an was revealed.[163] The Qur'an refers to jihad in twenty-four verses, most of which emphasize the spiritual and non-violent manifestations of jihad.[164] Only a few verses specifically address jihad as armed resistance to the enemies of Islam, and in those verses

[154] Sachedina, 'The Development of Jihad in Islamic Revelation and History', in Johnson and Kelsay (eds), *Cross, Crescent, and Sword*, 37; see also Pirzada, 'Islam and International Law' in Gauhar (ed), *The Challenges of Islam*, 196.

[155] Amin, *Reclaiming Jihad*, 80.

[156] Bassiouni, *The Sharia and Islamic Criminal Justice*, 201.

[157] Afsaruddin, Views of Jihad throughout History, 165; see also Shah N.A., *Islamic Law and the Law of Armed Conflict*, 31.

[158] Firestone, *Jihad*; see also Bonney, *Jihad*.

[159] Amin, *Reclaiming Jihad*, 82.

[160] Ibid.

[161] al-Khalafi cited in Amin, *Reclaiming Jihad*, 82.

[162] Bassiouni, *The Sharia and Islamic Criminal Justice*, 205.

[163] Ibid., 205.

[164] Bassiouni, Evolving Approaches to Jihad, 119; see also Kamali, 'Introduction' in Muhammad, Kalin and Kamali (eds), *War and Peace in Islam*, XIII.

resorting to the use of force as a jihad is contemplated as self-defence.[165] The source evidence suggests that jihad has been divided into four main varieties, each of which has been subdivided into four types and thereby resulting in a total of sixteen varieties.[166] The following figure demonstrates the varieties:

Among the sixteen varieties of jihad (see Fig. 3.2) the only four varieties when 'use of force' is allowed consist of the last type (by person). Therefore, jihad against the self, against the unbelievers, against the hypocrites, and the agents of corruption allow the use of force by a person. This is known as military jihad. However, such use of force is allowed only in a very limited circumstance which has been specifically circumscribed in the Qur'an and Sunna.[167] The overriding purpose of jihad is the quest for peace and justice.[168] The Qur'an obliged Muslims to make the world aware of the divine path and required humanity to obey the divine will manifested through the Prophet of Islam.[169] This obligation establishes a relationship between 'call to the faith' and jihad. The Qur'an authorizes the undertaking of jihad to establish or re-establish an ethical order in the world by calling to the divine path.[170]

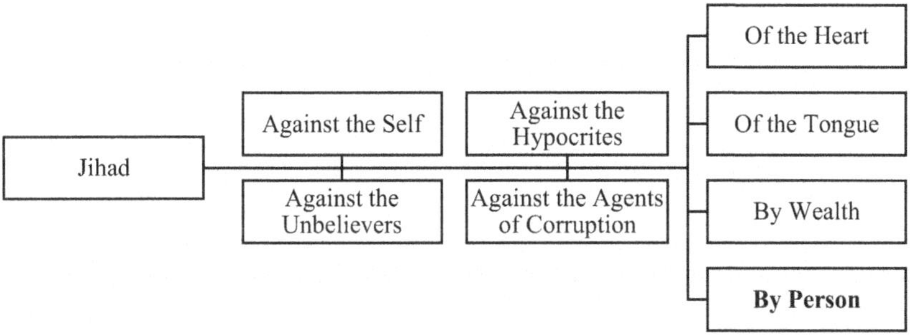

Fig. 3.2 Divisions and sub-divisions of jihad

[165] Shah, *Self-Defense in Islamic and International Law*, 15.

[166] www.islamicsupremecouncil.org/legal_rulings/Jihad/jihad-withadditions.pdf accessed 14 July 2020.

[167] Sonn, 'Irregular Warfare and Terrorism in Islam' in Johnson and Kelsay (eds), *Cross, Crescent, and Sword*, 129.

[168] Kamali, 'Introduction' in Muhammad, Kalin and Kamali (eds), *War and Peace in Islam*, XVI.

[169] Al-Qur'an 34:27, Abu Yusuf translation. "We have sent thee not, except to mankind entire, good tidings to bear, and warning; but most men do not know it."

[170] Khadduri, *War and Peace in the Law of Islam*, 56.

3.4.2 Evolution of the Meaning of Jihad

The meaning of Jihad has been evolving since the time of the Prophet and often reflects changing political realities. In the Qur'an, the term jihad has been used to denote both spiritual and forceful dimensions. Whereas the spiritual dimension of jihad was predominant during Islam's first twelve years, later it came to mean that the Muslims have an obligation to bear arms for the defence of the *ummah*.[171] This military aspect of jihad was subsequently redefined by state doctrine to legitimize the exercise of self-defence before an attack and justify conquest.[172] Over time, the political legitimization of force was transformed into a doctrine that supported the use of force in the attainment of political goals.[173]

In the formative period, jihad meant the defensive force against religious persecution and aggression against Muslims. In the Classical Period, the scholarships were divided between aggressive and defensive forces. However, in the Modern period jihad is used for justifying the use of force for multiple reasons such as the liberation of the Muslim world from European Imperialism and unlawful foreign occupation. This is because the one-state Caliphate abode of Islam was abolished in 1922, with the extinction of the Ottoman Empire.[174] Unlike the classical jurists who formulated their theory in a time when a state of war already existed in the absence of a specific peace treaty, modern scholars advocated their position in a post-United Nations world.[175] Modern Muslim scholars deal with new circumstances which often render the classical theory inoperative or even irrelevant.[176] In response, the modern scholars were confronted by the revivalists of the classical conception of jihad by calling Muslims to engage in individual as well as collective use of force. This call paved the way for the propagation of jihad by states and armed non-state actors as a call for every Muslim to fight non-Muslims in another state, foreign powers, or an apostate leader who carry out

[171] al-Nawawi, *Al-Alaqat al-Duwaliyya wa'l-Nuzum al-Qadaiyya*, 95; see also Bassiouni, *The Sharia and Islamic Criminal Justice*, 201.

[172] Shaban, *Islamic History*, 133; see also Bassiouni, Evolving Approaches to Jihad, 119.

[173] Peters, *Islam and Colonialism*, 131.

[174] Al-Dawoody, *The Islamic Law of War*, 77; see also Van Engeland, 'The Balance Between Islamic Law, Customary Law and Human Rights in Islamic Constitutionalism', 1321.

[175] Ibid., 82; see also Weeramantry, *Islamic Jurisprudence*, 150.

[176] Kelsay, *Islam and War*, 107.

their political goal in collusion with a foreign power. For example, the Iraq-Kuwait war, Iraq-Iran war, and jihad against the Western powers and the rulers or leaders of Muslim states who collude with the former.[177] In these instances, the states and armed non-state actors have claimed the legitimacy of the use of force based on jihad.[178]

Islamic jurisprudence has always been the subject of an interplay between the political and theological doctrines in different historical periods.[179] Despite the Shari'a requirement to wage legitimate war, the use of force in Islamic international law has not been free from the encroachment from political leaders who have temporal reasons to recourse to force. As James Turner Johnson pointed out that 'despite the invocation of the religious authority of war, the causes of the wars in question were essentially temporal; despite being termed jihad, they were wars of the state, not wars of religion.'[180] Throughout the centuries, competing claimants to the *khalifa* (leadership) resorted to the doctrine of jihad in their power struggles.[181] This doctrinal extension of jihad to political goals has increased dramatically over the past 200 years, during which time it has come to justify regime change and political opposition to rulers.[182]

Since politics became an integral part of Islamic law on the use of force the rulers like Ummayyad, Abbasid, Mongols, Seljuks, and the Turkish Ottoman Empire entertained a broader concept of military jihad together with the classical jurists like al-Shaf'i and his followers. The rulers and leaders very rarely used the spiritual nature of jihad. The transformation of jihad from spiritual to predominantly military has resulted in the wider recognition of jihad as a 'holy war', especially by the Western scholars. This was due to the interpretation of the classical exegetes that jihad is a permanent and total war against unbelievers.[183]

[177] For an account of recourse to force by the states and armed non-state actors, see Chap. 4.

[178] For an analysis of the legitimacy arguments made by the states and armed non-state actors, see Chap. 4.

[179] Copinger-Symes, Is Osama bin Laden's Fatwa Urging Jihad Against Americans, 44.

[180] Johnson, *The Holy War Idea in Western and Islamic Traditions*, 96.

[181] Bassiouni, *The Sharia and Islamic Criminal Justice*, 202.

[182] Ibid.; see also Bassiouni, Evolving Approaches to Jihad, 119.

[183] Van Engeland, 'Islam and the Protection of Civilians in the Conduct of Hostilities, 139.

3.5 Who Can Authorize the Use of Force in Islamic International Law?

Questions about who is legally entitled to call for or initiate use of force as jihad, in a world which no longer has Caliphs leading the *ummah*, are debated by Islamic scholars. A vast majority have argued that only state leaders in Islamic (or Muslim majority) lands are legitimately entitled to authorize the use of force if a genuine 'just cause' emerged.[184] However, the two major branches of Islam, the Sunni and Shi'a, differ sharply for doctrinal reasons on the necessary authority to wage war in the sense of jihad. The position of the Sunni jurists is that both offensive and defensive jihad could be waged by any Muslim authority in Islamic law against the abode of war.[185] The Shi'a position, on the other hand, has been that a divinely appointed person, the just Imam, who would unite political and religious sovereignty, is necessary for any jihad that is not defensive.[186] The last divine Imam, the Twelfth Imam, not being available, there is no legal authority to use offensive force until his return from a hidden position.[187] Consequently, the eminent Shi'a and Sunni authorities have respectively maintained that use of force, except for self-defence, is forbidden in the absence of the *ma'sum*, that is 'the inerrant Imam',[188] or the Caliph.[189] As a result, no offensive force or war of aggression is legal in Islamic international law since the disappearance of the hidden Imam and death of the last rightly guided Caliph, Ali.

Despite the sharp differences as to the authority to wage war the positions of Shi'a and Sunni schools of thought give a clear message that 'use of force is not legal in Islamic international law unless it is necessary for self-defence of a Muslim state.'[190] However, these positions are not definitive about who has the legal authority to decide on the use of force in self-defence and in what circumstances such force can be used. In Islamic

[184] Kelsay, *Arguing the Just War in Islam*, 101.

[185] Al-Buti, *Jihad in Islam*, 59; see also Shaltut, *Jihad in Mediaeval and Modern Islam*, 44.

[186] Mutahhari, *Jihad and Shahadat*, 103; see also Sachedina, 'The Development of Jihad in Islamic Revelation and History' in Johnson and Kelsay (eds), *Cross, Crescent and Sword*, 41.

[187] Sharastani, *Muslim Sects and Divisions*, 140; Cohlberg, *Belief and Law in Imami Shaism*, 78; Abedi and Legenhausen, *Jihad and Shahadat*, 15.

[188] Nasr, *The Heart of Islam*, 262.

[189] Hamidullah, *Muslim Conduct of State*, 151.

[190] Ibid.; see also Bennoune, 'As-salama 'alaykum? Humanitarian Law in Islamic Jurisprudence', 622.

international law, the use of force must be declared by a legitimate leader.[191] Hence, no group, party, or organization has the authority to take up arms in the name of jihad without authorization from the ruler of the state in which that group, party, or organization is based.[192] In this way, Islamic law has made provisions to control disorder and anarchy. A Sunna of the Prophet supports this position: 'A Muslim ruler is a shield [of his people], and a war can only be waged under him and people should seek his shelter [in war].'[193] As a result, it is the ruler who has the legal authority to declare jihad and make decisions on the use of force. Any use-of-force decision made by armed non-state actors is illegal in Islamic international law for the lack of their lawful authority to make such decision.

In addition to having a lawful authority to make decision on the use of force, a ruler must be satisfied that the reason for making such a decision is justified. This is because the legal authority of the ruler must correspond to a just cause. For example, a ruler who uses defensive force in circumstances which is inconsistent with the Qur'anic proscriptions is unlawful in Islamic law for the lack of 'just cause' element of use of force.[194] Therefore, the legality of use of force in Islamic law requires the satisfaction of both elements of use of force, namely right authority and just cause (see Fig. 3.3).

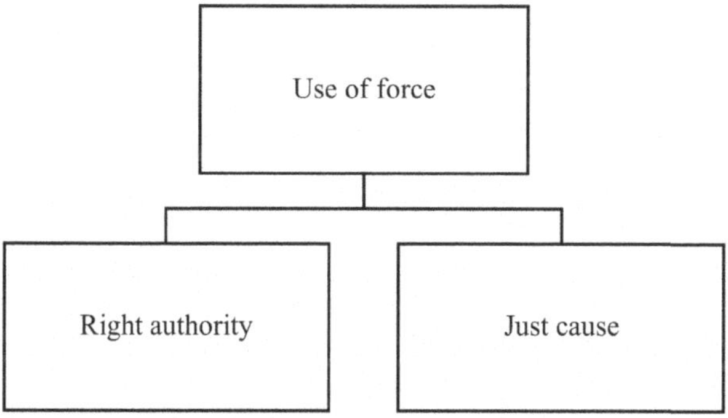

Fig. 3.3 Elements of use of force

[191] Hamidullah, *Muslim Conduct of State*, 151; see also Kamali, 'Introduction' in Muhammad, Kalim, and Kamali (eds), *War and Peace in Islam*, XIII.

[192] Asad, *The Principle of State and Government in Islam*, 35.

[193] Bukhari, *Sahih al-Bukhari*, hadith no. 2957.

[194] Khadduri, *Al-Shafi's Risala*, 112; see also Khan, Jurodynamics of Islamic Law, 231.

Another issue on the legality of use of force arises when a ruler abstains from making decisions on the use of force. For instance, if a ruler makes no call for jihad or use of force for self-defence even when it is necessary to do so. The majority of Muslim scholars and exegetes agree that if a head of state or government does not authorize the use of necessary force and his abstention amounts to a disregard of the Shari'a, such omission can give the undisputed leader of a Muslim state the authority to declare the use of defensive force to protect the Muslim community within that state.[195] The best example to illuminate the legality of this position is the Russian invasion of Afghanistan in 1979. The Afghan leaders declared jihad against both the invaders and the pro-communist ruler of Afghanistan. Muslims around the world joined the Afghan jihad. This kind of jihad was considered as a war in self-defence or defensive jihad, although it was not declared by a Muslim ruler.[196] Another example of this type of declaration is the letter written by 100 scholars addressing al-Baghdadi (the then leader of the so-called Islamic State in Iraq and Syria [ISIS]), which confirmed his lack of legal authority to declare the use of force under Islamic law as he was neither a ruler nor an undisputed leader of a Muslim state.[197]

The restriction on the authority to use force to the rulers, or in the absence of a ruler the undisputed leader of a Muslim state, is a very high requirement.[198] This is because the authority of a ruler, or in his absence the undisputed leader of a Muslim state, is always subject to dispute. As a result, it is a high requirement to establish lawful authority to use force without questioning the status of such authority as a legitimate ruler or an undisputed leader. Therefore, the leaders of any group or organization are not eligible to declare jihad or use force under Islamic international law.[199] These leaders of such group or organization are not representative of the Islamic belief or behaviour, and they do not have any recognized status as an authority in Islamic international law to make such decision and declaration. For example, the recent al-Azhar position has also confirmed that the declaration of use of force by Al-Qa'ida, ISIS (Islamic State in Iraq and Syria), ISIL (Islamic State in Iraq and Levant), QSIS or Al-Qa'ida Separatists in Iraq and Syria, and other similar groups or organizations are

[195] Shah, The Use of Force under Islamic Law, 343.

[196] Ibid.

[197] Allam, *The Ideological Battle*, 160.

[198] Asad, *The Principle of State and Government in Islam*, 59.

[199] Ibid., 36.

unlawful due to lack of right authority.[200] This position has been confirmed by the scholars of Mardin Declaration, who attended a Peace Summit Conference (Mardin: The Abode of Peace) that was convened in the Turkish city of Mardin at the Artuklu University campus on 27–28 March 2010.[201] Participating in the conference was a group of renowned Muslim scholars, from across the Muslim world, who brought with them diverse and relevant specializations. They gathered to collectively study 'jihad' as the most important juridical concept in Islamic law on the use of force. They have concluded that only leaders of Muslim states can issue a call for jihad and that no other individual has the right to wage war against a nation or population.[202] Taking direct aim at contemporary jihadists and their reliance on Ibn Taymiyya's fatwa, the scholars declared that 'anyone who seeks support from this fatwa for killing Muslims or non-Muslims has erred in his or her interpretation and has misapplied the revealed texts.'[203] Therefore, armed non-state actors are not allowed to recourse to force due to a lack of legitimate authority under Islamic international law.

The scholarly positions of Sunni and Shi'a schools of thought, outlined above, set out the legal position of Muslim states and the issues surrounding the legality of use of force in Islamic international law. This is because Muslim states in the world generally belong to Sunni and Shi'a schools of thought.[204] For example, the Kingdom of Saudi Arabia and the Islamic Republic of Iran are generally adherents of the Sunni and Shi'a schools of thought respectively. Moreover, these scholarly positions outline the political legacy of the use of force in the legal discourse of Islamic international law.[205] For instance, these scholarly positions also set out their understanding of the political history of Islam and the connections of the Qur'anic jihad with that history.[206] In this way, the political history of Islam has immensely influenced their understanding of jihad. On the one hand, the classical Sunni jurists influenced the political reality of war, and on the

[200] Allam, *The Ideological Battle*, 130.

[201] The New Mardin Declaration (27 April 2010); for *contra* see Michot, 'Ibn Taymiyya's "New Mardin Fatwa",130.

[202] Ibid.

[203] Ibid.

[204] Sharastani, *Muslim Sects and Divisions*, 70.

[205] Mandaville, *Islam and Politics*, 36.

[206] Al-Shaybani, *The Islamic Law of Nations*, 16; Sachedina, 'The Development of Jihad in Islamic Revelation and History', in Johnson and Kelsay (eds), *Cross, Crescent, and Sword*, 41.

other hand, the Shi'a jurists focused on the political ideology of war.[207] This political influence has made the classical Sunni jurists and their modern counterparts justify aggressive use of force based on historical conquests by Muslim rulers. They treated aggressive use of force (offensive jihad) as a divinely approved political tool for furthering the 'sphere of Islam' and keeping the 'sphere of war' in check.[208] However, the Shi'a jurists were able to question the legality of the conquests by the aggressive use of force and thereby making a strong claim that such use of force was opposed to the Qur'anic commands.[209] As a result, highly political legacies of the use of force were incorporated into Islamic jurisprudence by the Sunni and Shi'a jurists.

The political legacy of the use of force in Islamic international law can also be traced in the decision-making process of Muslim rulers. This decision is based on the knowledge and evidence available to the rulers and is not purely based on Islamic international law.[210] The only point that is relevant to the law is that such use of force must not be aggressive or for any other purpose than self-defence, and must be a measure of last resort. The ruler's permission is mandatory, and only then it is permissible to use force in self-defence.[211]

A further political legacy of the use of force can be found in the Qur'anic exegesis. The three words (with their derivatives) used in the Qur'anic context of the use of force are *qital* (fighting, murder, killing, infanticide), jihad (struggle, striving), and *harb* (war).[212] Islamic law developed its just war doctrine as early as the seventh and eighth centuries CE, which was before the just war tradition of the West began to coalesce into its classical form, based on the Qur'an and Sunna.[213] Al-Shaybani, an Islamic Jurist of the Classical period, developed a sophisticated concept of the use of force theory that governed the relationship between Muslim and non-Muslim

[207] Ibid.

[208] Khadduri, *War and Peace in the Law of Islam*, 63; see also Waddy, *The Muslim Mind*, 102.

[209] Asad, *The Principle of State and Government in Islam*, 35.

[210] Allam, *The Ideological Battle*, 160.

[211] Ibid., 175; see also Khadduri, *War and Peace in the Law of Islam*, 78.

[212] Al-Dawoody, *The Islamic Law of War*, 56; see also Shah, *Islamic Law and the Law of Armed Conflict*, 31.

[213] Johnson and Kelsey, *Cross, Crescent and Sword*, xiv.

nations.[214] It is the Classical jurists who differentiated between *harb* (war) and jihad (struggle, effort), and the only relationship between these two concepts was overlapping. The jurists outlined this overlap by setting up a connection between *harb* (war) and *qital* (fighting).[215] The connection suggests that the Qur'an allows the use of force or fighting (*qital*) only in the path of God (jihad) in a state of war (*harb*). In this connection, just war develops when jihad and *harb* merge together, and at that point, jihad enters the mode of *qital*. Therefore, the following theory applies to just war in Islam:

$$\text{Jihad} + \text{harb} = \text{Qital}$$

Whereas jihad requires religious authorization, *harb* requires political authorization and direction. Therefore, *qital* (fighting) is only just when both religious and political authorizations come from the right authorities.[216] Accordingly, the 'just cause' test is satisfied when the religious authority approve jihad and the political authority approve use of force. These authorizations do not necessarily need to emanate from the same person or institution as long as these are from a legal authority and consistent with the Shari'a (*Siyasa Shari'a*). For instance, a ruler of a Muslim state can authorize defensive force if the population of that country is under an actual or imminent attack from another state or under forceful invasion or occupation from a foreign power. If the political authority is responsible for the foreign invasion or occupation such as by colluding with a foreign power, the religious authority can alone authorize the use of force. For example, the 1882 British invasion of Egypt with an invitation from the legitimate ruler (a political authority) Khedive Tawfiq when defensive force was declared by the *Ulama* (religious authority) to save the country from non-Muslim invasion. As a result, a decision to recourse to defensive force may legitimately come from a religious leader where the political authority such as the state government has colluded with a foreign power to launch aggressive force.

[214] Al-Shaybani, *The Islamic Law of Nations*, 5.

[215] Shah, *Islamic Law and the Law of Armed Conflict*, 31.

[216] Allam, *The Ideological Battle*, 20; see also Shah, *Islamic Law and the Law of Armed Conflict*, 60.

3.6 Conclusion

This chapter has discussed the nature and extent of the use of force permitted in Islamic international law. The permission to use force only for defensive purposes and as a last resort is the fundamental provision of Islamic international law as validated by the Shari'a. However, due to the influence of politics on the ideology of Islam, the Shari'a has been subject to elaboration beyond the necessity of the common good. Self-interest gratification and political agenda have been the underlying motivation for abusing Islamic jurisprudence, which resulted in the invocation of ideologies, such as jihad, to represent religious duty to use force against Muslims and non-Muslims, and for the expansion of territory. Jihad has also been misused by a few Muslim and most non-Muslim scholars who denoted this term as synonymous with 'holy war'. Eventually, jihad has been misleadingly promoted by both state and armed non-state groups to facilitate international terrorism.

After examining the nature and extent of the use of force, this chapter has shown that Islamic international law does not permit the use of force beyond the necessity to defend the religion and people from persecution. In very exceptional circumstances it allows defensive force but never permits aggressive force. However, the use of defensive force requires 'right authority' and 'just cause', which are lacking in the status and ideologies of armed non-state actors. Although very few Muslim scholars and armed non-state actors have invoked the ideology of the classical juristic views of permanent war against non-Muslims, this does not represent contemporary Islamic international law as the Shari'a itself does not represent the dominant classical view in the modern world.

The overall analysis of this chapter concludes on the fundamental principles which are based on the modernists' view and represent the core values of Islamic international law. These principles confined the authority to decide on the use of force to the ruler or undisputed leader of a Muslim state. As a result, Islamic international law excluded armed non-state actors from having any legal or political authority to use force or declare the same. However, armed non-state actors claim that they have the authority to recourse to force against another state if and when the state authorities are unable or unwilling to use force to defend foreign aggression and when they collude with a foreign power to suppress political opponents and rebellion within the state. Islamic law allows recourse to defensive force to repel aggression but not to launch the same. Therefore, any claim of the legitimate use of force by states and armed non-state actors must be addressed from both within and beyond the law. Whereas the question of legality can be answered from the law, the question of legitimacy cannot be answered from this. As a result, the question of legitimacy must be answered from beyond the law such as by exploring the legal-political legacies of the use of force. This is because the legal-political legacies pave the way for a claim of the legitimacy of use of force to become the law. The next chapter discusses the legal-political legacies of use of force in Islamic international law.

References

Abedi M. and Legenhausen G., *Jihad and Shahadat* (The Institute for Research and Islamic Studies, 1986).

Abu Zahra M., *Concept of War in Islam* (Cairo: Ministry of Waqf, 1961).

Afsaruddin A., *Jihad and Martyrdom in Islamic Thought and History* (USA: Oxford University Press, 2016).

———., 'Views of Jihad throughout History' (2007) 1 Religious Campus 167.

Al-Buti M., *Jihad in Islam* (Munzer Adel Absi tr, Dar al-Fikr: Damascus, 1995).

Al-Ghunaimi M. T., *The Muslim Conception of International Law and the Western Approach* (Martinus Nijhoff, The Hague, 1968).

An-Na'im A., *Islam and the Secular State* (Harvard University Press, 2009).

———., An-Na'im, *Toward an Islamic reformation: civil liberties, human rights, and international law* (Syracuse University Press 1996) 158.

al-Nawawi A., *Al-Alaqat al-Duwaliyya wa'l-Nuzum al-Qadaiyya (International Relations and Judicial Systems)* (Beirut: Dar-al-Kitab al-Arabi, 1974).

al-Rahman 'Utham A. (ed), *Tuhfat al-Ahwazi bi-Sharh Jami' al-Tirmidhi* (Cairo: Maktaba' at al-Ma'rifah) Hadith No. 1671.

Ali S. A., *A Critical Examination of the Life and Teachings of Mohammed* (London: Williams and Norgate, 1983).

Allam S., *The Ideological Battle: Egypt's Dar al-Iftaa Combats Radicalization* (The Grand Mufti of Egypt, 2016).

al-Jawziyya I. Q., *Zad al-Ma'ad fi Hady Khayr al-'Ibad*, vol. 2 (Cairo: al-Babi al-Halabi, 1970).

al-Tabari M. J., *AL-Tabari's Book of Jihad: A Translation from the Original Arabic* (Yasir S. Ibrahim tr, The Edwin Mellen Press, 2007).

Amin E. M. A., *Reclaiming Jihad: A Qur'anic Critique of Terrorism* (UK: The Islamic Foundation, 2014).

Asad M., *The Principle of State and Government in Islam* (Dar al-Andalus: Gibraltar, 1985).

Badar M., 'Jus in bello under Islamic International Law' (2013) 3 International Criminal Law Review 593.
Bakircioglu O., *Islam and Warfare: Context and Compatibility with International Law* (Routledge, 2014).
Bassiouni M. C. and Guellali A. (eds.), *Jihad and its Challenges to International and Domestic Law* (The Hague Academic Press, The Hague, 2010).
Bassiouni M. C., *The Sharia and Islamic Criminal Justice in Time of War and Peace* (Cambridge University Press, 2014).
Bassiouni M. C., 'Evolving Approaches to Jihad: From Self-defense to Revolutionary and Regime-Change Political Violence' (2007) 8 Chicago Journal of International Law 119.
Bennoune K., 'As-salama 'alaykum? Humanitarian Law in Islamic Jurisprudence' (1993) 15 Michigan Journal of International Law 622.
Bonney R., *Jihad: From Qur'an to bin Laden* (New York: Palgrave, 2004).
Bowering G. (ed), *The Princeton Encyclopedia of Islamic Political Thought* (Princeton University Press, 2013).
Bsoul L. A., *International Treaties (Mu'ahadat) in Islam: Theory and Practice in the Light of Islamic International Law (Siyar) according to Orthodox Schools* (University Press America, 2008).
Calasso G. and Lancioni G. (eds), *Dar al-Islam/Dar al-harb: Territories, People and Identities* (Brill, 2017).
Cohlberg E., *Belief and Law in Imami Shaism* (Variorum Aldershot: Great Britain, 1991).
Copinger-Symes T. R., 'Is Osama bin Laden's Fatwa Urging Jihad Against Americans' dated 23 February 1998 Justified by Islamic Law?' (2003) 3 Defence Studies 44.
El Fadl K. A., *Reasoning with God: Reclaiming Shari'ah in the Modern Age* (Rowman & Littlefield, 2014).
Esposito J. L., *Islam: The Straight Path* (Oxford: Oxford University Press, 1994).
———., *Unholy War: Terror in the Name of Islam* (Oxford University Press, 2002).
Firestone R., *Jihad: The Origin of Holy War in Islam* (Oxford University Press, 1999).
Fyzee A.A., *Outlines of Muhammadan Law* (Fifth edn, Oxford University Press, 2008).
Gauhar A. (ed), *The Challenges of Islam* (London: Islamic Council of Europe, 1978).
Glubb J., *A Short History of the Arab Peoples* (Hodder and Stoughton: London, 1969).
Hamidullah M., *Muslim Conduct of State* (4th edn, Lahore: Ashraf Press, 1961).
Hasan F. A., 'The Sources of Islamic Law' (1982) 76 American Society of International Law Proceedings 65.
Haykal M. H., *The Life of Muhammad* (Crescent Publishing, Delhi, 1990).

Hisham I., *Sirat al-Nabi (The Life of the Prophet)*, vol. 3 (Cairo: al-Maktaba al-Tajariyya al-Kubra, n.d.).

Hitti P. K., *History of the Arabs* (New York, St. Martin's Press, 1970).

Ibrahim A. F., *Pragmatism in Islamic Law: A Social and Intellectual History* (Syracuse University Press, 2015).

Ishaq I., *The Life of Muhammad: Sirat Rasul Allah* (Alfred Guillaume tr, 1967 edn, Oxford University Press, 1955).

Johnson J. T. and Kelsay J. (eds), *Cross, Crescent, and Sword: The Justification and Limitation of War in Western and Islamic Tradition* (New York: Greenwood Press, 1990).

Johnson J. T., *The Holy War Idea in Western and Islamic Traditions* (Pennsylvania State University Press, 1997).

Kathir I., *Tafsir al-Qur'an al-'Azim*, vol.1, (Riyadh: Dar al-Salam, 1998).

Kamali M. H., *Principles of Islamic Jurisprudence* (The Islamic Texts Society, 1991).

Kelsay J., *Arguing the Just War in Islam* (Harvard University Press, 2009).

———., *Islam and War: A Study in Comparative Ethics* (John Knox: Westminster, 1993).

Khadduri M., *Al-Shafi's Risala: Treatise on the Foundations of Islamic Jurisprudence* (2nd edn, the Islamic Texts Society, 1961).

———., *The Islamic Law of Nations: Shaybani's Siyar* (Baltimore: John Hopkins Press, 1966).

———., *War and Peace in the Law of Islam* (Baltimore: The John Hopkins Press, 1955).

Sharastani M. A., *Muslim Sects and Divisions: The Section on Muslim Sects in Kitab al-Milal wa 'I-Nihal* (A.K. Kazi and J.G. Flynn tr, Kegan Paul International, 1984).

Khan L. A., 'Jurodynamics of Islamic Law' (2008) 31 Rutgers Law Review 231.

Kissling H. J., *The Muslim World: A Historical Survey* (F.R.C. Bagley tr, E.J. Brill: Leiden, Netherlands, 1969).

Kurdi A. A., *The Islamic State: A Study based on the Islamic Holy Constitution* (Mansell Publishing: London, 1984).

Mahmassani S., *Falsafat al-Tashri Fi al-Islam: The Philosophy of Jurisprudence in Islam* (Farhat J. Ziadeh tr, Leiden: Brill, 1961).

———., 'The Principles of International Law in the Light of Islamic Doctrine' (1966) 117 Recueil des Cours 205.

Mahmoudi S., 'The Islamic Perception of the Use of Force in the Contemporary World' (paper presented at the International Law and the Islamic World: Towards a Multipolar International Legal System, organised by Max Planck Institute for Comparative and International Public Law, Heidelberg and the Institute for Political and International Studies, Tehran, Iran, 3-5 April 2004).

Mandaville P., *Islam and Politics* (Routledge, 2014).

Michot Y., 'Ibn Taymiyya's "New Mardin Fatwa". Is genetically modified Islam (GMI) carcinogenic?' (2011) 101 The Muslim World 130.
Moaddel M., 'The Study of Islamic Culture and Politics: An Overview and Assessment' (2002) 28 Annual Review of Sociology 359.
Muhammad P. G., Kalin I. and Hashim Kamali M. H. (eds), *War and Peace in Islam: The Uses and Abuses of Jihad* (MABDA, 2013).
Mutahhari A. M., *Jihad and Shahadat* (The Institute for Research and Islamic Studies, 1986).
Nafi B., 'Fatwa and war: On the Allegiance of the American Muslim Soldiers in the Aftermath of September 11' (2004) 1 Islamic Law and Society 78.
Nasr S. H., *The Heart of Islam: Enduring Values for Humanity* (New York: Harper Collins Publishers, 2004).
Netton I. R., *A Popular Dictionary of Islam* (Curzon Press: London, 1992).
Peters R., *Islam and Colonialism: The Doctrine of Jihad in Modern History* (The Hague: Mouton Publishers, 1979).
Rabb I. A., '"We the Jurists": Islamic constitutionalism in Iraq' (2008) 10 University of Pennsylvania Journal of Constitutional Law 527.
Rahman A., *Encyclopedia of Seerah*, vol I (The Muslim School Trust: London, 1985).
Schacht J., *Origins of Muhammadan Jurisprudence* (Oxford: Clarendon Press, 1967).
———., *An Introduction to Islamic Law* (Oxford: Clarendon Press, 1982).
Shaban M. A., *Islamic History: A New Interpretation* (Cambridge University Press, 1971).
Shah N. A., *Self-Defense in Islamic and International Law* (UK: Palgrave Macmillan, 2008).
———., *Islamic Law and the Law of Armed Conflict: The Armed Conflict in Pakistan* (Routledge: London, 2011).
Shah N. A., 'The Use of Force under Islamic Law' (2013) 24 European Journal of International Law 343.
Shaltut M., *Jihad in Mediaeval and Modern Islam* (Rudolph Peters tr, E.J. Brill, Leiden, 1977).
Sharastani M., *Muslim Sects and Divisions: The Section on Muslim Sects in Kitab al-Milal wa 'l-Nihal* (A.K. Kazi and J.G. Flynn tr, Kegan Paul International, n.d.).
The New Mardin Declaration' (27 April 2010) http://iqra.ca/2010/the-new-mardin-declaration/ accessed 20 February 2020.
Thomas P. H., *Dictionary of Islam* (W.H. Allen & Co: London, 1992).
Van Engeland A., 'Statehood, Proto States and International Law: New Challenges, Looking at the case of ISIS' (2016) paper was presented at American Society of International Law (ASIL) Annual Conference.
———., 'The Balance Between Islamic Law, Customary Law and Human Rights in Islamic Constitutionalism Through the Prism of Legal Pluralism' (2014) 4 Cambridge Journal of International and Comparative Law 1321.

———., 'Islam as Religion of Peace: an Articulated Reply to Terrorism', in R. Barnidge Jr (ed), *The Liberal Way of War: Legal Perspectives* (Ashgate, 2013).

———., 'Islam and the Protection of Civilians in the Conduct of Hostilities: the Asymmetrical war from the Transnational Terrorist Groups' Viewpoints and from the Muslim Modernists' Viewpoints', in C. Bassiouni C. and Guellali A. (eds), *Jihad And The Challenges Of International And Domestic Law* (Cambridge University Press, 2010).

———., 'When Two Visions of a Just World Clash: International Humanitarian Law and Islamic Humanitarian Law' (2006) American Society of International Law Proceedings 156.

Vanhullebusch M., *War and the Law in Islamic World* (Brill 2015).

———., 'Islamic Law and the Responsibility to Protect' (2010) 4 Human Rights and International Legal Discourse, 191.

Waddy C., *The Muslim Mind* (Grosvenor: London, 1990).

Weeramantry C. G., *Islamic Jurisprudence: An International Perspective* (Palgrave Macmillan, 1988).

Yusuf H. O., 'Transitional Justice in the Middle East and North Africa' (2017) 14 Muslim World Journal of Human Rights 145.

Zawati H., *Is Jihad a Just War? War, Peace and Human Rights under Islamic and Public International Law* (Edwin Mellen, 2001).

Zebiri K., *Mahmud Shaltut and Islamic Modernism* (Oxford: Clarendon Press, 1993).

CHAPTER 4

Legitimacy of Use of Force in Islamic International Law: The Legal-Political Legacies

4.1 Introduction

The legitimacy of use of force by and against Muslim states has been a subject of contentious debate among states, armed non-state actors, academics, and politicians. This debate has evolved into a key question of 'the legitimacy of use of force' particularly in most Muslim states.[1] This is because most international and non-international armed conflicts in the twenty-first century have involved one or more Muslim states. For instance, the invasion of Afghanistan in 2001, the Iraq War in 2003, the conflict in Libya in 2009, the Syrian crisis that started in 2011, and the ongoing conflict in Yemen are among the gravest armed and humanitarian conflicts of the century. The international and internal armed conflicts devastatingly affected the Muslim states and armed non-state actors functioning within these states. As a result, they have raised the question of the legitimacy of use of force. Muslim states and armed non-state actors have answered this question with reference to their religious principles, legal framework, and political position.

[1] The term 'Muslim states' denotes those states where the majority of the population are Muslims. It does not connote that those states are necessarily governed by either Islamic law or Shari'a.

M. Z. Sabuj, *The Legitimacy of Use of Force in Public and Islamic International Law*,
https://doi.org/10.1007/978-3-030-77298-7_4

The place of Islam in Muslim states is not only a religion but also a source of law.[2] Most of these legal principles are sourced from the Shari'a law, which is the primary source of Islamic law. However, the power to apply these legal principles lies in political authorities such as the states and armed non-state actors. Hence the relationship between Islam as a religion and law as enforced by a political institution at the state level and inter-state level is an important one. In other words, Islamic law and politics go hand in hand not least when it comes to the use of force. In this relationship, Islamic law and politics play a significant role in the law-making process in Muslim states, and for this reason, these two cannot be separated.[3] As a result, the answer to the legitimacy question must be given within not only the purview of Islamic law but also the politics that shaped it.

As far as Islamic law is concerned the legitimacy question has been answered from the perspective of Shari'a, which sits at the core of Islam as a religion. The Shari'a principles primarily consist of the Qur'an and Sunna (narrations of the words and actions of Prophet Muhammad). Similarly, the legal position of Islamic international law about the use of force travelled beyond the Shari'a to include juristic works (*Fiqh*), arbitral awards, and *Siyar*, which is composed of treaties, pacts, and other state practice.[4] As a result, the legal position offers an analysis of the main sources of Islamic law, such as the Qur'an, Sunna, Ijma (consensus), Qiyas (analogy), and *Siyar*. This analysis shows a crucial interplay between the law and politics, which explains the legal and political legacies of the use of force in Islamic international law. This analysis also shows the vital role played by political Islam in the evolution and transformation of the legal-political legacies of use of force. These legacies have provided a productive basis to answer the legitimacy question which is 'where does the legitimacy of use of force lie—Public or Islamic international law?'

This chapter begins with a theoretical analysis of the role of political Islam. It shows the extent to which Islamic law and politics go hand in hand. It gives a detailed outline of the legal framework of use of force in Islamic international law from legal and political perspectives. It shows that a combination of the legal and political legacies can answer the legitimacy question, but that answer may not always provide a legitimate basis

[2] Rabb, '"We the Jurists", 527.

[3] Ibid.

[4] For a detailed analysis on 'the meaning and significance of *Siyar* in Islamic international law on the use of force' see Chap. 3.

for use of force. This chapter argues that the legitimacy of extraterritorial use of force, as claimed by armed non-state actors, mainly depends on the legitimacy of use of force in Public international law.

4.2 The Role of Political Islam in the Formation and Evolution of the Legitimacy of Use of Force

The use of force in Islamic international law is founded and developed on the Qur'anic text as well as the Sunna of the Prophet.[5] However, the history of Islam suggests that political Islam has a significant role to play in its evolution and transformation.[6] Following the death of Prophet Muhammad in 632 CE, the legal framework started to adopt the precedents of caliphs, rulers, and non-state actors that took place during the early Islamic history and were highly influenced by political considerations.[7] During this time, the political crises that occurred in resolving the issues surrounding leadership (Caliphate) in the Muslim community shaped the legal framework to a great extent.[8] The oppression or persecution (*fitna*) that resulted from these political crises supplied the key political tool to the legitimacy of use of force. As spreading *fitna* is prohibited in Islam and this can be caused by rulers as well as armed non-state actors,[9] the claim of the legitimate use of force to end persecution came from both.[10] Therefore, the legitimacy question has been answered by invoking a suitably tailored political tool to claim the reciprocal right to use force to end oppression and persecution by states and armed non-state actors respectively. In this way, political Islam played a very important role in the evolution and transformation of the legal framework. It influenced the multiple manifestations of the legitimate authority to use force by competing voices.

The role of political Islam also hugely influenced the answer to the legitimacy question at the inter-state level. In the formative period of Islam (between the seventh and twelfth century CE) peace treaties had

[5] An-Na'im, *Islam and the Secular State*, 12, 88.

[6] Fadel, 'State and Sharia', 93.

[7] Al-Dawoody, *The Islamic Law of War*, 149.

[8] al-Nawawī, *Al-Majmū'*, 337; al-Māwardī, 'Al-ahkām as-sultānīya wal-wilāyāt ad-dīnīya' in Mu'awwaḍ and al-Mawjūd (eds.), *Al-Ḥāwī al-Kabīr*, 104.

[9] al Shaybani, *Kitab al-Sunnah*, 507; see also Abi-Shayba, *Al-Musannaf*, 622.

[10] Asad, "Islamic Humanitarian Law" cited in Bassiouni, *The Sharia and Islamic Criminal Justice*, 166.

been concluded between Muslim and non-Muslim states.[11] Political considerations played a key role in the conclusion of many peace treaties.[12] These peace treaties took precedence over the Shari'a.[13] For instance, in the Treaty of *Hudaibiyya* Prophet Muhammad entered into a peace agreement with the Quraysh (a Meccan tribe that held political control in the city) whereby the Muslims were barred from going to pilgrimage (*hajj*) in Mecca despite the Qur'an and Sunna specifically required all able Muslims to go to pilgrimage as it is one of the five pillars of Islam.[14] Hajj was made obligatory long before the conclusion of the treaty of *Hudaibiyya* in 628 CE. It was provided as one of the mandatory pillars of Islam in chapter 3:97 of the Qur'an, which was revealed very shortly after the Battles of Badr and Uhud in 624 CE and 625 CE respectively.[15] The Qur'an proclaims that:

> And Hajj (pilgrimage to Mecca) to the house (Ka'bah) is a duty that mankind owes to Allah, those who can afford the expenses.[16]

Moreover, a hadith of the Prophet has been reported in 'Al-Bukhari and Muslim', which stated that:

> Al-Masjid al-Haram (in Mecca) was built by Ibrahim al-Khalil, whose religion the Jews and Christians claim they follow. However, they do not perform Hajj to the house that Ibrahim built by Allah's command, and to which he invited the people to perform Hajj.[17]

Furthermore, there are Qur'anic references that show that Hajj was made obligatory long before the treaty. For example, chapters 2:124–127 and 22:27–30 state that:

> Ibrahim, along with his son Ismael, raised the foundations of a house that is identified by most commentators as the Kaaba. After the placing of the Black Stone in the Eastern corner of the Kaaba, Ibrahim received a revelation

[11] Watt, *The Formative Period of Islamic Thought*, 19.

[12] Bsoul, *International Treaties (Mu'ahadat) in Islam*, 115.

[13] Ibid.

[14] The full text of the treaty can be found in Hamidullah, *Muslim Conduct of State*, 266–268.

[15] Shīrāzī, *Tafsīr-i Nimūnā*, 408.

[16] Al-Qur'an 3:97, Abu Yusuf translation.

[17] *Ibn Kathir*, 33.

in which Allah told the aged prophet that he should now go and proclaim the pilgrimage to mankind.[18]

Since then pilgrimage, although with disruption and irregularity, continued until the conquest of Mecca in 632 CE when its regularity was reinstated.[19] The pilgrimage season in 622 CE, the year when the Prophet migrated to Medina, was the thirteenth.[20] The Qur'anic provisions, hadith, and history of Islam suggest that Hajj was made obligatory before the conclusion of the treaty. However, despite it was made obligatory the Prophet agreed to suspend any pilgrimage to Mecca to avoid bloodsheds and aggression that Quraysh held towards Muslims, and this decision was based on political considerations such as public welfare (*Masalahah*) rather than religion.[21] Similarly, the Prophet honoured a provision of the treaty of *Hudaibiyya*, where he decided to make an exception to the Qur'anic provision which provided that 'persecution is worse than killing.'[22] One of the clauses of the treaty allowed the extradition of any male refugee from Medina to Mecca but not the other way around. Abu Jandal sought refuge in Medina and begged the Prophet to grant him asylum. The Prophet was aware of the dilemma that on the one hand Abu Jandal would be persecuted upon extradition and, on the other hand, if he was not extradited the peace treaty would be broken which could lead to loss of lives in both camps due to resumption of war.[23] The Prophet decided to extradite Abu Jandal according to the treaty.[24] Although this decision was inconsistent with the Qur'anic command which proffered killing over persecution, the Prophet honoured the treaty as a politically legitimate factor which is also backed in the Qur'an.[25] The Prophet chose to stick to the treaty provisions by pragmatically preferring one Qur'anic provision over the other based on 'public welfare'.[26] These are guidelines of the Prophet which the

[18] Al-Qur'an 2:124–127 and 22:27–30, Abu Yusuf translation.

[19] Salahi, *Muhammad*, 21.

[20] Ibid.

[21] For a discussion about the role of *Masalahah* in addressing the legitimacy argument, see Chap. 5.

[22] Al-Qur'an 2:217, Abu Yusuf translation.

[23] Pirzada, 'Islam and International Law' in Gauhar (ed), *The Challenges of Islam*, 196.

[24] Ibid.

[25] For a discussion on the Qur'anic provisions concerning the law of treaties, see Chap. 3.

[26] For a discussion on 'public welfare (*masalahah*)' please, see Chap. 5.

Muslim community is commanded to follow.[27] Therefore, public welfare is an established political practice in Islamic international law on the use of force that was transformed into Islamic legal methodology.[28] This example shows that political considerations have a crucial role to play in the evolution of Islamic international law and it may take precedence over a clear principle of religion. This has created a legal-political legacy illustrating a situation where politics and religion should be kept separate.

Further evolution of Islamic international law has taken place in the modern world since the struggle for decolonization and the resultant division of the world into nation-states. Reshaping of religious authority at the state level during and after the formation of modern nation-states has played a significant role in the creation of legal-political legacies by states and non-state actors. In Muslim states, the exercise of governmental authorities by political parties that promised to adopt Islam not only as a religion but also as a political means to the legitimate exercise of sovereign power was very popular since the struggle for decolonization.[29] For example, the invocation of jihad to legitimate armed struggle against colonial power became a very popular political agenda among Muslim leaders and rulers in the colonial period in places such as Egypt, Africa, and India.[30] This trend continued further even after decolonization.

Since the division of the Muslim community (*ummah*) into independent nation-states, contemporary discussion of the use of force in the context of Islamic international law is usually oriented towards the concept of jihad.[31] This concept has been used and abused by states and armed non-state actors in Muslim states to claim the legitimacy of use of force. Examples are the call for jihad by Afghan leaders during the Russian invasion of Afghanistan in 1979,[32] Iran's call for jihad to its citizens and beyond during the war against Iraq in 1980–1988.[33] Similarly, the then President of Iraq Saddam Hussein's call for jihad to Iraqi people against the

[27] The Qur'an has commanded all Muslims to follow the guidelines of the prophets. See Al-Qur'an 4:90.

[28] Opwis, *Masalaha and the Purpose of the Law*, 65.

[29] Peters, *Islam and Colonialism*, 86.

[30] Ibid., 86; see also Hitti, *History of the Arabs*, 145.

[31] Mahmoudi, The Islamic Perception of the Use of Force in the Contemporary World, page 2.

[32] Shah, The Use of Force, 343.

[33] Rezamand, Use of Religious Doctrine, 83.

imminent attack of the US in 2003.[34] These are notable examples where politics and religion concurrently created legal-political legacies on the use of force. These legacies have given rise to a dilemma between the religious principles of use of force and political necessity for the same. Whereas the religion recognizes the legitimacy of use of force to defend the Muslims from aggression such as that of the Russian invasion of Afghanistan in 1979, it does not recognize the legitimacy of use of force in situations such as the Iraq-Iran war. This is because the latter is a political call which the religion does not regard as legitimate. This religiopolitical scrutiny of the use of force applies indiscriminately against Muslim and non-Muslim states. Therefore, any recourse to force against another state, whether Muslim or non-Muslim, for which the religion does not provide the legitimate basis is purely political and illustrates the situation where religion and politics should not be kept separate. The religiopolitical legacy has created a fundamental principle of use of force in Islamic international law, which prohibits any recourse to force in promoting biased or partisan political interests. This situation is different from that of *Hudaibiyya*, stated above, where a legal-political legacy had been created that benefited both parties by avoiding unnecessary bloodsheds as opposed to the Iraq-Iran war, where it benefited only the party which invoked such use of force. Moreover, Islamic international law, as developed from *Siyar* to a great extent, does not allow the use of force by Muslim states against each other. The prohibition of use of force between Muslim states can also be found in the state practice between *Dar al-Islam* and *Dar al-Harb*.[35]

Following decolonization, the nature of modern nation-states in Muslim majority populated territories, as culturally and historically distinct from Europe where they emerged, developed a hybrid pattern that not only adopted Islam as a source of religious guiding principles of sovereign powers but also imported political trends from the West such as lobbying, the formation of political parties and their participation in elections, and entering into broad coalitions with non-Islamist groups and parties.[36] Whereas the ruling class was unable to obtain complete sovereignty from their previous colonial power on the one hand, they were under immense pressure from the local population to govern according to

[34] Mahmoudi, The Islamic Perception of the Use of Force in the Contemporary, 7.
[35] An-Na'im, Toward an Islamic reformation, 149.
[36] Mandaville, Islam and Politics, 66.

religious principles.[37] This situation had resulted in a dilemma as the ruling authorities needed support from both the former colonial power and local population during the infancy of the states.[38] For example, Egypt obtained its formal independence from the British rule in 1922, but the country was jointly governed with an Egyptian Monarch until the end of the Second World War.[39] Moreover, the new Egyptian ruler was under immense pressure from non-state actors such as Muslim Brotherhood that were demanding to govern according to religious principles as established by the Shari'a.[40] This pressure became very acute because of a wide gap between the rich and the poor, which resulted in social inequality and the deprivation caused by rapidly rising economic and political expectations that were not being met by the ruling authorities.[41] As a result, the religio-political legacies created in this relationship between the states and non-state actors in Muslim territories played a crucial role in the evolution and transformation of the legal framework on the use of force.

Following the formation of new nation-states, most of the ruling authorities faced huge challenges to take their respective nations to the desired directions of the local population. They did not effectively govern the states because of their failure in keeping social, economic, and political order. For example, the ruling authorities struggled to maintain economic stability following the Second World War due to the effect of the Cold war, civil conflict, and defeat in war in states such as Egypt and Pakistan.[42] As a result, they were accused of failing to govern effectively, and the reason for such failure was claimed to be the non-institutionalization of Islam in the political order of states. This situation witnessed a rise of Muslim Brotherhood in Egypt in the late 1950s and 1960s, which received huge support from the local population. A similar movement occurred in Algeria between 1962 and 2011.[43] These movements gave rise to the mobilization of non-state actors that aimed to pursue Islamic political order at the state level.

Armed non-state actors often challenged the legitimacy of use of force by state authorities on religious principles as outlined above. In response

[37] Roy, The Failure of Political Islam, 33.
[38] Pahuja, *Decolonising International Law*, 44.
[39] Mandaville, *Islam and Politics*, 74.
[40] Ibid., 94.
[41] Gurr, *Why Men Rebel*, 25.
[42] Black, *The History of Islamic Political Thought*, 16.
[43] Mandaville, *Islam and Politics*, 117.

to this challenge, the state authorities often claimed justification for such use of force on political grounds such as the government's power to use force to maintain stability.[44] With this claim of justified use of force together with the support from their foreign power, the state authorities often tried to suppress armed non-state actors as their political opponents.[45] However, this suppression also pressed for a necessity among non-state actors to institutionalize the religion by establishing an Islamic political order at the state level by removing the regime from political power.[46] The feel of this necessity was also bifurcated whereby some advocated for the totalization of Islam and others advocated for its application in limited areas such as personal law. For example, whereas Mohammad 'Abduh advocated for the totalization of Islam at the state level, his follower Rashid Ridā preferred the application of Islam in religious rituals and personal law rather than in the political affairs of the state.[47] Whilst the earlier advocated for a caliphate system the latter insisted to embrace the moral guidance of religion as a path to good governance and a solution to corruption.

Whereas the proponents of setting up an Islamic caliphate were revolutionary and prepared to use force against those ruling authorities who manifested Islam as a source of spiritual and moral principles, they were very tolerant to modern secular states.[48] The legal institutionalization of Islam at the state level was a political agenda, and the legacy created by recourse to force for this purpose was purely political. The legitimacy of use of force to institutionalize Islam at the state level or in a caliphate setting is questionable in the modern world. This is because modern nation-states had formed mainly on nationalism whereby their main purpose was to become independent from a colonial or foreign power.[49] This was a political agenda independent of religion.[50] In this setting, many of the armed non-state actors involved in the politics of forming nation-states

[44] An-Na'im, *Toward an Islamic reformation*, 150.

[45] Pahuja, *Decolonising International Law*, 44.

[46] Mandaville, *Islam and Politics*, 76.

[47] Ibid., 68; An-Na'im has also advocated against the totalization of Islam in a Muslim state.

[48] An-Na'im, *Islam and the Secular State*, 46.

[49] Moaddel, *Islamic Modernism, Nationalism, and Fundamentalism*, 211; see also Pahuja, *Decolonising International Law*, 44.

[50] Rabb, '"We the Jurists": Islamic constitutionalism in Iraq', 527; for contra see An-Na'im, *Islam and the Secular State*, 9.

had little interest in pursuing a totalization of an Islamic political order.[51] Therefore, seeking to invoke legitimacy from the religion where the underlying political force was to establish independent nation-states free from foreign intervention became problematic. This political legacy, independent from any religiopolitical agenda, failed to incorporate in the legal framework of Islamic international law and accordingly failed to create a legal-political legacy. As a result, the formation of a caliphate-style Islamic political order lost its popularity to a large extent among the Muslims of newly established nation-states.

The question of the legitimacy of pursuing Islamic political order by armed non-state actors and moral guidance by others involves a complementary analysis between religion and law. This is because both are within the sphere of religious principles which are the main sources of law and morality. For instance, the main sources of Islamic international law (as a body of laws) are composed of religious principles such as the prohibition of aggression and morality such as acting in unjust manner. The former has become law and the latter a moral principle, but both have emanated from the religion. In this setting, the legitimacy of use of force by armed non-state actors to end persecution at the state level and exercise their right to self-defence at the inter-state level is heavily dependent on Islamic international law, which allows the use of force against an unjust ruler who persecutes the non-state actors and colludes with foreign powers in that process.[52] However, this legal entitlement should be invoked and exercised in a just manner, which is purely a moral factor as opposed to legal. The combination of the legal position and moral considerations provides the legitimacy of such use of force in Islamic law. Therefore, in this situation law and religion should not be separated from each other to secure the legitimacy of use of force. For this reason, as long as the use of force by and against non-state actors is concerned, the legitimacy of such use of force requires an interplay between Islamic *jus ad bellum* (authority to use force as a legal principle) and *jus in bello* (recourse to use of force in a just manner). On this footing, it is important to note that the use of force in Islamic law does not differentiate between international and non-international armed conflicts; rather it makes the universal application of

[51] Mandaville, *Islam and Politics*, 76.

[52] El Fadl, 'Ahkam al-Bughat' in Johnson and Kelsay (eds), *Cross, Crescent and Sword*, 156; see also al-Mawardi, *al-Hawi al-Kabir*, XIII: 97; Al-Dawoody, *The Islamic Law of War*, 151; Badar and Sabuj, The Islamic Law of Rebellion, 365.

the rights and status of armed non-state actors on an equal footing with the rights and duties of the rulers.[53] However, the togetherness of the law and religion does not always provide the legitimate basis of use of force such as where the religion has commanded to use force without giving any consideration to moral factors. The recent movements to set up and expand an Islamic caliphate by recourse to violent measures by states and armed non-state actors are notable examples as discussed above. In these situations, the law and religion must be kept separate to draw the dividing line between legitimate use of force as recognized in Islamic law and illegitimate use of force which has not secured any place beyond the religion.

4.3 The Legal Framework of Use of Force in Islamic International Law

The use of force in Islamic international law may be studied from the viewpoints of Islamic jurisprudence and Muslim states' practice.[54] Whereas Islamic jurisprudence has developed surrounding the main sources of the religion such as the Qur'an, Sunna, Ijma, and Qiyas as well as the concomitant juristic opinions of different schools of legal thought (*Madhhab, pl. Madhahib*), the foundation of Islamic international law was built on *Siyar*.[55] The founding elements of *Siyar* have paved the way for political Islam to mingle with the legal framework.[56]

In this chapter, the reference to 'Political Islam' includes the process through which state actors pursue governmental power in the context of modern nation-states and armed non-state actors challenge such governmental power in the process of their establishment as political groups. This political process is mainly premised on the legitimacy argument. For instance, governments of Muslim states pursue governmental authorities in the context of nation-states to exercise sovereign power at the state level and inter-state level. Similarly, non-state actors challenge such sovereign power for their lack of legitimate authority to use force nationally and

[53] Okon, Islam, War and International Humanitarian Law, 100; This has also been argued by de Vattel, 'The Law of Nations' cited in McConnell, *Extracting Accountability from Non-State actors*, 133.

[54] Mahmoudi, The Islamic Perception of the Use of Force in the Contemporary World, 13.

[55] For an outline of the components of *Siyar*, see Chap. 3.

[56] For a discussion on the connection between 'time of the caliphs' and other Muslim rulers' foundation for Siyar and the political element in Siyar contested by nation-states and non-state actors in the nineteenth and twentieth century', see Chap. 3.

internationally. As a result, both states and non-state actors challenge each other for lack of legitimate authority to use force. However, the challenges posed by them show a crucial interplay between religion and politics. It is apparent that state authorities robustly challenge armed non-state actors about the legitimacy of use of force for their lack of political authority. It is also evident that armed non-state actors challenge the authority of states to use force for their arbitrary exercise of political power and lack of religious authority for the same. These challenges have developed counter-claims of the legitimate use of force against each other by states and armed non-state actors.

The state authorities claim that armed non-state actors do not have any legitimate authority to use force against them according to the main source of Islamic law. For instance, they claim that the Qur'anic provisions authorize state authorities to use force against the non-state actors to maintain stability.[57] They also refer to one of the jurists of the Sunni school,[58] Ahmad Ibn Hanbal, who had reportedly stated that Muslims should obey their rulers and leave any decision as to 'use of force' at their disposal.[59] Similarly, armed non-state actors counterclaim that they have legitimate authority to use force against the state authorities because the Qur'an commands to 'enjoin good and forbid evil'.[60] For example, in the *Al Mahdi* case before the International Criminal Court (ICC) the accused relied on the principle of 'enjoining what is right and forbidding what is wrong' (*al-amr bi'l-ma'ruf wa'l-nahy'an al-munkar*) as a justification for the destruction of cultural property in Mali.[61]

In addition, they also relied on the Prophet's Sunna where he was reported to have said that 'to hear and obey the ruler is obligatory, so long as one is not commanded to disobey God for if one is commanded to disobey God, he shall not hear or obey.'[62] Moreover, while the Qur'an and Sunna do not explicitly command the use of force against unjust rulers, most non-state actors make reference to the following Qur'anic verse which creates a powerful symbolic construct to justify the use of force against state authorities:

[57] Al-Qur'an 49:9–10. Abu Yusuf translation; see also Johnson and Kelsey (eds.), *Cross, Crescent and Sword*, 152.

[58] A school of thought which most Muslims adhere to.

[59] Hanbal., *Musnad*, 279.

[60] Al-Qur'an 3:104, 9:71, 9:112, 22:41, 3:114, 7:157, 9:67, 31:17, Abu Yusuf Translation.

[61] *Prosecutor v. Al Mahdi* (2017) 17 International Criminal Law Review 486–516.

[62] al-'Asqalani, *Fath al-Bari bi Sharh Sahih al-Bukhari*, 121.

Would not you fight in the way of Allah for *al-mustadafin* (the oppressed socially weak Muslims) from men, women, and children who pray: Our Lord! Take us from this city of the oppressive people and appoint for us from Your side a guardian and appoint us from Your side a protector.[63]

In addition to referring to the main sources of Islamic law in support of using force against the state authorities, there were practices and conduct of many of the Prophet's companions and several of the early jurists who took part in, supported, or sympathized with the use of force by armed non-state actors.[64] For example, some versions of the Sunna of the Prophet have stated that a ruler should be obeyed as long as he implements the book of God or, in some versions, as long as he leads Muslims according to the book of God.[65] Other versions make the duty of blind obedience applicable only in the time of the Prophet.[66] A set of widely cited Sunna explicitly states that a ruler should not be obeyed if he commands a sin or that he should be obeyed only to the extent that he commands what is good and just.[67] These Sunna promote or encourage armed resistance to rulers in one form or another. A common form of this genre states that the best form of jihad is a word of truth spoken before an unjust ruler.[68] Moreover, Caliph Ali reportedly said that if the Kharijites[69] rebel against

[63] Al-Qur'an 4:75, Abu Yusuf translation.

[64] Badar and Sabuj, The Islamic Law of Rebellion, 365.

[65] al Shaybani, *Kitab al-Sunnah*, 492; see also Hanbal, *Musnad*, VI:451; al-Hajjaj, *Al-Fami' al-Sahih*, VI:15; Ibn Maja, *Sunan*, II:955; al-Qastalani, *Irshad al-Sari Sharh Sahih al-Bukhari*, X:170; see also al-Nawawi, *Al-Majmu'*, XII:468.

[66] Hanbal, *Musnad*, II:279.

[67] Dawud, *Sunan*, IV:94; al-Bazzar, *Al-Bahr al-Zakhkhar*, II:204; al-Hajjaj, *Al-Fami' al-Sahih*, VI:15; Ibn Maja, *Sunan*, II:956.

[68] al-Tirmidhi, *al-Fami' al-Sahih*, 409.

[69] The Kharijites [or Khawarij] were the first identifiable sect of Islam. Their identity emerged as followers of [Prophet] Muhammad attempted to determine the extent to which one could deviate from ideal norms of behaviour and still be called Muslim. The extreme Kharijite position was that Muslims who commit grave sins effectively reject their religion, entering the ranks of apostates, and therefore deserve capital punishment. This position was considered excessively restrictive by the majority of Muslims, as well as by moderate Kharijites, who held that a professed Muslim could not be declared an unbeliever (*kafir*). The Kharijites believed it was forbidden to live among those who did not share their views, thus acquiring the name by which they are known in mainstream Islamic historiography—*khawarij* means 'seceders' or 'those who exit the community'. Radical Kharijites, on the other hand, declared those who disagreed with their position to be apostates, and they launched periodic military

an unjust ruler, then Muslims should not fight them because, in this situation, they may have a legitimate cause for their rebellion.[70]

4.3.1 Justification of the Use of Force by States

The use of offensive force under the banner of defensive jihad is not relatively new in the practice of Muslim states. Such practice can be traced back to the thirteenth century CE when Ibn Taymiyya declared offensive jihad against the Crusaders and Mongols who threatened Islam.[71] Similarly, Muslim religious scholars declared jihad against the British during the Indian Sepoy Mutiny in 1857–1858.[72] In addition, when Sultan Abd al-Hamid (1878–1909), the then Head of the Ottoman Empire, was declared Caliph of Islam, which entitled him to invoke jihad against European intervention or pressure, both the Sultan and rulers of countries that were separated from the Empire after the First World War often sought to use jihad as a weapon against British and French domination in the Middle East and other Asiatic and African countries.[73]

Since then jihad had invoked to support political goals, such as when the Ottoman Empire went to war against Britain and France in 1914, the Caliph declared jihad and called upon Muslims in the Middle East and India to rise against the British and their allies.[74] Sharif Husayn of the

attacks against mainstream Muslim centres until they ceased to be a military threat in the late eighth century CE. See Sonn and Farrar, "Kharijites" in Oxford Bibliographies.

[70] Abi-Shayba, *Al-Musannaf*, 737. 'During the fourth Caliph 'Ali's reign (656–661 CE), the Khawarij and Shi'a movements split from the Sunni majority. The Battle of Siffin (657 CE) had pitted Mu'awiya, the then governor of Syria, against 'Ali, with the former charging 'Ali with not bringing the third Caliph Uthman's killers to justice. However, 'Ali refused to fight his Muslim brothers, and so they agreed to settle their dispute through arbitration. A civil war nevertheless ensued, as 12,000 of 'Ali's supporters (who subsequently became the Khawarij) disagreed with settling the matter by means of human arbitration. They contended that 'Ali should have turned to divine judgement and applied the law of retaliation, as prescribed by the Qur'an. Citing their slogan *la hukma illa lillah* ('Authority belongs to God alone'), the Khawarij called upon all Muslims to follow the Qur'an to the letter. This was the first occurrence in Islamic history of a sect appropriating the right to declare *takfir* against fellow Muslims, and the rise of the Khawarij.' See Badar et al., The Radical Application of the Islamic Concept of *Takfir*, 134.

[71] Khadduri and Ghareeb, *War in the Gulf*, 230.

[72] Ahmed, 'Role of the Ulema in Indo-Muslim History' XXXI Studia Islamica, 1, 10, cited in al-Ghunaimi, *The Muslim Conception of International Law*, 142.

[73] Khadduri and Ghareeb, *War in the Gulf*, 231.

[74] Toynbee, *Survey of International Affairs*, 43.

Hijaz (an ally of the British) counteracting the Caliph's declaration invoked jihad as an Arab ruler.[75] Similarly, jihad had been used as a weapon to propagate the use of force by state authorities regularly when they needed to use force extraterritorially. Majid Khadduri and Edmund Ghareeb aptly noted the following occurrence of events when jihad had been invoked by states:

> During the inter-war years, the Syrian leaders invoked jihad in their struggle against the French in 1920 and 1928. In 1936, the Mufti of Jerusalem invoked jihad against the British. In Iraq, nationalist opposition to the British in the revolt of 1920 and the military uprising in 1941 were legitimised by the invocation of jihad in order to provide public support against foreign intervention.[76]

In the 1980s Ayatollah Khomeini's revolutionary call for jihad shaped the attitude of Iranian people and their view of Iraq.[77] His radical revolutionary-style government in Iran was felt as a threat by Saddam Hussein in Iraq and his Western allies.[78] Conversely, Iraq's occupation of few territories of Iran was the focal point for propagating jihad against Iraq and its supporters.[79] This call for jihad also became popular among the Shi'a population, the Kurdish population, and other secular opposition groups residing in Iraq. In addition, an Iranian-backed organization committed to the imposition of strict Islamic rule throughout Iraq, the Supreme Assembly of Islamic Revolution in Iraq, was active from 1986 aiming for regime change in Baghdad.[80] Iran had also facilitated extraterritorial use of force through a jihadist group in Beirut, Lebanon, against the American and French Military Personnel in October 1983 and in France in December of the same year.[81] All these attacks were carried out based on liberation jihad against foreign interference. This had possibly given Osama bin Laden and his followers a platform to propagate

[75] Ibid., 44.

[76] Khadduri and Ghareeb, *War in the Gulf*, 231.

[77] Kepel, *Jihad*, 109.

[78] Johnson, 'Mustazafin and Taughatti' in Ashton and Gibson (eds), *The Iraq-Iran War*, 59.

[79] Ibid., 60.

[80] Ibid., 66.

[81] Razoux, 'France's Involvement in Iraq-Iran War' in Ashton and Gibson (eds) *The Iraq-Iran War*, 220.

defensive jihad in an offensive nature but from the viewpoint of armed non-state actors.

In the Iraq-Kuwait war, Iraq's invocation of jihad against foreign power (in this case the Security Council and the Western states and their allies) which intervened in the dispute between Iraq and Kuwait had resulted in division among the Muslim scholars. Saddam Hussein certainly sought to mobilize Islamic sentiment behind him, calling for jihad and placing the Islamic credo *la Allah ila Allah* ('there is no God but God') on the Iraqi flag.[82] Some supported Iraq's call of jihad on the ground that the foreign powers are unbelievers, and their interference would deprive the Muslims of the opportunity to resolve their disputes by peaceful means according to the Islamic standards.[83] On the other hand, others backed Kuwait's argument that Iraq's invasion of Kuwait was the reason for foreign intervention, and Iraq was solely responsible for this.[84]

Although Iraq's call for jihad had been supported by few Muslim states like Algeria, Tunisia, Libya, Sudan, and Yemen, Saddam Hussein's appeal to Muslims and the declaration of jihad was considered hypocritical, intended to create dissension among the coalition powers and to extract concessions before withdrawal from Kuwait.[85] This situation was similar to that of the First World War (stated above) when the Ottoman Sultan (an ally of Germany) and the ruler of Saudi Arabia (an ally of Britain) declared jihad against each other. As a result, the use of force for jihad became the subject of a popular political agenda rather than purely Islamic.

4.3.2 The Justification of the Use of Force by Armed Non-state Actors

Relying on the religious authority, discussed above, non-state actors like Al-Qa'ida have been trying to justify their violent actions. They claim that, they can legitimately exercise their religious authority to declare defensive actions against aggression by non-Muslim states which constructively resort to aggressive force for their benefit and in doing so often collude with the rulers of Muslim states who abstain from exercising their political

[82] Dumay, 'La "guerre sainte" comme arme ideologique', *Le Monde*, 20–21 January 1991 cited by Halliday, The Gulf War 1990–1991, 109.

[83] al-Khalij' cited in Khadduri and Ghareeb, *War in the Gulf*, 237.

[84] Ibid., 238.

[85] Ibid., 241.

authority to declare the use of force to respond to aggression.[86] Also, these groups claim the legitimacy of use of force against Muslim rulers who they accuse of assisting and even supporting the non-Muslim Western powers in their influence on Muslim states and as a result subjecting God's command to them.[87] However, these justifications are not free from scrutiny for being influenced by political agenda.

Non-state actors are known to have invoked different ideologies to justify their violent use of force. They have claimed individual responsibility for armed jihad even in modern days. They are known as the 'revivalists' who lean more strongly towards the expansionist doctrines stressing that the clear message of later Qur'anic revelations was to spread the word of God by use of force.[88] According to them the nature of fighting is such that one might consider it analogous to the historical notion of the imposed war, so that the duty to fight is in some way an individual duty.[89] They say that the most pressing task for the revivalists is the replacement of un-Islamic regimes within Muslim countries, whose hypocrisy must be overcome before the external jihad can be resumed.[90] In this respect, three examples of the militant argument are instructive, namely the Neglected Duty (1981), the Charter of Hamas (1988), and the Declaration on Armed Struggle Against Jews and Crusaders (1998).

'The Neglected duty' is a testament to the assassination of the then President of Egypt Anwar Sadat in 1981. The writer of the testament was Muhammad abd el Salam Faraj, who was himself accused of this assassination. This testament appealed to the rise of militant Islam. According to al-Faraj 'a well-established rule of the Islamic law that the punishment of an apostate will be heavier than the punishment of someone who is by origin an unbeliever.'[91] The background of the text is set upon the precedent set by classical Ulama and the political situation posed by Sadat's policies. Of the latter, the most important concerns were with the recognition and establishment of formal relations between Egypt and the state of

[86] Amin, *Reclaiming Jihad*, 119.

[87] Mawdudi, *Towards Understanding the Qur'an*, 199; Khatab, Hakimiyyah and Jahiliyyah, 145.

[88] Afsaruddin, *Jihad and Martyrdom*, 11; see also Copinger-Symes, Is Osama bin Laden's Fatwa, 53.

[89] Ibid., 10; see also Kelsay, *Arguing the Just War in Islam*, 128.

[90] Copinger-Symes, 'Is Osama bin Laden's Fatwa, 53.

[91] Faraj, *al-Faridah al-Ghaibah*, 169.

Israel.[92] Besides, Sadat's policies towards Egyptian Christians and his readiness to open Egypt to foreign investments also suggested a willingness to compromise the Islamic character of Egyptian society.[93]

Muhammad abd el Salam Faraj and his followers judged President Anwar Sadat an apostate who must repent or be killed. The testament promulgated that 'the Rulers of this age are in apostasy from Islam … They carry nothing from Islam but their names.'[94] It also promulgated that 'an apostate leader no longer has the qualification of a leader; to obey such a person is no longer obligatory, and the Muslims have the duty to revolt against him and depose him, to put a just leader in his place when they are able to do so.'[95] As the title of the testament hints, the 'neglect' of the duty to fight is itself a sin, at least of omission.[96] This testament, therefore, focuses on the near enemy, which is the leader or ruler.

The Charter of Hamas (1988) reflects the struggles between Israelis and Palestinians, where the movement established by Hamas believed that Islam is the solution to all political ills. The charter conceives armed struggle as resistance to the taking of land entrusted to the Muslim community.[97] The Islamic Resistance Movement believes that:

> The land of Palestine is entrusted to the Muslims until the Day of Resurrection. It is not right to give it up in whole or in part. No Arab state … no King or Leader … no organization, Palestinian or Arab, has such authority.[98]

The charter also heavily stresses the responsibility of fighting by every individual in circumstances where Muslim lands have been usurped by the foreign power. According to the charter:

> There is no higher peak in nationalism, no greater depth of devotion than this: When an enemy makes incursions into Muslim territory then struggle and fighting the enemy becomes an obligation incumbent upon every individual Muslim (male) and Muslimah (female).[99]

[92] Kelsay, *Arguing the Just War in Islam*, 130.
[93] Ibid., 131.
[94] Faraj, *al-Faridah al-Ghaibah*, 169.
[95] Ibid., 191.
[96] Kelsay, *Arguing the Just War in Islam*, 133.
[97] Ibid., 134.
[98] The Charter of Hamas, sec. 22.
[99] Ibid., sec. 12.

The World Islamic Front Declaration on Armed Struggle Against Jews and Crusaders (1998) was signed by five different militant groups from Egypt, Afghanistan, Pakistan, and Bangladesh.[100] The message sent by this declaration was that US military presence in Arabian Peninsula following the Gulf War in 1991 is an imposed war on Muslims, and it is an individual duty of every Muslim to fight this war. The declaration provided that:

> Ulama throughout Islamic history has unanimously agreed that armed struggle is an individual duty if the enemy destroys the Muslim countries ... The ruling to fight the Americans and their allies, civilians and military, is an individual obligation for every Muslim who can do it in any country in which it is possible to do it ... We call on every Muslim who believes in God and wishes to be rewarded to comply with God's order to fight the Americans and plunder their money wherever and whenever they find it. We also call on Muslim 'ulama', leaders, youths, and soldiers to launch the raid on the adversary's U.S. troops and the satanically inspired supporters allying with them, and to displace those who are behind them so that they may learn a lesson.[101]

This declaration focuses on the far enemy, such as the U.S. and its allies, and accordingly claims justification for both internal and extraterritorial use of force irrespective of the enemy's presence. However, this analogy gained so much popularity among extremists to cause violence all over the world. Shari'a precedents cast the duty to fight in an imposed war as an individual duty, but that terminology does not appear to suggest a popular uprising.[102] The arguments advanced and actions claimed to be justified by such scholars and authorities are subject to serious criticism on Shari'a grounds.[103] Authors of the testament, charter, and declaration do not have the right authority to declare the use of force in Islamic law. The cause may be just, which is the defensive use of force against foreign usurpation, but the Shari'a requirement of 'just and legitimate authority' is lacking.

As a result, the Shaykh al-Azhar has criticized 'the Neglected Duty' for causing widespread harm than good.[104] Saudi scholars suggested the

[100] Mahmoudi, The Islamic Perception of the Use of Force in the Contemporary World, 8.

[101] http://www.fas.org/irp/world/para/docs/980223-fatwa.htm accessed 17 August 2020.

[102] Kelsay, *Arguing the Just War in Islam*, 129.

[103] Ibid.

[104] Ibid., 133.

operations carried out in accordance with the declaration as without precedent in the history of Islam, and the participants might best be judged as 'mere' suicide.[105] Both Muslim scholars and Shaykh al-Azhar issued opinions against Al-Qa'ida-sponsored bombings of US embassies in Kenya and Tanzania in 1998.[106] Their action is opposed to the Shari'a notion of honourable combat. According to Shari'a precedents fighting should be the last resort even in self-defence, and any claim of imposed war must be responded to first by preaching and then by diplomacy before using force.[107] The fundamental problem with the militant versions of Shari'a reasoning is that they confuse their views with those of the Qur'an and Sunna.[108]

Following the presentation of 'The Clash of Civilization' theory by Samuel Huntington in 1993,[109] the West has related the cause of terrorist attacks including the 9/11 to Islamic religious extremism and particularly to jihad.[110] This claim from the West is very serious and therefore requires scholarly investigation. These are very common trends among few modern exegetes who support the classical view of jihad. Amongst these exegetes, Sayyid Qutb, Abu'l A'la Mawdudi, and Bin Laden were very influential.

According to Mawdudi, military jihad is a 'perpetual revolutionary struggle' whose aim is to bring the whole world into conformity with the ideals of Islam.[111] Similarly, Sayyid Qutb advocated for the abrogation of non-violent verses of the Qur'an, which is a common denominator in the classical theory, and came up with a distinctive and revolutionary vision of jihad as a permanent struggle.[112] This view of Qutb is not radically different from classical theory. He inclined to support offensive jihad and rejected defensive jihad and named the proponents of the latter as 'defeatists' and 'apologists'.[113]

[105] Ibid., 140.
[106] Ibid., 142.
[107] Ibid., 147.
[108] El Fadl, *And God Knows the Soldiers*, 37.
[109] Huntington, *The Clash of Civilization*, 81.
[110] Al-Dawoody, *The Islamic Law of War*, 3.
[111] Mawdudi, 'Shari'at al-Islam' cited in Amin, *Reclaiming Jihad*, 93.
[112] Ibid., 99.
[113] Qutb, 'Zilal' cited in Amin, *Reclaiming Jihad*, 100.

On the other hand, leaders of Al-Qa'ida considered their jihad purely defensive.[114] Those scholars attempting to disassociate Islam from the policies of Al-Qa'ida were said to be 'ostensible' Muslims, lacking in conviction, untrustworthy, or unrepresentative of the faith.[115] However, this claim of defensive jihad cannot be lawfully declared by Al-Qa'ida under Islamic law because such a claim is opposed to the Shari'a. They do not have the 'right authority' and 'just cause' to declare the use of force according to Islamic law.[116] The Western powers did not invade any Muslim country at the time of the declaration made by Al-Qa'ida in 1998.

The above discussion suggests that the term 'jihad' is very powerful in the Muslim psyche.[117] The classical jihad is still invoked by today's extremists, such as Sayyid Qutb, Abu'l A'la Mawdudi, and Bin Laden, who insist on practising terrorism in the name of Islamic jihad.[118] The interpretation of the Qur'an as applied by some of the classical exegetes and their modern extremist followers has had its impact on the formulation of modern Western understanding of jihad in Islam.[119] Although few extremists and terrorist groups have invoked the ideology of classical juristic views of permanent war against non-Muslims, this does not represent contemporary Islamic law as the Shari'a itself does not represent the dominant classical view in the modern world. Shari'a is a living mechanism that evolves, but such evolution does not include the invocation of any legal principle that is inconsistent with its core elements, namely the Qur'an and Sunna.

Hence, the current position is that if the cause is just, armed non-state actors may use force against their ruler, and similarly, a ruler may suppress such use of force only if it is unjust and illegitimate. As a result, the legitimacy question involves a dilemma between the use of force by and against armed non-state actors. This dilemma lies in the fact that if the use of force by non-state actors is permissible in Islamic law, the state authorities or rulers have a corresponding duty that entitles them to use force against armed non-state actors to maintain order in the society. However, both states and non-state actors cannot claim the legitimacy of their respective use of force against each other at the same time and on the same cause. As a result, both states and non-state actors often turned to political

[114] Amin, *Reclaiming Jihad*, 119.
[115] Kelsay, *Arguing the Just War in Islam*, 3.
[116] For a discussion about 'right authority and just cause' in Islamic law, see Chap. 3.
[117] Bassiouni, *The Sharia and Islamic Criminal Justice*, 221.
[118] Amin, *Reclaiming Jihad*, 124.
[119] Ibid.

considerations in their attempts to address this dilemma and answer the legitimacy question.

4.4 The Legal-Political Legacies of Use of Force: A Dilemma Leading to Reconciliation

The separation of religion from the law-making process has been a contentious issue in the modern world. Both Muslim states and armed non-state actors have questioned the legitimacy of a legal framework, which is inconsistent with religious principles. This is because the role of religion in the law-making process is undeniable particularly during the formative period of Islamic thought.[120] As a result, the use of force based on religion often seems legitimate. However, such use of force may not be legitimate and therefore requires examination. Whilst evidence of the separation between religion and law is available in the law-making process, evidence of the interplay between the same is also available. This has resulted in a dilemma which is 'where the religion should be kept separate from law and where it should not'.

The use and abuse, as the case may be, of religious principles by those who emphasize the legitimacy of use of force as a means of promoting political interest have a significant impact on the question of the legitimate use of force. On the one hand, if a religious principle is invoked to manifest the legitimacy of use of force that principle creates a religiopolitical legacy, on the other hand, if force is used according to the law that principle not only secures legitimacy but also confirms it. Whilst the former is purely based on religion which was revealed a long time ago and, in a society, very different from the modern ones, the latter passed through a process where it had been thoroughly tried and tested.[121] Therefore, in the former case the religiopolitical legacy created may be a dangerous one and accordingly may not have become law through a political process; so in this case, it is desirable to keep religion separate from the law. However, in the latter case it is undesirable to keep the religion separate from the law.

The religious principles that were revealed a long time ago under different social conditions cannot be the sole legitimate basis of use of force due to the inconsistency between history and present circumstance or

[120] Watt, *The Formative Period of Islamic Thought*, 22.

[121] al-Raziq, 'The Problem of the Caliphate' in Moaddel and Talattof (eds), *Modernist and Fundamentalist Debate*, 95.

between approved texts and new contexts, and non-transformation into law in any relevant social condition as well as lack of potential for such transformation in the modern world. In this situation, the religion must be kept separate from the law, and this is because the legitimacy has not obtained through a political process that created the legal-political legacy. However, laws that emanated from religious principles were often benefited from their sources which can provide further guidance as to interpretation and application in novel situations. Conversely, religious principles which had not passed through a political process of becoming the law are often susceptible to dangerous and innovative (*bid'a*) political interpretation. Therefore, it is vital to keep the law and religion separate, where it is necessary to reconcile the dilemma that may occur from their interplay, that is 'where the religion should be kept separate from the law and where it should not'.

Islamic international law has gone through a political process that has been tried and tested since the early days in Islam, which had been manifested as a religion.[122] This body of laws is already established its legal principles through a political process whereby it had invoked and also disregarded religious principles in this process. Therefore, religion is relevant only where it can offer further guidance as to the interpretation and application of the law in novel situations. If the religion cannot offer such guidance, then it will offer nothing but an innovative interpretation of the religion leading to the creation of dangerous religiopolitical legacies. In such situations, religion should be kept separate from the law.

Islamic international law manifestly proclaims the legitimacy of use of force to fend off aggression as an established legal principle.[123] However, the legitimacy of this legal principle has been provided by an interplay between religion as a source of this legal principle and politics as a tool to establish this principle into law. This interplay has provided a legal-political legacy. However, this interplay between religion and law cannot provide the legitimacy of use of force in all circumstances. For instance, where a legal-political legacy outweighs a religious principle that is claimed to represent the law, it is the former which prevails over the latter. In those circumstances, the legitimacy of use of force is obtained through a political

[122] Ibid.

[123] Al-Qur'an 2:190, 194; 4:91; 9:36; and 22:39 (Abu Yusuf tr.); see also Sabuj, 'Islamic international law', 1–17.

process whereby it is transformed into the law. Therefore, religion should be kept separate from the law in those circumstances.

On the contrary, the numerous examples of legal principles in Islamic international law that developed through an interplay between religion and law have been emphasizing by Muslim states and armed non-state actors to support the ultimate necessity of this interplay in the law-making process in modern nation-states. The integral part played by religion generally in the law-making process and particularly in the formative period of Islam has strengthened this emphasis as it has been robustly argued that Islam and law cannot be kept separate.[124] These scholarly positions have also set out their understanding of the political history of Islam and the connections of the Qur'anic jihad with that history.[125] On this footing, both states and non-state actors questioned the legitimacy of use of force in Islamic law, where any of its principles are inconsistent with the religion in general and according to their interpretation of the religion in particular. This questioning often led the way to gain political interests for the benefit of states and non-state actors. As a result, the proponents of an interplay between religion and law to pursue a biased political interest often created dangerous religiopolitical legacies.

Invocation of jihad (a religious principle) to pursue purely political purposes became very common among states and non-state actors since the beginning of decolonization. The call for jihad to legitimize armed struggle against colonial power became a very popular political agenda of the Muslim leaders and rulers in that period.[126] For example, the invocation of jihad to legitimize armed struggle against colonial power became a very popular political agenda of Muslim leaders and rulers in the colonial period in places such as Egypt, Africa, and India. This purely political, as opposed to religious, agenda has been described by James Turner Johnson as 'essentially temporal'. He pointed out that 'despite the invoking of religious authority of war, the causes of the wars in question were essentially temporal; despite being termed as jihad, they were wars of the state, not wars of religion.'[127]

Although most of these movements mainly focused on the institutionalization of Islamic political order based on nationalism, few movements

[124] Asad, *Genealogies of Religion*, 1; See also Johnson, *The Holy War Idea*, 96.
[125] For an account of the political history of jihad, see Chap. 3.
[126] Sabuj, Islamic international law, 16.
[127] Johnson, *The Holy War Idea*, 96.

were based on ethno-religious identities such as the political movements in Saudi Arabia led by activists like Muhammad Ibn Abdul Wahhab. His main concern was the danger posed on Islam by innovation (*bid'a*). His political movement eventually collaborated with that of the Saud family, which led Wahhabism to strongly establish a political institution in the Kingdom of Saudi Arabia that is currently ruling the country.[128] This movement began to politicize Islam by bringing the religion into scrutiny such as differentiating the true believers from infidels (*Kafir*). This led to an emphasis on the practice of excommunication (*Takfir*) of an infidel or apostate from Islam.[129] This differentiation was purely political as its main purpose was to pursue a claim of legitimacy to rule the Kingdom of Saudi Arabia. However, this political legacy has not been adopted as a principle of Islamic law due to its inconsistency with the fundamental principle of religion which is 'prohibition of aggression'. Therefore, its legal status is questionable from within the religion.

The political legacy created by *Takfir* has played a vital role in this categorization. However, such categorization does not have the support of religion. As a result, *Takfir* is a dangerous political legacy that must be kept separate from the law due to being inconsistent with the religion. This can be clear from what has evolved in the twentieth and twenty-first centuries. For example, the invocation of *Takfir* as a legitimate basis of use of force as advocated by Sayyid Qutb in Egypt in the 1960s as a leader of the Muslim Brotherhood.[130] Similarly, labelling the Shi'a Muslims as infidels and holding them responsible for *Takfir* is evident in the ongoing enmity between the Saudi Arabia ruling authority (the Saudi Royal Family) and the Islamic Republic of Iran, where most of the population are Shi'a Muslims. This is known as Wahhabism, and its self-proclaimed legitimacy of the use of force against other Muslims based on religious belief has led the ongoing airstrikes by Saudi Arabia in Yemen. Saudi Arabia claims legitimacy of their airstrikes to suppress the Houthi rebels who the former categorizes as infidels and spreaders of *fitna* (persecution).[131] Similarly, Iran claims legitimacy for supporting the Houthi rebels in Yemen (who are Shi'a Muslims) based on their effort to save the Muslims from aggression and persecution. So, where does the legitimacy lie? Both Saudi Arabia's

[128] Mandaville, *Islam and Politics*, 50.
[129] El Fadl, *Rebellion and Violence in Islamic Law*, 281.
[130] Khatab, Hakimiyyah and Jahiliyyah, 145.
[131] BBC News Desk, 'Yemen Crisis: Who Fights Whom?' (28 March 2017).

claim and Iran's claim are religiopolitical. Therefore, both religion and politics must play a key role in deciding these contrasting claims of legitimacy. Moreover, as aggression and persecution are questions of fact and law, their legitimacy must be decided based on the guidance given by the religion as a source of law and political consideration as a process to make that law. In this way, the legitimacy question will be answered by creating a legal-political legacy. Applying this method to the contrasting claims of the legitimate use of force by Saudi Arabia and Iran, it can be argued that both of their claims lack legitimacy. These religiopolitical claims cannot become law since in this case the religion must not be kept separate from law. This is an example where the argument to intermingle the law with religion is very strong as the latter can guide to answer the legitimacy question.

The above discussion has shown that a combination of the law and religion can answer the legitimacy question, but that answer may not always provide a legitimate basis for the use of force. This chapter has shown that there are circumstances where religiopolitical and purely political legacies can produce a dilemma between the law and religion concerning the use of force. Reconciliation of this dilemma is a necessary precondition to answer the legitimacy question. This section has suggested a solution to this dilemma by offering a reconciliation outlining the situations 'where the religion should be kept separate from law and where it should not'.

4.5 The Legitimacy of an Islamic Caliphate in the Modern World

A reconciliation between the law and religion, as suggested in the above section, is an approach to 'use of force' in Islamic law that can potentially answer the legitimacy question. However, the revival of a new legitimacy argument that has been made by armed non-state actors at the beginning of the twenty-first century needs further analysis. As a convincing argument has been made about the necessity of an Islamic caliphate in the modern world, it is very crucial to analyse the legitimacy of this argument. Therefore, this section offers a critical analysis of the legitimacy of an Islamic caliphate in the modern world.

After independence from the colonial power, the Muslims were divided into independent states and there was no prospect or necessity to form a unified Islamic caliphate at that time.[132] Following the abolition of the caliphate in 1922 at the end of the Ottoman Empire,[133] the effect of decolonization underpinned by the notion of national self-determination drifted over most of the Middle East, India, West Africa, and Southeast Asia.[134] While the Sunni-Shi'a tensions had been part of the political legacies generally in most Muslim states and particularly in the Middle East, the upsurge of the use of force by armed non-state actors in the twenty-first century has taken the legitimacy question in a different direction.[135] The 9/11 terrorist attack by Al-Qa'ida, the Iraq War in 2003, and the rise of ISIS (Islamic State in Iraq and Syria) in the aftermath are key examples of non-state actors' claiming for an Islamic caliphate in the modern world.

The legitimacy of use of force to establish an Islamic caliphate has been profoundly claimed by Al-Qa'ida, ISIS, ISIL (Islamic State in Iraq and Levant), QSIS, or Al-Qa'ida Separatists in Iraq and Syria. However, this claim of the legitimacy of use of force has been subjected to huge criticism. Scholars from al-Azhar have questioned the legitimacy of such use of force.[136] Moreover, scholars from all around the world have written an open letter to Baghdadi, the then leader of ISIS, declaring that the use of force to pursue a caliphate-style regime is illegitimate in Islamic law.[137] On the contrary, the legitimacy of such use of force has been claimed to be rooted in the religion as argued by the proponents of an Islamic caliphate.[138] In other words, this claim of a legitimate Islamic caliphate is based on an interplay between the law and religion. However, the lack of the legitimacy of use of force to pursue a caliphate-style regime and the denial of such a regime following the end of the Ottoman Empire in 1922 do not support this claim. Moreover, the legal-political legacies created by the history of Islam since its manifestation as a religion do not provide any legitimate basis for an Islamic caliphate in the modern world.

In the early days of Islam, a caliphate was essential to institutionalize the religion by setting up a political entity. Such a political entity set up an

[132] Afsaruddin, Views of Jihad, 167.

[133] Van Engeland, 'The Balance Between Islamic Law, Customary Law and Human Rights in Islamic Constitutionalism Through the Prism of Legal Pluralism, 1321.

[134] Al-Dawoody, *The Islamic Law of War*, 77.

[135] Nasr, *The Shi'a Revival*, 65.

[136] Allam, *The Ideological Battle*, 130.

[137] The New Mardin Declaration (27 April 2010); for contra see Michot, 'Ibn Taymiyya's "New Mardin Fatwa", 130.

[138] Black, *The History of Islamic Political Thought*, 161.

Islamic caliphate and institutionalized the religion by invoking it into the legal corpus. As a result, Islamic law established and evolved as a body of legal principles at the state level and inter-state level. Since the formation of Islamic international law through the political process this system has been tried and evaluated in different institutional settings over a long time. However, there is no political force for setting up a caliphate-style regime in the modern world. Moreover, following the death of the rightly guided Caliphs,[139] the later Caliphs, including the Ummayyads and the Abbasids, there was no authority left on any states or armed non-state actors to use force to establish an Islamic caliphate.[140] In the absence of a rightly guided Caliph, most of the political authorities to decide on the use of force have passed on to the ruler or state government of modern nation-states. However, no such authorities have conferred on them to establish an Islamic caliphate.

Since the institutionalization of Islam as a religion and sources of law, different schools of thought (*Madhhab, pl. Madhahib*) have emerged. These schools of thought have developed complex juristic work (*Fiqh*) based on different methods of interpretation (*Ijtihad*) adopted by these schools.[141] These schools represent a strong sense of diversity in religion in terms of juristic work. In the presence of different schools of thought in Islamic jurisprudence, the religion has grown to adapt to the legal and political settings of modern nation-states.[142] Moreover, the nature of modern nation-states in Muslim majority populated territories has changed their pattern that not only adopted Islam as a source of religious guiding principles of sovereign powers but also imported political trends such as lobbying, the formation of political parties and their participation in elections, and entering into broad coalitions with non-Islamists groups and parties.[143] Furthermore, the mass migration of Muslims to non-Muslim and Western states together with their practice of the religion all over the world has made the argument for a caliphate very week. This is because the legality of use of force is promoted in the Qur'an, where Muslims are being persecuted.[144] However, such persecution is more evident in Muslim

[139] The rightly guided caliphs are known as the first four caliphs of Islam namely, Abu Bakr, Uthman, Umar, and Ali.

[140] Crone and Hinds, *God's Caliphs*, 56.

[141] Sharastani, *Muslim Sects and Divisions*, 10.

[142] Asad, *The Principle of State and Government*, 35.

[143] Mandaville, *Islam and Politics*, 66.

[144] Al-Qur'an 22:39–40, Abu Yusuf translation; see also Chap. 3.

states than in non-Muslim or Western states, where protection is available for Muslims under state, regional, and international human rights law.[145]

Whereas an Islamic caliphate was an integral part of the survival of the religion in its infancy, such a caliphate is neither necessary nor legitimate in the modern world. The legal principles that have formed Islamic international law have developed in course of time from the legal-political legacies. Religion has played its role in the formation of these legacies as far as the use of force is concerned. There is not much left for the religion itself to legitimately contribute to the law except offering valuable guidance in its application and interpretation in novel situations. Any religious principle, whether accurate or controversial, which has not been adopted or may not so adopt in the corpus of the law lacks legitimate authority. Such religious principles are either religiopolitical or simply political. Religious principles become religiopolitical where the religion is a source of those principles, but they have not converted or may not convert into the law through a political process. Such principles are purely or simply political where neither the religion is a source nor they have become law through a political process.

4.6 Conclusion

In Muslim states, the place of Islam is not only a religion but also a source of law. Most of these legal principles are sourced from Shari'a law, which is the primary source of Islamic law. The power to apply these legal principles lies in political authorities such as states and non-state actors. Hence the relationship between Islam (as a religion) and law (as enforced by a political institution at the state level and inter-state level) is an important one. In this relationship, it is arguable that law and religion are integral parts in the law-making process in Muslim states, and for this reason, these two should not be separated where a political institution such as a state enacts and enforces the law. However, this argument lacks most of its strength when the interplay between the law and religion cannot provide the legitimacy of use of force such as where a political process can provide the best solution by keeping the religion separate from law. This process often creates valuable legal-political legacies, at the state level and international level, which eventually have or can become law.

[145] Shah, The Use of Force under Islamic Law, 343.

The legal-political legacies created through a political process have been challenged by states and armed non-state actors. They challenged each other's legitimate political authority for being inconsistent with the religion. These states and non-state actors have referred to 'jihad' from the Qur'an and used it as a political tool to claim the legitimacy of their use of force as outlined in this chapter. They have made this reference to pursue a religiopolitical or purely political agenda that has failed to become law through a political process. As a result, their claim to the legitimacy of use of force has failed to create a legal-political legacy on the use of force.

Whereas religion has played a key role in these contrasting claims of legitimacy made by states and armed non-state actors in Muslim states, politics has played the leading role here. As a result, the legitimacy question reached a vantage point where on the one hand non-state actors claim the legitimacy of recourse to force against their rulers and foreign states that collude with those rulers to use force against them, and on the other hand, the latter claim legitimacy of such use of force, namely intervention by invitation, national security, and self-defence. Although non-state actors are not the immediate subjects of Islamic international law, the collusion of Muslim rulers with foreign powers brings the legitimacy question within its remit. The extension of the remit of Islamic international law to include non-state actors gains further strength from the Muslim rulers' collusion with foreign states as tantamount to the revival of the former colonial trend.[146] Moreover, although foreign intervention by invitation from the rulers of Muslim states is legitimate in Public international law, the same is not in Islamic international law.[147] As a result, intervention by invitation is an illegitimate collusion in Islamic international law. This is a legal-political legacy developed by the law. Furthermore, according to Islamic international law, a Muslim state is under an obligation to be readily available to provide armed support to other Muslim states. However, Islamic international law allows a non-Muslim state to intervene in a Muslim state by invitation only when no Muslim states are willing and able to offer armed support. Regarding non-Muslim states an invitation is necessary, or in the absence of such invitation, the Islamic law of treaties will

[146] For a discussion about the colonial influence on Muslim states in the modern world, see Chap. 3.

[147] For a discussion about the legality of intervention by invitation in Public and Islamic international law, see Chaps. 2 and 3.

apply.[148] Islamic law of treaties binds the Muslim states to follow the UN Charter, which they have signed and ratified. On this footing, it can be argued that Islamic international law should accept the legitimacy of intervention based on invitation, national security, and self-defence. However, from the discussion and findings in the preceding chapters, it can also be argued that Islamic international law should accept the legitimacy of these uses of force if they are consistent with the UN Charter, which most Muslim states have signed and ratified. In other words, any claim of the legitimacy of extra-Charter use of force is not legitimate in Islamic international law when it exceeds the terms of the treaty (UN Charter) to which the latter agreed.

In these circumstances, the conflicting claims of legitimacy by non-state actors in Islamic international law, on the one hand, and states in Public international law on the other hand reach a vantage point. At this point, the answer to these claims depends on a coherent approach between these regimes. If extra-Charter force is not being used there is no risk of collusion between the rulers of Muslim states and foreign states or breach of Public and Islamic international law. This position can turn down the claims of the legitimacy of extra-Charter use of force based on intervention by invitation, national security, and self-defence. This can also turn down the claims of the legitimate use of force made by armed non-state actors against their rulers based on collusion and extra-Charter use of force. As a result, only a coherent approach to the legitimacy of use of force between the Public and Islamic international law can overcome the legitimacy deficits.

References

Abi-Shayba A A. M. I., *Al-Musannaf fi al-Ahadith wa al-Athar* (Beirut: Dar al-Fikr, Vol.VIII, 1989).

al-'Asqalani A. I. H., *Fath al-Bari bi Sharh Sahih al-Bukhari* (Beirut: Dar al-Fikr, 1993).

al-Bazzar A. B. A., *Al-Bahr al-Zakhkhar* (Medina: Maktabat al-'Ulum wa al-Hikam, 1988).

Al-Dawoody A., *The Islamic Law of War: Justifications and Regulations* (Palgrave Macmillan, 2011).

[148] For a discussion about the Islamic law of treaties, see Chap. 3.

Afsaruddin A., *Jihad and Martyrdom in Islamic Thought and History* (USA: Oxford University Press).
———, 'Views of Jihad throughout History' (2007) 1 Religious Campus 167.
al-Ghunaimi M. T., *The Muslim Conception of International Law and the Western Approach* (Martinus Nijhoff: The Hague, 1968).
al-Hajjaj A M., *Al-Fami' al-Sahih* (Beirut: Dar al-Ma'rifa, n.d.).
Allam S., *The Ideological Battle: Egypt's Dar al- Iftaa Combats Radicalization* (The Grand Mufti of Egypt, 2016).
al-Mawardi A., *al-Hawi al-Kabir Sharh Mukhtasar al-Muzani* (Beirut: Dar al-Kutub al-Ilmiyya, 1994).
al-Nawawi A. M., *Al-Majmu' Sharh al-Muhadhdhab* (Beirut: Dar al-Fikr, n.d.).
al-Qastalani A., *Irshad al-Sari Sharh Sahih al-Bukhari* (Cairo: Dar al-Fikr, 1304 AH).
al Shaybani A. B., *Kitab al-Sunnah* (Beirut: al-Maktab al-Islami, 1993).
Asad M., *The Principle of State and Government in Islam* (Dar al-Andalus: Gibraltar, 1985).
Asad T., *Genealogies of Religion: Disciplines and Reasons of Power in Christianity and Islam* (Baltimore, MD: John Hopkins University Press, 1993).
Amin E. M. A., *Reclaiming Jihad: A Qur'anic Critique of Terrorism* (UK: The Islamic Foundation, 2014).
An-Na'im A., *Islam and the Secular State* (Harvard University Press, 2009).
Ashton N. and Gibson B. (eds), *The Iraq-Iran War: New International Perspectives* (Routledge, 2013).
al-Tirmidhi A. I. M., *al-Fami' al-Sahih* (Cairo: Dar al-Hadith, Vol.IV, 1987).
Badar M. E. and Sabuj M., 'The Islamic Law of Rebellion and Its Potential to Complement Public International Law on the Use of Force' (2019) 6(2) Journal of International and Comparative Law 365.
Badar M. E. et al., 'The Radical Application of the Islamic Concept of *Takfir*' (2017) 31 Arab Law Quarterly 134.
Bassiouni M. C., *The Sharia and Islamic Criminal Justice in Time of War and Peace* (Cambridge University Press, 2014).
BBC News Desk, 'Yemen Crisis: Who Fights Whom?' (28 March 2017) http://www.bbc.co.uk/news/world-middle-east-29319423 accessed 18 September 2020.
Black A., *The History of Islamic Political Thought: From the Prophet to the Present* (2nd edn, Edinburgh University Press, 2011).
Bsoul L. A., *International Treaties (Mu'ahadat) in Islam: Theory and Practice in the Light of Islamic International Law (Siyar) according to Orthodox Schools* (University Press America, 2008).
Copinger-Symes T.R., 'Is Osama bin Laden's Fatwa Urging Jihad Against Americans' dated 23 February 1998 Justified by Islamic Law?', (2003) 3 Defence Studies 53.

Crone P. and Hinds M., *God's Caliphs: Religious Authority in the First Centuries of Islam* (Cambridge University Press, 1986).

Dawud S. A., *Sunan* (Cairo: Dar al-Hadith, 1988).

Fadel M., 'State and Sharia' in Peters R. and Bearman P. (eds), *The Ashgate Research Companion to Islamic Law* (Ashgate Publishing, 2014).

El Fadl K. A., *And God Knows the Soldiers: The Authoritative and the Authoritarian in Islamic Discourses* (Lanham, Md.: University Press America, 2001a).

———, *Rebellion and Violence in Islamic Law* (Cambridge University Press, 2001b).

Faraj M. S., *al-Faridah al-Ghaibah: The Neglected Duty* (Johannes J.G. Jansen tr, New York: Macmillan, 1986).

Gauhar A. (ed), *The Challenges of Islam* (London: Islamic Council of Europe, 1978).

Gurr T., *Why Men Rebel* (NJ: Princeton University Press, 1969).

Halliday F., 'The Gulf War 1990–1991 and the study of international relations' (1994) 20 Review of international studies 109.

Hamidullah M., *Muslim Conduct of State* (4th edn, Lahore: Ashraf Press, 1961).

Hanbal A. I., *Musnad* (Beirut: al-Maktab al-Islami, Vol.VII, 1993).

Hitti P. K., *History of the Arabs* (New York, St. Martin's Press, 1970).

Huntington S., *The Clash of Civilization and the Remaking of World Order* (New York: Simon & Schuster, 1996).

Ibn Kathir, part 4 (Muhammad Saed Abdul-Rahman tr, MSA Publication, 2009).

Ibn Maja A. A. M, *Sunan* (Beirut: Dar Ihya' al-Kutub al-'Arabiyya, n.d.).

Johnson J. T. and Kelsey J. (eds.), *Cross, Crescent and Sword: The Justification and Limitation of War in Western and Islamic Tradition* (New York: Greenwood Press, 1990).

Johnson J. T., *The Holy War Idea in Western and Islamic Traditions* (Pennsylvania State University Press, 1997).

Kelsay J., *Arguing the Just War in Islam* (Harvard University Press, 2009).

Kepel G., *Jihad: The Trial of Political Islam* (London: Tauris, 2008).

Khatab S., 'Hakimiyyah and Jahiliyyah in the Thought of Sayyid Qutb' (2002) 38 Middle Eastern Studies 145.

Khadduri M. and Ghareeb E., *War in the Gulf: The Iraq-Kuwait Conflict and its implications* (Oxford University Press, 1997).

Mahmoudi S., 'The Islamic Perception of the Use of Force in the Contemporary World' (paper presented at the International Law and the Islamic World: Towards a Multipolar International Legal System, organized by Max Planck Institute for Comparative and International Public Law, Heidelberg and the Institute for Political and International Studies, Tehran, Iran, 3–5 April 2004, page 13).

Mandaville P., *Islam and Politics* (Routledge, 2014).

McConnell L., *Extracting Accountability from Non-State actors in International Law* (Routledge, 2017).

Michot Y., 'Ibn Taymiyya's "New Mardin Fatwa". Is genetically modified Islam (GMI) carcinogenic?' (2011) 101 The Muslim World 130.
Moaddel M. and Talattof K. (eds), *Modernist and Fundamentalist Debate* (New York: Palgrave Macmillan, 2000).
Moaddel M., *Islamic Modernism, Nationalism, and Fundamentalism: Episode and Discourse* (Chicago, IL: University of Chicago Press, 2005).
Mu'awwaḍ A. M. and al-Mawjūd A. A. (eds.), *Al-Ḥāwī al-Kabīr: Fī Fiqh Madhhab al-Imām al-Shāfi 'ī Raḍī Allah 'anh wa huwa Sharḥ Mukhtaṣar al-Muznī* (Beirut: Dār al-Kutub al-'Ilmiyyah, Vol.13, 1999).
Mawdudi S. A. A., *Towards Understanding the Qur'an* (Zafar Ishaq Ansari tr, The Islamic Foundation, 1995).
Nasr V., *The Shi'a Revival: How Conflicts Within Islam Will Shape the Future* (New York: Norton, 2006).
Okon E. E., 'Islam, War and International Humanitarian Law' (2014) 10 European Scientific Journal 100.
Opwis F., *Masalaha and the Purpose of the Law: Islamic Discourse on legal Change from the 4th/10th to 8th/14th Century* (Leiden: Brill, 2010).
Pahuja S., *Decolonising International Law* (Cambridge University Press, 2011).
Peters R., *Islam and Colonialism: The Doctrine of Jihad in Modern History* (The Hague: Mouton Publishers, 1979).
Rabb I. A., '"We the Jurists": Islamic constitutionalism in Iraq' (2008) 10 University of Pennsylvania Journal of Constitutional Law 527.
Rezamand A., 'Use of Religious Doctrine and Symbolism in the Iraq-Iran War' (2009) 9 Journal of the Centre for Studies in Religion and Society 83.
Roy O., *The Failure of Political Islam* (London: I.B. Tauris, 1994).
Sabuj M., 'Islamic international law: an emerging branch of law which answers the contentious question of 'authority to use force' in Islamic law and politics' (2019) *British Journal of Middle Eastern Studies*, pp. 1–17.
Salahi A., *Muhammad: His Character and Conduct* (Islamic Foundation, 2013).
Shah N. A., 'The Use of Force under Islamic Law' (2013) 24 European Journal of International Law 343.
Sharastani M. A., *Muslim Sects and Divisions: The Section on Muslim Sects in Kitab al-Milal wa 'I-Nihal* (A.K. Kazi and J.G. Flynn tr, Kegan Paul International, 1984).
Shīrāzī M., *Tafsīr-i Nimūnā*, vol 2 (Tehran: Dār al-Kutub, 2008).
Sonn T. and Farrar A., "Kharijites" in Oxford Bibliographies, available at https://www.oxfordbibliographies.com/view/document/obo-9780195390155/obo-9780195390155-0047.xml (visited 25 October 2020).
The Charter of Hamas (M. Maqdsi tr, Dallas: Islamic Association for Palestine, 1990).

'The New Mardin Declaration' (27 April 2010) http://iqra.ca/2010/the-new-mardin-declaration/ accessed 30 August 2020.

Toynbee A. J., *Survey of International Affairs*, vol 1 (London: Oxford University Press, 1925).

Van Engeland A., 'The Balance Between Islamic Law, Customary Law and Human Rights in Islamic Constitutionalism Through the Prism of Legal Pluralism' (2014) 4 Cambridge Journal of International and Comparative Law 1321.

Watt M., *The Formative Period of Islamic Thought* (Oneworld Publications, 1998).

CHAPTER 5

Answer to the Legitimacy Question: A Coherent Approach

5.1 Introduction

The legitimacy of use of force in Public and Islamic international law, as discussed in the preceding chapters, is based on justifications of the authority to use force. The justifications offered by states and armed non-state actors are from religious, legal, and political perspectives. In this setting, the justifications offered by elite and powerful states are mainly based on their institutional political position at the state and inter-state levels such as national security and geopolitical interest.[1] Similarly, the justifications offered by states and armed non-state actors in Muslim states are based on religion as well as politics at the state and international levels such as states' invitation of foreign powers to intervene and armed non-state actors' accusation of collusion with those foreign powers.[2] As a result, the legitimacy debate has reached a vantage point where the key issue is whether the justifications based on the religion and institutional political position as proffered by Public and Islamic international law on the use of force can be reconciled. Whereas these justifications challenge each other's legitimacy of the use of force by Public and Islamic international law, a coherent approach can reconcile the justifications and overcome the challenges.

[1] For a discussion of these justifications, see Chap. 2.

[2] For a discussion of these justifications, see Chap. 4.

M. Z. Sabuj, *The Legitimacy of Use of Force in Public and Islamic International Law*,
https://doi.org/10.1007/978-3-030-77298-7_5

Moreover, a coherent approach is vital to answer the legitimacy question. This is because, as shown in the earlier chapters and argued in this chapter, the legitimacy of use of force in the modern world lies neither in Public international law nor in Islamic international law as a mutually exclusive legal framework. This chapter argues that a coherent approach to both Public and Islamic international law can overcome the challenges and answer the legitimacy question.

This chapter provides an outline of the coherent approach and how it can operate in overcoming the challenges of the legitimate use of force as a matter of justification in Public and Islamic international law. It focuses on the processes applicable to these legal regimes in overcoming the legitimacy deficits. This chapter concludes by answering the legitimacy question where it shows that the legitimacy of use of force in Public and Islamic international law lies in a joint setting of these two legal systems. In this setting, the legitimacy of use of force is found in a descriptive sense, where the subjects of Public and Islamic international law perceive the use of force as legitimate.

5.2 The Coherent Approach

The religious, legal, and political legacies of use of force and their legitimacy in Public and Islamic international law mean justification of authority to use force. Therefore, legitimacy is generally understood as the equivalent of having the authority to make binding decisions or to prescribe binding rules.[3] This authority emanates from a source and grows in a manner acceptable to be legitimate. Therefore, the legitimacy of use of force is generated from a source and a process. The source and process are not the same for Public and Islamic international law, but they must operate coherently. In other words, this is a coherent approach that can run in a combined setting of the sources and processes of Public and Islamic international law. The sources can provide a legitimate basis for use of force, and the processes can justify that basis. As a result, the combination between the sources and processes can pave the way for recognizing valid sources of law and addressing the claims of the legitimate use of force as a matter of procedural justification. In other words, the sources will provide for the legitimacy of the substantive law and the processes will provide for

[3] Wolfrum, 'Legitimacy in International Law' in Wolfrum and Roben (eds.), *Legitimacy in International Law*, 6.

justification of claims of legitimacy of that substantive law.[4] In this setting, a coherent approach will recognize each other's law and address the claims of legitimacy.

The legitimacy of use of force in Public international law is rooted in the classical natural law tradition.[5] This tradition is often said to have treated substantive moral justifiability, which is a concept of legitimacy for philosophers, as an essential element of legal validity.[6] Thomas Aquinas, for instance, is often quoted as stating that 'if in any point [human law] deflects from the law of nature, it is no longer a law but a perversion of the law.'[7] Likewise, William Blackstone estimated that 'no human laws are of any validity, if contrary to the law of nature.'[8] This position held by the natural lawyers suggests that moral justifiability constitutes an inextricable aspect of legal validity, which is likely to result in the legitimacy of an action, rule, actor, or system.[9] However, Public international law has developed further over time to include the law-making process as a legitimate basis of the use of force. For example, sovereign equality between the states in their participation at the international level as provided by the UN Charter.[10] However, sovereign equality between member states has not been implemented in the decision-making process on the use of force. For instance, although UN Charter has recognized the principle of sovereign equality of its member states in article 2(1), this principle has not been implemented in the decision-making process at the Security Council, where major decisions on the use of force are made.[11]

Similarly, the legitimacy of Islamic international law on the use of force is rooted in a source called the Shari'a.[12] The Shari'a is an authentic source of law that provides religious validity from the Qur'an, Sunna, Ijma, and Qiyas. In addition to Shari'a, the exemplary role that jurisconsults play in

[4] Rabb, *Doubt in Islamic Law*, 59.

[5] Johnson, 'Threats, Values and Defense' in Elshtain (ed), *Just War Theory*, 57; see also Chesterman, *Just war or Just Peace*, 7.

[6] Thomas, The Uses and Abuses of Legitimacy, 729.

[7] Aquinas, *Summa Theologica*, Art II.

[8] Blackstone, *Commentaries*, 41.

[9] Austin, *The Province of Jurisprudence*, lecture V; see also Kelsen, The Natural Law Doctrine, 485; Hart, *The Concept of Law*, 208; Raz, Kelsen's Theory of the Basic Norm, 100.

[10] UN Charter, art 2 (1); see also Henderson, 'The Arab Spring and the Notion of External State Sovereignty in International Law', 175.

[11] Henderson, 'The Arab Spring and the Notion of External State Sovereignty in International Law', 175.

[12] For a discussion on the Shari'a as a source of Islamic law see Chap. 3.

society is often explained in terms of Prophetic legacy. Muhammad was the first jurisconsult of the Muslim community, and later jurisconsults have continued to play the very role he played.[13] As a result, the Shari'a is a living mechanism of the Islamic law, which has been continuing its legitimate authority through Ijtihad as entertained by the jurisconsults.[14] Therefore, the legitimacy of use of force in Islamic international law lies in the Shari'a as a source that shapes the process through Ijtihad to keep pace with the time and social changes.[15] Unlike Public international law, Islamic international law has not developed further to include the law-making process as a legitimate basis of the use of force. The processes that the jurists of Islamic law claimed to be legitimate are controversial. Moreover, the division between the Shi'as and Sunnis in the eighth century CE and the birth of other schools of legal thoughts within these divisions gave rise to ideological differences among religious leaders and jurists.[16] As a result, the processes observed by the religious leaders and jurists were not uniform and proven contradictory to each other. In these circumstances, innovative and diverse interpretations of law by many self-declared authorities with the added influence of politics have resulted in religiopolitical claims of legitimate authority to make decisions on the use of force.[17] These claims of legitimate authority continued as an integral mission of political Islam. From the emergence of transnational networks pursuing global militant agendas in the name of Islam to the persistence and transformation of traditional Islamic political parties, and to the appearance in the global media claiming to speak as authorities and authentic Islamic voices: the influence of political Islam is very extensive in the modern world.[18] Furthermore, the closure of Ijtihad in ninth century CE stimulated the situation further.[19] Consequently, Islamic international law remained predominantly a source-led legal system as opposed to a process-led legal system.[20]

[13] Hallaq, *A History of Islamic Legal Theories*, 204.

[14] An-Na'im, *Islam and the Secular State*, 12.

[15] Rabb, 'Against Kadijustiz', 343.

[16] Sharastani, *Muslim Sects and Divisions*, 70; see also Mandaville, *Islam and Politics*, 36–38.

[17] For a discussion on 'authority to use force in Islamic international law', see Chap. 3.

[18] Mandaville, *Islam and Politics*, 1.

[19] For a discussion about the closure of Ijtihad and its effect in the legal process, see Chap. 3.

[20] Rabb, *Doubt in Islamic Law*, 59.

In Chap. 4, it has been shown that the legitimacy of use of force in Islamic international law lies in the legal-political legacies that have developed by an interplay between the religion and political process. In this process the religion has played a key role in providing the source, hence contributed towards the satisfaction of the source-oriented legitimacy of the use of force. As a result, only those religious principles have the credentials to become the law which are clearly articulated in the source such as the Qur'an and Sunna. As a result, those laws are inherently legitimate due to their direct reference to the text. Moreover, these credentials are obtained or given by developing the law from the source not only through direct references but also through undergoing a process, which involves debates and disagreements among jurists and scholars, such as discovering legal solutions to problems that have not been dealt with by the source. Therefore, the legitimacy of Islamic international law lies in the process which is known as Ijtihad (exertion of intellectual reasoning). In other words, any law that has developed through the process of Ijtihad is legitimate. So, on the one hand, the Qur'an and Sunna provided the source-oriented legitimacy, and on the other hand, Ijtihad provided the process legitimacy. Consequently, the legitimacy of use of force in Islamic international law lies in a joint setting of the source and process. Although the role of the Qur'an and Sunna as sources of Islamic international law is vital to understand the source-oriented legitimacy, the role of Ijtihad is also vital to understand the process legitimacy. Discussing Ijtihad is crucial in finding the legitimate process and addressing the contradictory claims of 'the authority to use of force' in a coherent manner. For this purpose, the following section discusses the process followed in Ijtihad to overcome the process legitimacy deficits of Islamic international law on the use of force.

5.3 The Process Legitimacy of Ijtihad from the Lens of Shari'a

Ijtihad is a process for developing legal provisions to comprise new cases as well as a strong factor in the development of Islamic law according to the needs of different countries and the conditions of changing times.[21] It has been concluded, in Chap. 4, that the existence of legitimacy deficit in a claim for an Islamic caliphate in the modern world and the emergence of

[21] Mahmassani, 'Adaptation of Islamic Jurisprudence' in Donohue and Esposito (eds), *Islam in Transition*, 145.

Muslim territories in modern nation-states setting show the need for Islamic international law to adapt to keep pace with the conditions of changing times. The method of Ijtihad can play a key role in this process. The barrier that was posted on the development of Islamic international law by arbitrary closure of Ijtihad in the twelfth century CE may be lifted to a great extent through this process.[22] Moreover, reopening the gate of Ijtihad will be a starting point to identify the legitimate authority to decide about the use of force in Islamic international law. Furthermore, this will recognize the legitimate authority to decide on the use of force by those jurisconsults who are authorized to do so in Islamic law and those who had not abstained rightfully from engaging in Ijtihad. For example, one of the influential jurists, Abū Ishāq al-Shātibī, of the fourteenth century advanced the case of purposive approach to Ijtihad arguing that the purposes (*maqāsid*) of the Shari'a can be established by way of juristic induction.[23] One of the unforeseen outcomes of purposive interpretation was that it accentuated Qur'anic intertextuality where the interpretive process itself was guided by the primary values of the Qur'an, derived inductively.[24] Like al-Shātibī, many other jurists had continued to engage in Ijtihad after its closure. As a result, Ijtihad has rescued and led to the flourishing of Islamic jurisprudence in the time of crisis such as in the Abbasid period.[25] As Subhi Mahmassani observed:

> When Baghdad fell in the middle of the Seventh Century A.H., intellectual activities diminished, and Arab civilization began to decline. This took place after the Sunni jurists unanimously agreed to close the door of Ijtihad and to be contented with the four known Sunnite schools … The result was that Islamic thought met a dead end, and imitation and stagnation in jurisprudence.[26]

The closure of Ijtihad violated the provisions and concepts of Islamic jurisprudence and condemned all Muslims to permanent stagnation and exclusions from the application of the laws of evolution. It imposed upon

[22] For a discussion on the closure of Ijtihad and its effect on the development of Islamic international law, see Chap. 3.

[23] Moosa, The Poetics and Politics of Law, 1.

[24] Ibid.

[25] Mahmassani, 'Adaptation of Islamic Jurisprudence' in Donohue and Esposito (eds), *Islam in Transition*, 145.

[26] Ibid., 146.

them to maintain the same conditions prevailing at the time of ancient jurists, and to follow the pattern they had set for themselves and for the Muslims of their days and the days that would follow.[27] As a result, a gap has been created between the laws that were applicable before the closure of Ijtihad and their applicability in modern times. The most effective way to fill this gap is by reopening the gate of Ijtihad with immediate effect for the juristic inductions to address the challenges of Islam in the modern world.[28] The door should be thrown wide open for anyone juristically qualified.[29]

The decision-making authority to use force in Islamic International law, in modern nation-states setting, is confined to the rulers or governments.[30] The rulers and governments must make any decision in relation to use force according to Islamic law, and for that purpose, they must consult with those who are qualified to take part in Ijtihad. This process has become the theoretical discipline of 'roots of law' (*usūl al-fiqh*) in Islamic jurisprudence.[31] Historically, the general purpose of *usūl al-fiqh* in Islamic jurisprudence was not so much to generate new laws as it was to provide a post hoc rationalization and justification for the legal practices that were already in circulation in the post-prophetic period.[32] The *usūl al-fiqh* emerged to dominate Islamic jurisprudence after the demise of Prophet Muhammad mostly through the role of *Muftīs* (jurisconsults who are capable of exercising legal reasoning independent of the schools of law)[33] as purveyors of the construction of Shari'a.[34] These purveyors continued to develop this role among others learned in Islamic jurisprudence known as the Mujtahids. Mujtahids are Islamic legal experts who make new legal pronouncements through Ijtihad.[35] The science of *usūl al-fiqh* has developed a methodology that enables the Mujtahids to infer, deduce, and discover rules of law from the two main sources, namely the Qur'an and the

[27] Ibid.

[28] An-Na'im, 'Toward an Islamic Hermeneutics for Human Rights', 229.

[29] Mahmassani, 'Adaptation of Islamic Jurisprudence' in Donohue and Esposito (eds), *Islam in Transition*, 146.

[30] Those who are qualified in Islamic international law to decide on the use of force have been discussed in Chap. 3.

[31] Nasr, *The Heart of Islam*, 124.

[32] Moosa, The Poetics and Politics of Law, 8.

[33] Esposito (ed), *Oxford Dictionary of Islam*, 85.

[34] Masud, 'Pluralism and International Society' in Hashmi (ed), *Islamic Political Ethics*, 136.

[35] Johnston, Maqāsid al-Shari'a, 149.

Sunna. It also enables them to provide individual reasoning through Ijtihad where the two main sources are silent on an issue of law.[36] For instance, the Qur'an and Sunna have not provided detailed guidance for each circumstance which the human being in general, and Muslims in particular, would encounter. As a result, there are circumstances where Muslims will have to go beyond the periphery of these two main sources to find out solutions to the legal issues.

The development of Shari'a had continued through sources that represent either consensus of juristic opinion (*Ijma*) or analogy (*Qiyas*).[37] Ijma is a process whereby the creative jurists, the Mujtahids, representing the community at large, are considered to have reached an agreement, on a technical legal ruling, thereby rendering it as conclusive and as epistemologically certain as any verse of the Qur'an.[38] On the other hand, Qiyas involves a process whereby the Mujtahids decide legal cases based on similar legal cases together with its rulings which had been adjudicated earlier by the Qur'an or Sunna or Ijma. As a result, in both Ijma and Qiyas, the Mujtahids, authorized by divine revelation, are capable of transforming a ruling reached through human legal reasoning into a textual source by the very fact of their agreement on its validity.[39] However, the overriding objective is to utilize methods of interpretation and reasoning while maintaining the fundamental position that law derives from the divine will.[40] As a result, Mujtahids have developed an Islamic jurisprudence through a process of legitimacy intending to fill the gap between the laws that were applicable before the closure of Ijtihad and their applicability in modern times. On the contrary, many other jurists offered interpretations without any discrimination or examination in the light of the original principles and text, and without the criteria of reason and thought.[41] As a result, the link between source and interpretation became very weak as well as distant from each other. Consequently, the interpretation given by these other jurists often contradicts the reasoning of Mujtahids in legal matters. In

[36] Kamali, *Principles of Islamic Jurisprudence*, 86; see also Khan, The Reopening of the Islamic Code, 341.

[37] Ibid., 168, see also Bakircioglu, *Islam and Warfare*, 27.

[38] Hallaq, *A History of Islamic Legal Theories*, 1.

[39] Ibid.

[40] Khadduri, *Al-Shafi's Risala*, 179; see also Kamali, Methodological Issues in Islamic Jurisprudence, 3.

[41] Mahmassani, 'Adaptation of Islamic Jurisprudence' in Donohue and Esposito (eds), *Islam in Transition*, 145.

these circumstances, contradictory claims of the legitimate use of force are being made. The most controversial issue remains 'the legitimacy of use of force', which the jurists must take on to answer in line with the spirit and purpose of Shari'a (*maqāsid al-Shari'a*).

5.3.1 *Maqāsid al-Shari'a*

Shari'a is a living mechanism. In addition to the Qur'an and Sunna, it equally refers to the spirit and method of extracting laws such as Ijtihad. Whereas the Qur'an and Sunna form the content of laws, the spirit of interpreting those laws emanates from *Maqāsid al-Shari'a* (the spirit and purpose of Shari'a), and the method of extracting the laws lies in Ijtihad. In this setting, Shari'a as a living mechanism legitimately operates through Ijtihad. Therefore, the legitimacy of use of force in Islamic international law must welcome Ijtihad, which is the most suitable method of interpretation of Shari'a, to accommodate the needs of modern society, public interest, and principles of justice and equity.[42] The growth of Ijtihad in line with the spirit and purpose of Shari'a is the only way forward to the legitimacy of use of force in Islamic international law in the twenty-first century. For this purpose, Ijtihad must include the text (Qur'an and Sunna), spirit, and an approved method. Building on these points, this section professes an interpretive strategy which superficially might be seen as utilization of the legal tool of public interest (*masalahah*), but if drawn to its logical conclusion, it often becomes a significant hermeneutical turn away from the letter of the law to a focus on its spirit—away from the specific injunctions of the text to the purpose behind them, *Maqāsid al-Shari'a*.[43]

The purposive approach of Shari'a (*maqāsidī*) is a very important Islamic legal theory that can overcome the legitimacy deficits of Islamic international law. It provides the foundation for an aspiration to use wisdom and safeguard people's welfare.[44] This approach is supported by an-Na'im as a possible way to reconcile Islamic tenets and respect for Public international law.[45] However, a better approach has been suggested by

[42] Van Engeland, 'When Two Visions of a Just World Clash, 156; see also An-Na'im, 'Toward an Islamic Hermeneutics for Human Rights' in An-Na'im and others (eds), *Human Rights and Religious Values*, 229.

[43] Johnston, Maqāsid al-Shari'a, 157.

[44] Mahmassani S., *Falsafat al-Tashri Fi al-Islam*, 106.

[45] an-Na'im, *Toward an Islamic Reformation*, 137.

Sachedina, who emphasized the role of epistemology in the reconciliation process. He has rightly identified 'many apologetic works and the call to create a Shari'a-based state' as potential barriers, which overlooked the need to take a fresh look at a religious epistemology requiring extensive rethinking before it can guide decisions affecting the lives of Muslims in a modern nation-state.[46] On this footing, it can be argued that the search for adaptability in Islamic jurisprudence of the modern world emphasizes a hermeneutical tool of *Maqāsid al-Shari'a*. For example, the first constitution to be drafted in a Muslim state (the Tunisian Constitution) signals this shift of emphasis. Its preamble begins with the phrase, 'God… who has given justice as a guarantee of the preservation of order in the world, and has given the revelation of law in accordance with human welfare'.[47] Similar wording is found in the opening paragraphs of the 'Pact of Security' promulgated by the then Tunisian ruler, Muhammad Brey, three years earlier which stated that:

> Praise be to God who has opened up for truth a way and brought about justice as a guarantor of the world's order and sent down the laws according to people's needs.[48]

The hermeneutical approach to law, as stated above, shows that the process legitimacy of Islamic international law on the use of force can legitimately link to the purpose and spirit of Shari'a. This process promotes the avoidance of harm and adopts a positive as well as proactive enhancement of benefit.[49] This is not to say that one could come up with an application that would contradict a known injunction in the text such as the Qur'an and the Sunna.[50] This method can be seen in the writings of Muhammad 'Abduh and Rashīd Ridā, who had incorporated elements of both the text and spirit.[51] However, to conform to the process legitimacy

[46] Sachedina, *The Islamic Roots of Democratic Pluralism*, 13.

[47] The Constitution of Tunisia 1860, preamble.

[48] Mansūr, and Marzūkī, *al-Qutr al-tūmisī fi safwat al-I tibār bi-mustawda*, 128.

[49] Kamali, Have We Neglected the Shari'ah doctrine of Masalahah?, 287.

[50] Ahmed, 'Which Comes First?' in Ahmed, Nassery, and Tatari (eds.), *The Objectives of Islamic Law*, 239; see also Johnston, Maqāsid al-Shari'a, 149; for *contra* see Kamali, Issues in the Understanding of Jihad and Ijtihad, 617; see also Younes, Islamic Legal Hermeneutics, 585.

[51] Martin and Woodward, *Defenders of Reason in Islam*, 137; see also al-Sayyid, Contemporary Muslim Thought, 27; see also Kerr, *Islamic Reform*, 55.

certain amount of pragmatism is necessary. For instance, the categorization of Muslim rulers by armed non-state actors as *Kafir* (apostates) who are pro-Western or colluding with foreign powers to intervene in the internal affairs of a Muslim state is often claimed to be legitimate according to the purpose and spirit of Shari‘a.[52] However, according to the *maqāṣid*, there are two possible interpretations on this issue, namely (a) no rulers act against the Shari‘a by collaboration with Western powers as long as such collaboration is inevitable between state governments in the modern world, and (b) colluding with foreign powers is illegitimate as it would result in persecution of the people. These contradictory interpretations of the purpose and spirit of Shari‘a give rise to the question about the scope of *maqāṣid*. This is because *maqāṣid* cannot be both legitimate and illegitimate at the same point and on the same matter.

The legitimate scope of *maqāṣid* is determined by an epistemological turn towards relative empowerment of reason over revelation supplemented by the hermeneutical decision to follow the spirit of the sacred text.[53] This is confined to the purpose of the text such as the Qur'an and Sunna.[54] Process legitimacy is not compromised as long as the purpose is aligned with the text. Therefore, the fine line between the purposive approach and inconsistent innovation (Bidyāt) lies in the text. In this way, a pragmatic interpretation of the text is very important to determine the scope of *Maqāsid al-Shari‘a*. This is because *maqāsid* cannot be used as a gateway to invoke innovative interpretation which is inconsistent with the clear proscriptions of the text. The fundamental principle of use of force is provided by the text (the Qur'an and Sunna) that prohibited the spreading of *fitna* (persecution) in the world.[55] Based on this fundamental principle it can be argued that intervention by invitation of a non-Muslim foreign power to intervene in the internal affairs of a Muslim state is illegitimate, except where such collaboration is inevitable in the inter-state affairs of states and no Muslim state is willing and able to collaborate, as this collusion would result in persecution that is prohibited in the text. Moreover, there is no precedent of collusion of this nature in Islamic international law.[56] As a result, the text can legitimately set out the scope

[52] For a discussion on 'Kafir' please, see Chap. 4.

[53] Johnston, Maqāsid al-Shari‘a, 149.

[54] Ibid., referred Muhammad Talbi.

[55] For a discussion on 'fitnah' with reference to the Qur'an and Sunna, see Chap. 3.

[56] For a discussion about 'collusion', see Chap. 4.

of *maqāsid* to avoid innovative and inconsistent interpretation. Furthermore, intervention by invitation lacks legitimate authority in Public international law due to the issues of uncertainty over legitimate consent.[57] Therefore, by adopting a coherent approach between Public and Islamic international law on 'intervention by invitation', it can be concluded that *maqāṣid* is a very potent tool for promoting one view of Islam as objectively true while impugning others for following a corrupt purpose which is prohibited by the fundamental principles of law. This amount of pragmatism is objectively legitimate as the spirit of Shari'a strongly conforms to the notion of public welfare (*masalahah*).

5.3.2 Pragmatic Eclecticism

Pragmatic eclecticism is a logical way to conclude. It considers the current world and its affairs to make a pragmatic decision. This decision is then compared with the text and past Ijtihad. However, past Ijtihad may not always uphold the common good, as they often value the theoretical coherence of the past over the practicality of the present.[58] As a result, any decision taken in the past must be reviewed by exercising pragmatic eclecticism and comparing it with the sources such as the Qur'an, Sunna, Ijma, and Qiyas. A connection between the sources, Shari'a, and Ijtihad was a common picture in courts and among Islamic scholars between the eighth and twelfth century CE.[59] Judges and scholars had regularly practised pragmatic eclecticism despite the almost unanimous opposition of jurists in the first four centuries of Islam when interpretive freedom was the norm inside the courtroom and outside of it.[60] This practice had developed a dialogic interaction between author-jurists from outside the courtroom and the judges inside of it.[61] The interaction granted the judges and jurists

[57] Heyns, Akande et al., 'The International Law Framework Regulating the Use of Armed Drones', 791; see also Vanhullebusch, 'Do Non-State Armed Groups Have a Legal Right to Consent to Offers of International Humanitarian Relief?' (2020) 25 (2) Journal of Conflict & Security Law 317.

[58] Ahmed, 'Which Comes First?' in Ahmed, Nassery, and Tatari (eds.), *The Objectives of Islamic Law*, 239.

[59] Ibrahim, *Pragmatism in Islamic Law*, 16.

[60] Ibid.

[61] For a discussion about the importance of a dialogical approach for achieving coherence see Baderin, *International Human Rights and Islamic Law*, 5.

the power to adjudicate and interpret laws respectively in line with the socio-political needs of their time.[62]

Pragmatic eclecticism views the law as a consequentialist. It focuses on the flexibility and dynamics of law while paying due regard to stability. For example, abrogation of offensive Jihad by later Qur'anic verses on defensive Jihad is a conclusion reached by exercising pragmatic eclecticism. The consequence of not exercising this is to legitimize permanent and total war against non-Muslims as arbitrarily claimed by few Muslim scholars and armed non-state actors.[63] These scholars and non-state actors advocated for the abrogation of non-violent verses of the Qur'an, which is a common denominator in the classical theory, and came up with a distinctive and revolutionary vision of jihad as a permanent struggle.[64] In this situation, the scholars and judges applied pragmatic eclecticism horizontally to take into account the principle of abrogation and its consequence in the modern world.[65] Moreover, pragmatic eclecticism's approach to the dynamics of the Qur'an as a source of Islamic law paved the way for Shari'a to reject the dominant classical opposition to the principle of abrogation by adopting flexibility in the process of the legitimacy of use of force in Islamic international law without giving up its stability.

The scope of exercising pragmatic eclecticism in Islamic international law is very narrow as argued by Jalāl al-Dīn al-Suyūtī. He argued that pragmatic eclecticism must be exercised for a pragmatic worldly reason (*amr dunyawī*) such as to redress any tension between the legal interpretations but not arbitrarily (*mujaraddan 'an al-qasd*).[66] By the word 'arbitrary', he meant that question of law must be interpreted by qualified persons such as Mujtahids according to the text.[67] Pragmatic eclecticism must be utilized by qualified legal actors, namely judges (qādīs), Mujtahids (legal scholars who are experts in exercising Ijtihad), and author-jurists (jurists who compile law books, creating, justifying, modifying, and codifying legal doctrine).[68] However, as far as pragmatic eclecticism is exercised by these qualified people, it is permissible to depart from any rules of

[62] Ibrahim, *Pragmatism in Islamic Law*, 23.

[63] For a discussion about 'total and permanent war' against the non-Muslim and the West, see Chap. 3.

[64] Amin, *Reclaiming Jihad*, 99.

[65] Ibrahim, *Pragmatism in Islamic Law*, 85.

[66] Ibrahim, Al-Sha'rānī's Response to Legal Purism, 112.

[67] Ibid.

[68] Khadduri, *Al-Shafi's Risala*, 365; see also Kamali, *Principles of Islamic Jurisprudence*, 169.

legal methodology (*usūl*).[69] The transplantation of legal rules by the qualified people through pragmatic eclecticism emanates from surveys of the text (the Qur'an and Sunna), Ijma, and Qiyas.[70] Whilst the survey of the text must be made by analogical reasoning (Qiyas), the same is not viable for consensus of opinion (Ijma).[71] This is because any consensus on a legal issue and methodology adopted to reach a conclusion that was agreed upon centuries ago may not always be suitable in different social and political contexts.[72] As a result, legal interpretation can be free from methodologies developed in the formative period. The method of Ijtihad, judicial decisions, and compilation of law through pragmatic eclecticism are objective and free from arbitrariness as emphasized by al-Suyūtī.[73] Moreover, the objectivity in legal reasoning and connectivity with the text make a strong opposition to arbitrariness.[74] The objectivity and arbitrariness were questioned in the tenth century CE, where it was argued that Ijtihad had given much freedom and flexibility in exercising analogical reasoning by mobilizing a mix of precedents, text, and social welfare as part of their process.[75] It was also argued that because of this freedom and flexibility entertained by jurists of the formative period and the resulting disconnection with the contents Ijtihad became arbitrary.[76] On the contrary, connectivity and objectivity were seen in the practices of legal scholars, where they exercised Ijtihad.[77] For example, through the mix of Ijtihad and pragmatic eclecticism al-Ghannūshī concluded that the articles of the Universal Declaration of Human Rights (UDHR) are largely in line with Islamic law.[78] These practices have maintained the continuity of legitimate Ijtihad following the closure of its gate, and consequently, the Shari'a emerged as a living mechanism.[79] According to Ahmed Fekry Ibrahim:

[69] Sadeghi, *The Logic of Law Making in Islam*, 76.

[70] For a discussion on 'Ijma and Qiyas', see Chap. 3.

[71] Qarāfī S., *al-Ihkām fī Tamyīz al-Fatāwā*, 88.

[72] Griffiths, 'Preface' in Dupret B., Berger M., and al-Zwaini L. (eds), *Legal Pluralism*, xii.

[73] Schacht and MacDonald, 'Idjtihad' in Bearman P. and Bianquis Th. et al. (eds), *Encyclopaedia of Islam*, 1965.

[74] Ibid.

[75] Ibrahim, *Pragmatism in Islamic Law*, 35.

[76] Ibid.

[77] Jackson, *Islamic Law and the State*, 77.

[78] Opwis, Masalaha, 187.

[79] For a discussion about the closure of the gate of Ijtihad and the evolution of Shari'a, see Chap. 3.

> Pragmatic eclecticism within Ijtihad has been much more dominant in modernist discourse because their exponents have succeeded in making the argument that their approaches have the backing of the authoritative premodern legal tradition.[80]

The continuation of pragmatic eclecticism within Ijtihad, since the official closure of its gate in the twelfth century, has been making a legal continuum in Islamic jurisprudence. The judges, Mujtahids, and author-jurists exercised pragmatic eclecticism beyond the formative period and throughout the centuries to mitigate tensions between the law and socio-political situations. During colonialism in the nineteenth century pragmatic eclecticism played a vital role in the modernization of Islamic international law. Moreover, with the emergence of modern nation-states scholars have adopted pragmatic eclecticism to examine the legitimacy of Public and Islamic international law. This examination was conducted not because of their methodological consistency but according to their utility to the modern nation-states that were striving to claim the legitimacy of use of force. In the twenty-first century claims of the legitimate use of force have reached a vantage point where the legitimacy of use of force in Public and Islamic international law is dependent on a coherent approach of these two legal systems where the use of force must be perceived as legitimate by those who are affected by such force. Thus, legitimacy in the descriptive sense must be the key aim of both Public and Islamic international law. Pragmatic eclecticism can play a vital role in discharging this aim.

5.3.3 *Public Welfare (*Masalahah*)*

Islamic jurisprudence is the science that identifies the methods devised by the scholars who are engaged in Ijtihad in their inferring and exploration of Islamic legal injunctions from the text, and their construction based on efficient causes that stand behind their revelation.[81] These injunctions, in turn, are related to public welfare (*masalahah*) that Islamic law aims to accomplish.[82] As a result, public welfare has a special place in Islamic law.[83] An Islamic scholar exercising Ijtihad must consider public welfare as a key

[80] Ibrahim, *Pragmatism in Islamic Law*, 200.
[81] Zahra, *Usūl al-Fiqh*, 3.
[82] Ibid.
[83] Van Engeland, 'Contextualisation of Humanitarian Assistance and Its Shortcomings, 169.

element to the process. For instance, a Mujtahid may conclude on the prohibition or permission of use of force based on 'whether it serves the public benefit or welfare'. The concept of public welfare can be immensely helpful in cases that are not regulated by the Quran, Sunna, Ijma, and Qiyas.[84] Therefore, equitable consideration in the process of Ijtihad can override the results of strict analogy, taking into account public welfare.[85]

Many jurists, both classical and modern, have recognized public welfare as a legitimate factor to consider in analogy (Qiyas) and Ijtihad. However, these jurists have emphasized considering public welfare in line with the text. Imam Abu Hanifa (the founder of the Hanafi school of thought) employed a procedure where he looked for law in the text, and when he could not find any regulation, he or his associates extended the existing rules by the process of analogy.[86] Similarly, the exercise of Ijtihad to promote public interest as a general purpose of the Shari'a was accepted by Imam Malik (the founder of the Maliki school) subject to the condition that the interest should be in harmony with the spirit of Shari'a (*maqāsid*) and should not conflict with any of its sources.[87] He accommodated public interest by the device of *istislah* while applying the Sunna of the Prophet.[88] In the absence of explicit text, he would have incorporated the analogy and a source of law unique to his school known as *masalahah* (public interest).[89] He regarded public interest as the object and purpose of Islamic law.[90] Moreover, the Hanbali school went further than that and advocated for placing public welfare before the text and consensus.[91] Ibn Hanbal (the founder of the Hanbali school) used this principle to seek the best solution to serve the general interest of the Muslim community. Although Imam Shafi (the founder of the Shafi school) supported following of analogy on the strength and spirit of the text, he did not allow juridical opinions based on *maslahah*.[92] He was concerned about the possibility of reliance on

[84] Esposito (ed), *Oxford Dictionary of Islam*, 261.

[85] Ibid.

[86] al-Mehdi, 'The Concept of an Islamic State' in Gauhar A. (ed), *The Challenges of Islam*, 114.

[87] al-Shātibi, *Al-I'tisām* (Cairo: 1332) 95 cited in Mahmassani, *Falsafat al-Tashri Fi al-Islam*, 88.

[88] al-Mehdi, 'The Concept of an Islamic State' in Gauhar A. (ed), *The Challenges of Islam*, 114.

[89] Mahmassani, *Falsafat al-Tashri Fi al-Islam*, 27.

[90] Ibid.

[91] Ibid., 116.

[92] Ibid., 27.

unrestricted subjective human opinions and because public interests vary according to context and time.[93] However, the Shafi school recognizes the sanctity of human life and enjoins human beings to take action against suffering and injustice.[94] For instance, Imam al-Gazzāli, a Shafi scholar, advocated the notion of public interest as *istislah*.[95]

Whilst concluding according to consideration of public welfare the jurists often provided multiple solutions to a single issue. As a result, it was necessary to find legitimate solutions to any given legal issue. In order to identify the legitimate basis of use of force from multiple juristic findings, Muslim scholars resorted to *istihsan* (juristic preference). The word 'istihsan' is the gerund of the verb 'istahsana', which denotes to prefer or to consider a thing commendable.[96] The Hanafi school liberally used analogy by a process of *istihsan*, which led to a measure of preference for reasoning.[97] Therefore, *istihsan* is a process used to broaden legal rules by means of analogy.[98] It allows jurists to abandon a strong precedent for a weaker precedent in the interests of justice.[99] Although there is no doubt that many jurists preferred to give priority to the text and stronger bases of law over the weaker, few jurists rejected to recognize this as a method of interpretation.[100] For example, Imam Abu Hanifa, Imam Malik, and Imam Ibn Hanbal had accepted *istihsan* and subscribed to take into account public welfare (*masalahah*), but Imam Shafi rejected it.[101] Imam Shafi stated that 'he who practices preference assumes unto himself the power of law-making which only belongs to those whom God and the prophet have ordained.'[102] On the contrary, the proponents (who are the majority of the Muslim jurists) of *istihsan* quoted from the Qur'an to support their stand. They referred to chapter 39 verse 18, which provided that 'who hear advice and follow the best thereof are those whom the God guides and

[93] Esposito (ed), *Oxford Dictionary of Islam*, 152.

[94] Ibid.

[95] al-Ghazzāli, *Al-Mustafa min 'Ilm al-Usūl* (Cairo: 1937) 137 cited in Mahmassani, *Falsafat al-Tashri Fi al-Islam*, 89.

[96] Mahmassani, *Falsafat al-Tashri Fi al-Islam*, 85.

[97] Ibid.

[98] Ibid., 19.

[99] Ibid., 27.

[100] Ibid., 85.

[101] al-Shātibi, *Al-I'tisām* (Cairo: 1332) 116 cited in Mahmassani, *Falsafat al-Tashri Fi al-Islam*, 86.

[102] al-Ghazzāli, *Al-Mustafa min 'Ilm al-Usūl* (Cairo: 1937) 137 cited in Mahmassani, *Falsafat al-Tashri Fi al-Islam*, 86; see also al-Shaf'i, *Kitab al-Umm*, 273.

such are men of understanding.'[103] However, there is a limit to the expansion proffered by Abu Hanifa, Imam Malik, and Imam Ibn Hanbal. If there were two analogies on a point of law they would set aside the one which was unsupported by the text and adopt instead the one which is so supported based on *istihsan* (juristic preference).[104] The further limit was imposed by rejecting any preference which a jurist found agreeable by reasoning and towards which he inclined through opinion.[105] This method of *istihsan* is invalid because it is often based upon mere whim and inclination.

Modern jurists such as Muhammad 'Abduh and Muhammad Rashīd Ridā resurrected al-Shātibi's scholarship and argued that common good constitutes the prime purpose of Islamic law (*maqāsid*) in modern times.[106] They called for the unification of any disagreements between different schools of thought and advocated the return to the sources and the true spirit of Shari'a, and the advance of the Shari'a in the field of progress and civilization at the national and international levels.[107] Sachedina called for a theology that would give the ethics of Qur'an its rightful place: 'the time has come for a fresh start from the points in the normative tradition where the system of Islamic law makes extensive use of judgements of equity through juristic preference (*istihsan*) and public interest (*maslahah*) for the common good and where ethical theology encourages human reasoned judgments of right and wrong.'[108] Moreover, in the nineteenth century, Tunisia '*Khayr al-Dīn al-Tūnisī's Aqwam al-masālik*' (The Surest Path) affirmed the principle of public interest as the supreme guiding principle of governments in Muslim states.[109] Muhammad Abū Zahra, an influential Egyptian jurist, emphasized that 'human welfare' should be the key consideration for Islamic jurisprudence in the modern world.[110] Furthermore, the necessity to uphold public welfare has also been found in the writings of Shaykh Muhammad al-Ghazālī, an al-Azhar scholar who later became a Grand Mufti of Algeria in the 1980s. He stated that:

[103] Al-Qur'an 39: 18, Abu Yusuf translation.

[104] Mahmassani, *Falsafat al-Tashri Fi al-Islam*, 85.

[105] al-Shātibi, *Al-I'tisām* (Cairo: 1332) 116 cited in Sobhi Mahmassani, *Falsafat al-Tashri Fi al-Islam*, 87.

[106] Esposito (ed), *Oxford Dictionary of Islam*, 290.

[107] Mahmassani, *Falsafat al-Tashri Fi al-Islam*, 92.

[108] Sachedina, *The Islamic Roots*, 45.

[109] Brown, *The Surest Path*, 61.

[110] Johnston, *Earth, Empire and Sacred Text*, 30.

> The Shari'a does not stipulate all the means necessary to enforce justice... But it has left that to people's independent legal judgment (*Ijtihad*) and the development of the times. And as long as justice, as seen by the Legislator, is an objective pursued for its own sake, then everything that strives to reach it is Shari'a—even if the Legislator does not mention it or lay down its details.[111]

The propositions of Sachedina for 'common good', Abū Zahra for 'human welfare', and al-Ghazālī for 'public welfare' support for adopting a pragmatic approach to Islamic jurisprudence including Ijtihad. This common approach built an interconnection between the religiopolitical and legal-political legacies. For instance, those religiopolitical legacies are legitimate which have or can become the law through a political process and hence transformed into the legal-political legacies.[112] Therefore, in upholding public interest the legitimacy of legal-political legacies must be considered as a key criterion. This is because those religious principles which have not or may not become law are promoting religiopolitical interests only as opposed to legitimacy. Therefore, religion should be kept separate from the law when it is useful for the common good. The role that Islamic international law can play in finding common good in the modern world is vital to the legitimacy question. As public welfare is the fundamental principle of legitimacy in Islamic international law, it is necessary and reasonable that Shari'a rules are interpreted to suit changing times.[113] Tariq Ramadan suggested that juristic interpretation of the text in the modern context is congenial to Islamic jurisprudence.[114] Times have changed, he argued: 'it is becoming necessary today to go back to the Qur'an and Sunna and, in the light of our environment, to deepen our analysis to develop a new vision appropriate to our new context to formulate suitable legal opinions.'[115] He refers to the Shari'a to resource from provisions of the text, consensus, analogy, and develop through Ijtihad that caters for considerations of the purpose of Shari'a, pragmatic eclecticism, and public welfare.

[111] Ibid.

[112] For a discussion about the legal-political legacies and their legitimacy in Islamic international law, see Chap. 3.

[113] An-Na'im, 'Toward an Islamic Hermeneutics for Human Rights', 229.

[114] Ramadan, *Western Muslims and the Future of Islam*, 69.

[115] Ibid.

5.4 The Place of Islamic International Law in Public International Law on the Use of Force

The universal application of Public international law on the use of force based on indiscriminate application to all nations in the world has been contested by the advocates of cultural relativity according to whom it is a Western idea not compatible with the norms and values of many non-western cultures.[116] However, this claim of Public international law to speak for people all over the world has been contested by the descriptive legitimacy deficit which requires the law to be perceived as legitimate by its subjects.[117] According to most Muslim states and non-state actors operating therein, Public international law is following its colonial trend where it is developed to promote the interests of colonial powers and there is no place for Islamic international law.[118] Moreover, colonial history suggests that Public international law treated other legal systems as unfit and uncivilized.[119] As a result, it can be argued that Public international law does not have a place for Islamic international law.

The legitimacy of Public international law is being questioned for its imperial characteristic. It lacks legitimacy in the descriptive sense where most of the more than 1.5 billion Muslims do not perceive the use of force in the modern world as legitimate.[120] This is because almost every armed attack in this century involved one or more Muslim states. Therefore, a coherent approach to the legitimacy of use of force requires recognition of the law of those people who are going to face the actual impact of such use of force.[121] In these circumstances, the call for the legitimacy of Public international law on the use of force has become a particularly important matter in current world affairs. In order to overcome the legitimacy deficits

[116] Freeman, *Human Rights*, ch 6.

[117] For a discussion about 'descriptive legitimacy deficits', see Chap. 2.

[118] For a discussion about the claims of state and armed non-state actors regarding Islamic international law, see Chap. 4.

[119] Nazzo, 'Territory, Sovereignty, and the Construction of the Colonial Space' in Koskenniemi, Rech and Fonesca (eds), *International Law and Empire*, 272; see also Anghie, *Imperialism, Sovereignty and the Making*, 58; Brownlie, 'The Expansion of International Society' in Bull and Watson (eds), *The Expansion of International Society*, 357; Elias, *Africa and the Development of International Law*, 6; Alexandrowicz, *An Introduction to the History*, 14.

[120] For a discussion on descriptive legitimacy deficits of Public international law, see Chap. 2.

[121] Franck, *The Power of Legitimacy Among nations*, 209.

of Public international law on the use of force, it has been argued that it must recognize Islamic international law as a source of the applicable law at the international level and ensure equal participation of every Muslim state in the decision-making process at international institutions such as the Security Council.[122] In this way, both source-oriented and process legitimacy of the use of force in Public international law can be obtained without side-lining a major legal system such as Islamic international law. This is a coherent approach to overcome the existing legitimacy deficits of Public international law on the use of force. The coherence between two radically different legal systems, such as Public and Islamic international law, within the global legal framework, is possible by emphasizing the importance of descriptive legitimacy.

5.4.1 General Principles of Law Recognized by Civilized Nations

Public international law has not officially recognized Islamic international law as a source of law despite there were and currently are scopes for this. Article 38 (1) (c) of the Statute of the International Court of Justice recognizes 'the general principles of law recognized by civilized nations' as a source of Public international law. This principle has established the notion that 'a principle which is found to be generally accepted by established legal systems may fairly be assumed to be so reasonable as to be necessary to the maintenance of justice under any system.'[123] Such principle of law is generally due to its roots and ranks in the legal system rather than its scope of application.[124] Therefore, it is arguable that Islamic international law can be a potential source of Public international law on the use of force despite its scope of the application being limited to the Muslim states only. Moreover, article 38 (1) (b) of the Statute recognizes 'international customs, as evidence of general practice accepted as law' as a source of Public international law. The Sunna of the Prophet, supported by the Qur'an, embodying the Arabian *jus gentium* is equivalent to international customs and accordingly falls into this category.[125] Furthermore, article 38(1) (d)

[122] This argument has been made by the author in Chap. 4.

[123] Clapham, *Brierly's Law of Nations*, 64.

[124] Abi-Saab, *Cours General de Droit International Public* cited in Clapham, *Brierly's Law of Nations*, 64.

[125] Pirzada, 'Islam and International Law' in Gauhar A. (ed), *The Challenges of Islam*, 196.

of the Statute recognizes 'judicial decisions and the teachings of the most highly qualified publicists of various nations, as subsidiary means for the determination of rules of law'. The methodologies such as *Maqāsid al-Shari'a*, pragmatic eclecticism, and *Masalahah* as entertained by the Judges, Mujtahids, and jurists in Muslim states are potentially very good sources of Public international law on the use of force.

The history of Islamic international law suggests that it came into existence in the Middle Ages and has developed since then.[126] It developed many principles of inter-state practices regarding diplomacy, the sanctity of alliances, and the limits of warfare more than a millennium before Public international law.[127] 'Speaking of the history of Public international law, writers habitually begin with the Greek City-States, describe the Roman period as immediately following, and then all of a sudden talk of modern times, neglecting the gap of almost a thousand years that intervenes.'[128] Islamic international law had intervened in the millennium between Antiquity and the Age of Discovery, that is the creating and sustained existence of a self-encompassing system of inter-state law meant to govern relations of the Islamic world and its 'other'.[129] Despite the claim that the basic tenets of Public international law which hold today are grounded in the European experience of not only the 1648 Peace of Westphalia but also the age of discovery inaugurated by the voyages of Columbus and de Gama,[130] there is a gap of Public international law through the Middle Ages.[131] In this gap, the Islamic international law took from its predecessors and, through acculturation, gave to those who came after it, so that the echoes of the law are to be recognized as having been heard in the development of the Christian law of nations continuing through to contemporary Public international law.[132] Therefore, it appears that Islamic international law has contemporary relevance in modern Public international law both historically and normatively.

[126] Allain, 'Acculturation through the Middle Ages' in Orakhelashvili A. (ed.), *Research Handbook*, 395.

[127] Ibid.

[128] Hamidullah, *Muslim Conduct of State*, 63.

[129] Allain, 'Acculturation through the Middle Ages' in Orakhelashvili A. (ed.), *Research Handbook*, 395.

[130] Ibid., 394.

[131] Pirzada, 'Islam and International Law' in Gauhar (ed), *The Challenges of Islam*, 196.

[132] Ibid.

Although disregarded by the European dominant system of Public international law, Islamic international law offers a set of laws on the use of force to follow by modern nation-states. The life of Prophet Muhammad (570–632 CE) was the catalyst that precipitated Arab conquest 'whose scale was unparalleled in world history' and which, by the early eighth century, 'encompassed the largest empire the world had yet seen'.[133] Islam was for the millennium under consideration, 'the greatest and most influential of the world monotheistic religions', constituting the leading civilization of the epoch, and including 'many of the world's great cities and some of its most productive agriculture'.[134] Some 800 years before Grotius brought together the various tenets of European public law *qua* Christian law of nations into one text, and several Islamic Jurists had devoted themselves to the regime of Islamic international law which, like its European counterpart some 800 years later, had aspirations of universal application.[135]

The political history of Islam suggests that incorporation through agreement rather than military conquest transpired, in 638 CE, under the reign of the second successor to Prophet Muhammad, Umar Ibn al-Khattab (the Second Caliph of Islam).[136] The law of treaties developed to agree with states (both Muslims and non-Muslims) and that this formed an impressive part of Islamic doctrine.[137] Whereas the crusaders proceeded on the principle that no faith need to be kept with infidels, Islamic international law required Muslims to strictly adhere to treaties even with non-Muslims, and 'these virtues of civilization were all on the side of the Saracens [re Muslims].'[138] The only known law of nations, beyond the one currently in force, which had a universal application and was fully operational was Islamic international law.[139] Moreover, the development of an international legal framework between the abode of Islam (*Dar al-Islam*) and the abode of war (*Dar-al-Harb*) during the imperial and colonial periods had formed Islamic international law as the most tried and tested law

[133] Ponting, *World History*, 305–306.

[134] Ibid., 301.

[135] Allain, 'Acculturation through the Middle Ages' in Orakhelashvili A. (ed.), *Research Handbook*, 397; for a critical analysis of the criticisms of the Muslim Qadis (Muslim judges) by the Western judges see Rabb, 'Against Kadijustiz, 343.

[136] Kennedy, *The Great Arab Conquest*, 91–92.

[137] Nussbaum, *A Concise History of the Law of Nations*, 53.

[138] Ibid., 54.

[139] Allain, 'Acculturation through the Middle Ages' in Orakhelashvili A. (ed.), *Research Handbook*, 407.

of nations.[140] Furthermore, the emergence of Muslim states and their acceptance of legal responsibility under Public international law by signing international treaties such as the UN Charter show that these states recognize the legality of use of force in Public international law as they have agreed under a treaty which is binding on them under both Public and Islamic international law. Consequently, Muslim states adopted systems of law that were foreign to them such as the French Jurisprudence in North Africa, the Soviet laws in Central Asia, the English Common law in India, the Dutch law in Indonesia, and above all modern Public international law in most Muslim states which are propounding by influencing not only the body of laws but also the meaning of legitimacy as it affects the Muslims.[141] This is a coherent approach that Islamic international law commands Muslim states to adopt. Similarly, Public international law must adopt the same or similar approach to overcome the descriptive legitimacy deficit by recognizing Islamic international law as a legitimate source of law on the use of force under article 38 of the Statute of the International Court of Justice.

5.4.2 *Sovereign Equality and the UN Collective Security System*

The Charter system has aimed to establish an international community based on co-existence and co-operation through a strong collective security system.[142] 'If the world of states is to be recognized as a community, each state must treat discrete obligations that arise only under special circumstances, like the obligation to help a friend [ally] who is in need, as derivative from and expressing a more general responsibility active throughout the association in different ways.'[143] The different ways to deliver responsibility of states must be coherent. However, the charter system has substantially failed to develop a coherent system of general obligation by or on behalf of states irrespective of any special relationship with each other.[144] For example, the co-operation between states within a

[140] For a discussion about 'abode of Islam and abode of war', see Chap. 3.

[141] Fyzee, 'The Reinterpretation of Islam' in Donohue and Esposito (eds), *Islam in Transition*, 151; see also Henderson C., 'The Arab Spring and the Notion of External State Sovereignty in International Law', 175.

[142] Charter of the United Nations, art 53.

[143] Dworkin, *Law's Empire*, 200.

[144] For a discussion about the failure of the UN Charter to develop a coherent international legal relationship between the states, see Chap. 2.

regional organization (such as NATO) is much stronger and frequent than outside of it. To overcome the legitimacy deficits of Public international law, a more coherent approach in the co-operation between states beyond a single regional organization is needed. This is because increased co-operation among a large number, if not all, of states would strengthen the co-existence of states within the international community and thereby its legitimacy. However, considering the preference of national and geopolitical interests among elite and powerful states, it is not viable to seek coherence among other states to fulfil their general obligation of co-operation under the UN Charter. This is because most foreign interventions in the twenty-first century were motivated mainly by the political interests of the elite and powerful states and their allies rather than discharging their underlying legal responsibility under Public international law on the use of force. As a result, it is crucial to implement sovereign equality under article 2 (1) of the UN Charter.[145] This will overcome the process legitimacy deficits of Public international law on the use of force by enabling the member states of the United Nations to take part equally in the decision-making process.

5.4.3 *Islamic International Law in the International Courts and Tribunals*

The International Court of Justice (ICJ) stands at the apex of international legal development.[146] Therefore, it shall play a key role in overcoming the existing legitimacy deficits of Public international law on the use of force. For this purpose, ICJ shall consider Islamic international law in deciding international disputes before them. Consideration of Islamic international law in the ICJ jurisprudence would play a key role in obtaining legitimacy of Public international law in the descriptive sense.[147] It will also uphold the legitimacy of results that the court may reach. However, ICJ jurisprudence to date has largely ignored Islamic international law. From its operation in 1946 through July 2020 the court issued 139

[145] Henderson, 'The Arab Spring and the Notion of External State Sovereignty in International Law', 175.

[146] Franck, *Fairness in International Law*, 318; see also Shaw, The International Court of Justice, 831.

[147] For a discussion on the legitimacy of use of force of Public international law in the descriptive sense, see Chap. 2.

judgements in contested cases and 28 advisory opinions.[148] Many of these judgements and advisory opinions are either involved or directed to one or more Muslim states.[149] However, in most of these judgements and opinions, Islamic law was neither considered nor applied. As a result, the ICJ has rarely or occasionally referred to Islamic law in the decisions and opinions. On the rare occasions where the ICJ referred to Islamic law, only in very few instances a majority of the court was convinced that references to Islamic law should be discussed. For instance, between 1946 and 2006 those few judges who argued that references to Islamic law 'should be discussed' had only twice been able to convince a majority of the Court to follow their lead.[150]

Relegating Islamic international law by the court has contributed to the legitimacy deficits of Public international law. As the court's statute allows it to consider Islamic international law in several different ways, the ICJ can argue that their decisions and opinions are legitimate if they apply Islamic international law to the disputes.[151] The court can consider Islamic international law in two ways, namely (a) as a source of international legal norms and (b) as an application of international legal norms—particularly in resolving disputes involving one or more Muslim states and non-state actors.[152] Whereas the former can be supported by article 38 of the ICJ statute, there are precedents in the ICJ jurisprudence for the latter. Islamic law was referred by the ICJ in the *United States Diplomatic and Consular Staff in Tehran* case to address Iran's challenge of the legitimacy of the Court.[153] Similarly, in the *Western Sahara* case, the Kingdom of Morocco made an argument in support of its claim of territorial sovereignty against the Mauritanian Entity (a quasi-state to which Mauritania was the successor).[154] Likewise, in the *Lockerbie case* judge Ahmed Sadek El-Kosheri, an ad hoc judge appointed by Libya, argued for the application of Islamic law in determining provisional measures for the extradition

[148] Available at https://www.icj-cij.org/en/decisions/ accessed 22 July 2020.

[149] Ibid.

[150] Lombardi, Islamic law in the Jurisprudence, 85.

[151] For a discussion on the ways that the ICJ Statute allows the court to apply Islamic law, see above.

[152] Lombardi, Islamic law in the Jurisprudence, 85.

[153] *United States Diplomatic and Consular Staff in Tehran (US v Iran)*, 1980 ICJ at 40 (May 24, 1980).

[154] *Western Sahara*, 1975 ICJ at 42–44 (summarizing and analyzing Morocco's arguments in support of its claim).

of the accused.[155] These cases and article 38 of the ICJ statute suggest that the legitimacy of Public international law necessitates appointing judges in the court among those who are learned in Islamic international law. This appointment is legally recognized by the ICJ statute. Article 9 of the Statute instructs that, in voting for the judges, electors should strive to ensure that 'in the body as a whole the representation of the main forms of civilization and the principal legal systems of the world should be assured.'[156] This article provides for a regional diversity of judges.[157] One might plausibly question whether the presence of judges from these regions can give the international community of states confidence that the diversity of the world's legal cultures is being adequately represented since these regions each comprise numerous states which represent different legal cultures.[158] This is because recruiting judges from diverse regions would not, by itself, guarantee that representation of Islamic international law is made. Therefore, it is essential that judges with a strong familiarity with Islamic international law must be appointed in the ICJ.

Similarly, Islamic international law shall be applied by other international courts and tribunals such as the International Criminal Court (ICC). Due to the occurrences of armed conflicts in Muslim states and allegations of international crime such as genocide being made in those countries, namely Iraq, Syria, and Yemen, the ICC must prepare itself for investigating and legitimately deciding these allegations. Moreover, the involvement of the ICC in recent cases such as *Al Mahdi* makes a strong proposition for recognition and application of Islamic international law by the court.[159] Furthermore, prosecuting the alleged member of Ansar Eddine (an armed non-state actor) and *de facto* chief of Islamic police Al Hassan Ag Abdoul Aziz, having just opened an investigation into the crimes committed against the Rohingya Muslims in Myanmar as well as the crimes committed in Afghanistan, prosecuting ISIS leaders for committing crimes in Iraq and Syria, and seeking a ruling on the Court's territorial jurisdiction in respect to Palestine, all urge for the necessity to

[155] *Questions of Interpretation and Application of the 1971 Montreal Convention Arising from the Aerial Incident at Lockerbie (Libyan Arab Jamahirya v US)*, 1992 ICJ 114 (Apr 14, 1992) at 217 (separate opinion of Judge El-Kosheri).

[156] Statute of the International Court of Justice, art 9.

[157] Lombardi, Islamic law in the Jurisprudence, 85.

[158] Ibid.

[159] *Prosecutor v. Al Mahdi* (2017) 17 International Criminal Law Review 486–516.

incorporate Islamic law in the proceedings of ICC.[160] As an international court, the ICC should represent the whole world, not only all geographical regions but also all legal traditions.[161] Article 36 of the Rome Statute states that 'the States Parties should consider "the representation of the principal legal systems of the world" in electing judges.'[162] Article 21 also indirectly refers to the Islamic legal tradition stating that 'national laws of legal systems of the world' should be examined in developing general principles of law.[163] Although the common law/civil law divide at the ICC has been extensively discussed, one legal tradition always seems to have been forgotten: the Islamic legal tradition. Islamic legal system can be considered as a 'major legal system' as it meets the two conditions, namely (a) it is geographically widespread and (b) its influence has been long-lasting.[164] There are 57 Muslim states which are members of the Organization of Islamic Cooperation (OIC) as well as the UN and consisting of over 1.5 billion Muslims.[165] These states apply and use Islamic law either as their main legal system or in addition to another one.[166] Although the application of Islamic law in these states is not uniform, yet Islamic principles and norms constitute a principal legitimizing factor for cultural-legal norms in most parts of the Muslim world.[167] For this purpose, the ICC must appoint its prosecutors and judges from those who are learned in Islamic law. The same applies to other international courts and tribunals such as the Permanent Court of Arbitration and other arbitral tribunals such as the International Tribunal for the Law of the Sea.

5.5 Conclusion

This chapter concludes that the legitimacy of use of force cannot be obtained by overcoming the existing legitimacy deficits of Public and Islamic international law separately as an independent legal system. Instead, these two legal systems must complement each other by filling

[160] Tiedrez, 'On the International Criminal Court's lack of Islamic law representation'.

[161] Ibid.

[162] Rome Statute of the International Criminal Court, art 36.

[163] Ibid., art 21.

[164] Mitchell and Powell, *Domestic Law Goes Global*, 68.

[165] http://www.oic-oci.org/oicv3/page/?p_id=52&p_ref=26&lan=en accessed on 20 July 2020.

[166] Mitchell and Powell, *Domestic Law Goes Global*, 68.

[167] Baderin, *International Human Rights and Islamic Law*, 6.

the gaps created by their existing legitimacy deficits. This chapter has answered the legitimacy question, that is where does the legitimacy lie, with an emphasis on the coherent approach between Public and Islamic international law. It has argued that the legitimacy question reached a vantage point where it has driven the question to a new direction which has taken it to two particularly important questions, namely (a) source-oriented legitimacy deficits of Pubic and Islamic international law and (b) process legitimacy deficits of the same. At this point, the legitimacy of use of force lies in the invocation of a coherent approach between Public and Islamic international law.

The source-oriented legitimacy of Public and Islamic international law emanates from their origins in the natural and divine law, respectively. However, a coherent approach between these two legal systems requires Public international law to recognize Islamic international law as a valid source of law.[168] This chapter has argued that this can be adopted under the framework statutes that set up international courts such as the ICJ and ICC. Public international law must adopt this coherent approach to overcome the existing legitimacy deficits. Whereas Public international law has moved away from the natural law, which is originated in Christianity, to facilitate a secular legal system based on legal and political theories such as the rule of law and sovereignty of states, the legitimacy of Islamic international law still lies on its sources and the Shari'a. The sources of Islamic law are the text (Qur'an and Sunna), Ijma, and Qiyas. However, the Shari'a is a living mechanism derived from these sources. The Shari'a continued to develop through the methods of Islamic jurisprudence such as Ijtihad. Ijtihad has been serving as a method of deduction of rules from the sources of Islamic law, the purpose of the Shari'a (*maqāsid*), pragmatic eclecticism, and public welfare (*masalahah*). Despite the closure of Ijtihad in the twelfth century CE Muslim scholars continued resorting to this method of deduction in the absence of guidance from the text, Ijma (consensus), and Qiyas (analogy). As a result, Ijtihad has been and is an essential ingredient for the growth of Shari'a. It has been nurturing the Shari'a to keep pace with the social, legal, and political changes in the modern world. Moreover, from a historical perspective, the Shari'a has never been in conflict with its

[168] Van Engeland has argued this under the theoretical basis of 'legal pluralism', see Van Engeland, 'The Balance Between Islamic Law, Customary Law and Human Rights in Islamic Constitutionalism', 1321.

evolution. Therefore, it is capable and ready to adopt the coherent approach of Public international law as suggested in this chapter.

The process legitimacy of Public and Islamic international law on the use of force has been subject to controversies. This chapter has discussed these controversies and concluded that the process legitimacy of the use of force in these two legal systems can be overcome by taking a coherent approach that seeks to answer the legitimacy question regarding their process legitimacy deficits. According to this approach, the process legitimacy of Islamic international law on the use of force can be overcome by exercising Ijtihad in line with the sources and purpose of the Shari'a (*maqāsid*), pragmatic eclecticism, and public welfare (*masalahah*). This process will reassure that Ijtihad is explaining rather than deviating from the text and sources. In this way, Ijtihad will function to promote the purpose of Shari'a in the modern world by overcoming the process legitimacy deficits and thereby freeing Islamic international law from the perceived taint of modern innovation. Similarly, concerning Public international law, this chapter argued that a coherent approach requires the implementation of sovereign equality of states in the decision-making process at international institutions such as the Security Council and applying Islamic international law in matters where one or both parties are Muslim states or armed non-state actors. These can be adopted under article 2(1) of the UN Charter and by applying Islamic law in international courts and tribunals such as the ICJ and ICC. This approach will overcome the process legitimacy deficits of Public international law on the use of force.

Public international law must adopt this coherent approach to overcome the existing legitimacy deficits that challenge this global framework. Overcoming these legitimacy deficits will secure the source-oriented, process, and descriptive legitimacy, that is the perception of any use of force as legitimate by those who are affected by it. As most of the armed conflicts in the twenty-first century involved one or more Muslim states it is time for Public international law to recognize Islamic international law as its source and incorporate this in the decision-making process at international institutions, courts, and tribunals. Relegating Islamic international law and its jurisprudence by holding them incompatible with Public international law, without recognizing their potential to provide enhanced legitimacy of the latter, is fatal in overcoming the legitimacy deficits. Whereas Islamic international law has provided the basis for regulating the use of force in the modern world through its progressive methods of jurisprudence such as Ijtihad, maqāsid al-Shari'a, pragmatic eclecticism, and masalahah, the time has come for Public international law to incorporate and apply Islamic international law as suggested in this chapter. This coherent approach of Public international law on the use of force will secure legitimacy in the descriptive sense and lead the way to its recognition as objective, neutral, and universal.

References

Ahmed R., Nassery I., and Tatari M. (eds.), *The Objectives of Islamic Law: The Promises and Challenges of the Maqasid al-Shari'a* (Lanham: Lexington Books, 2018).

Alexandrowicz H., *An Introduction to the History of the Law of Nations in the East Indies* (Oxford: Clarendon Press, 1967).

al-Sayyid R., 'Contemporary Muslim Thought and Human Rights' (1995) 21 Islamo-christiana 27.

al-Shaf'i M. B. I., *Kitab al-Umm*, vol 7 (Beirut: Dar al-M'rifa, 1973).

Amin E. M. A., *Reclaiming Jihad: A Qur'anic Critique of Terrorism* (UK: The Islamic Foundation, 2014).

Anghie A., *Imperialism, Sovereignty and the Making of International Law* (Cambridge University Press, 2005).

An-Na'im A., *Islam and the Secular State* (Harvard University Press, 2009).

———, 'Toward an Islamic Hermeneutics for Human Rights' in An-Na'im A. A. and others (eds), *Human Rights and Religious Values: An Uneasy Relationship?* (William B Eerdmans 1995).

———, *Toward an Islamic Reformation: Civil Liberties, Human Rights and International Law* (Syracuse University Press, 1990).

Aquinas T., *Summa Theologica* (Treatise on the Theological Virtues) Quest 95.

Austin J., *The Province of Jurisprudence Determined* (First published 1832, Wilfrid E Rumble ed, Cambridge University Press, 1995).

Baderin M. A., *International Human Rights and Islamic Law* (Oxford University Press, 2003).

Bakircioglu O., *Islam and Warfare* (Routledge, 2014).

Bearman P. and Bianquis Th. et al. (eds), *Encyclopaedia of Islam* (2nd edn, Leiden: Brill, 2011).

Blackstone W., *Commentaries on the Laws of England*, vol 1 (Clarendon, 1766).

Brown C. L., *The Surest Path: The Political Treatise of a Nineteenth-Century Muslim Statesman* (Harvard University Press, 1967).

Bull H. and Watson A. (eds), *The Expansion of International Society* (New York: Oxford University Press, 1984).

Chesterman S., *Just War or Just Peace* (Oxford University Press, 2001).

Clapham A., *Brierly's Law of Nations: An Introduction to the Role of International Law in International Relations* (Seventh edition, Oxford University Press, 2012).
Donohue J. and Esposito J. (eds), *Islam in Transition: Muslim Perspectives* (New York: Oxford University Press 2007).
Dupret B., Berger M., and al-Zwaini L. (eds), *Legal Pluralism in the Arab World* (The Hague: Kluwer Law International, 1999).
Dworkin R., *Law's Empire* (Harvard University Press, 1986).
Elias T., *Africa and the Development of International Law* (Leiden: A.W. Sijthoff, 1972).
Esposito J. (ed), *Oxford Dictionary of Islam* (Oxford University Press, 2004).
Franck T., *Fairness in International Law and Institutions* (Oxford: Clarendon Press, 1995).
———, *The Power of Legitimacy Among Nations* (Oxford University Press, 1990).
Freeman M., *Human Rights: An Interdisciplinary Approach* (Cambridge, UK: Polity, 2002).
Gauhar A. (ed), *The Challenges of Islam* (London: Islamic Council of Europe, 1978).
Hallaq W. B., *A History of Islamic Legal Theories* (Cambridge University Press, 1997).
Hamidullah M., *Muslim Conduct of State* (4th edn, Lahore: Ashraf Press, 1961).
Hart H. L. A., *The Concept of Law* (2nd edn, Oxford University Press, 1994).
Hashmi S. (ed), *Islamic Political Ethics: Civil Society, Pluralism, and Conflict* (Princeton University Press, 2002).
Henderson C., 'The Arab Spring and the Notion of External State Sovereignty in International Law' (2014) 35 Liverpool Law Review 175.
Heyns C., Akande D, Hill-Cawthorne L., and Thompson C., 'The International Law Framework Regulating the Use of Armed Drones' (2016) 65 (4) International and Comparative Law Quarterly 791.
Ibrahim A. F., *Pragmatism in Islamic Law: A Social and Intellectual History* (Syracuse University Press, 2015).
———, 'Al-Sha'rānī's Response to Legal Purism: A Theory of Legal Pluralism' (2013) 20 Islamic Law and Society 112.
Jackson S., *Islamic Law and the State* (Leiden: Brill, 1996).
Johnson J.T., 'Threats, Values and Defense' in Elshtain J.B. (ed), *Just War Theory* (Blackwell, 1992).
Johnston D., 'Maqāsid al-Shari'a: Epistemology and Hermeneutics of Muslim Theologies of Human Rights Authors' (2007a) 47 Die Welt des Islams 149.
———, *Earth, Empire and Sacred Text: Muslims and Christians as Trustees of Creation* (London: Equinox, 2007b).
Kamali M. H., 'Have We Neglected the Shari'ah doctrine of Masalahah?' (1988) 27 Islamic Studies 287.
———, *Principles of Islamic Jurisprudence* (Islamic Texts Society: Cambridge, 1991).

———, 'Methodological Issues in Islamic Jurisprudence' (1996) 11 Arab Law Quarterly 3.

———, 'Issues in the Understanding of Jihad and Ijtihad' (2002) 41 Islamic Studies 617.

Kelsen H., 'The Natural Law Doctrine before the Tribunal of Science' (1949) II West Pol Q 481.

Kennedy H., *The Great Arab Conquest: How the Spread of Islam Changed the World We Live In* (UK: Weidenfeld and Nicolson, 2007).

Kerr M., *Islamic Reform: The Political and Legal Theories of Muhammad 'Abduh and Rashīd Riḍā* (University of California Press, 1966).

Khan A., 'The Reopening of the Islamic Code: The Second Era of Ijtihad' (2003) 1 University of St. Thomas Law Journal 341.

Khadduri M., *Al-Shafi's Risala: Treatise on the Foundations of Islamic Jurisprudence* (2nd edn, the Islamic Tests Society, 1961).

Koskenniemi M., Rech W. and Fonesca M. J. (eds), *International Law and Empire* (Oxford University Press, 2017).

Lombardi C., 'Islamic law in the Jurisprudence of the International Court of Justice: An Analysis' (2008) 8 Chicago Journal of International Law 85.

Mahmassani S., *Falsafat al-Tashri Fi al-Islam: The Philosophy of Jurisprudence in Islam* (Farhat J. Ziadeh tr, Leiden: Brill, 1961).

Mandaville P., *Islam and Politics* (2nd edn, Routledge, 2014).

Martin R. and Woodward M., *Defenders of Reason in Islam: Mu'tazilism from Medieval School to Modern Symbol* (Oxford: Oneworld, 1997).

Mitchell S. and Powell E., *Domestic Law Goes Global* (Cambridge University Press, 2011).

Moosa E., 'The Poetics and Politics of Law after Empire' (2002) UCLA Journal of Islamic and Near Eastern Law 1.

Nasr S. H., *The Heart of Islam: Enduring Values for Humanity* (New York and San Francisco: Harper San Francisco, 2002).

Nussbaum A., *A Concise History of the Law of Nations* (New York: The Macmillan Company, 1962).

Opwis F., 'Masalaha in Contemporary Islamic Leal Methodology' (2005) Islamic Law and Society 187.

Orakhelashvili A. (ed.), *Research Handbook on the Theory and History of International Law* (Edward Elgar Publishing, 2011).

Qarāfī S., *al-Ihkām fī Tamyīz al-Fatāwā 'an al-Ahkām wa-Tasarrufāt al-Qādī wa'l-Imām* (Beirut: Maktabat al-Matbū 'at al-Islāmiyya bi-Halab, 1995).

Ponting C., *World History: A New Perspective* (UK: Chatto and Windus, 2000).

Rabb I. A., *Doubt in Islamic Law: A History of Legal Maxims, Interpretation, and Islamic Criminal Law* (Cambridge University Press 2015a).

———, 'Against Kadijustiz: On the Negative Citation of Foreign Law' (2015b) 48 Suffolk University Law Review 343.

Ramadan T., *Western Muslims and the Future of Islam* (London & New York: Oxford University Press, 2004).
Raz J., 'Kelsen's Theory of the Basic Norm' (1974) 19 Am J Juris 94.
Sachedina A., *The Islamic Roots of Democratic Pluralism* (New York: Oxford University Press, 2001).
Sadeghi B., *The Logic of Law Making in Islam* (New York: Cambridge University Press, 2013).
Sharastani M. A., *Muslim Sects and Divisions: The Section on Muslim Sects in Kitab al-Milal wa 'I-Nihal* (A.K. Kazi and J.G. Flynn tr, Kegan Paul International, 1984).
Shaw M. N., 'The International Court of Justice: A Practical Perspective' (1997) 46 International & Comparative Law Quarterly 831.
Thomas C., 'The Uses and Abuses of Legitimacy in International Law' (2014) 34 Oxford Journal of Legal Studies 729.
Tiedrez J., 'On the International Criminal Court's lack of Islamic law representation' available at https://voelkerrechtsblog.org/time-for-an-islamic-legal-scholar-at-the-icc/ accessed 22 August 2020.
Van Engeland A., 'Contextualisation of Humanitarian Assistance and Its Shortcomings in International Human Rights Law' (2016) 49 Israel Law Review 169.
———, 'The Balance Between Islamic Law, Customary Law and Human Rights in Islamic Constitutionalism Through the Prism of Legal Pluralism' (2014) 4 Cambridge Journal of International and Comparative Law 1321.
———, 'When Two Visions of a Just World Clash: International Humanitarian Law and Islamic Humanitarian Law' (2006) American Society of International Law Proceedings 156.
Vanhullebusch M., 'Do Non-State Armed Groups Have a Legal Right to Consent to Offers of International Humanitarian Relief?' (2020) 25 (2) Journal of Conflict & Security Law 317.
Wolfrum R. and Roben V. (eds.), *Legitimacy in International Law* (Heidelberg: Springer, 2010).
Younes S., 'Islamic Legal Hermeneutics: The Context and Adequacy of Interpretation in Modern Islamic Discourse' (2002) 41 Islamic Studies 585.
Zahra M. A., *Usūl al-Fiqh* (Cairo: Dār al-Fikr al-'Arabī, 1958).

CHAPTER 6

Conclusion

The legitimacy of use of force in Public international law is rooted in classical natural law tradition. This tradition satisfied the source-oriented legitimacy of Public international law. Philosophers and legal scholars like Thomas Aquinas and William Blackstone treated this body of law as legitimate due to its origin from the law of nature. Similarly, the legitimacy of Islamic international law is rooted in the sources such as the Qur'an, Sunna, Ijma, and Qiyas. As a result, both Public and Islamic international law satisfied the source-oriented legitimacy. However, these two legal systems have developed independently from each other since their origin. These systems have been developing and refining through processes that are also independent of each other. Whereas Public international law has moved further from its source and developed to pursue a secular legal system, Islamic international law has not moved from its source. In this setting, on the one hand, Public international law has developed a system that claims to be objective, neutral, and universal, but on the other hand, Islamic international law has developed a system that claims to be based on the Shari'a. The issue with the legitimacy of these two legal systems lies in the process that they follow in the decision and law-making processes concerning the use of force. This is because on the one hand Public international law follows an institutional process that professes the legitimacy of use of force decisions taken by the Security Council, and on the other hand Islamic international law follows an Islamic jurisprudential process to

M. Z. Sabuj, *The Legitimacy of Use of Force in Public and Islamic International Law*,
https://doi.org/10.1007/978-3-030-77298-7_6

profess the legitimacy of use of force. In this process, the jurists of Islamic law exercise Ijtihad (exertion of intellectual reasoning) as a legitimate process of developing Islamic jurisprudence in line with the Shari'a that includes the text (Qur'an and Sunna), Consensus (Ijma), and analogy (Qiyas). As a result, the Muslim jurists play an exemplary role in explaining and interpreting the legitimacy of use of force to keep pace with time and social changes. However, the processes that Public and Islamic international law have followed are subject to legitimacy deficits. For example, the decision-making process at the Security Council and abuse of the juristic authority to interpret the Shari'a.

Both armed non-state actors and state authorities have been making use of Islamic and Public international law to justify their respective use of force as just and legitimate. Armed non-state actors such as the Muslim Brotherhood, Hamas, and militant groups such as Al-Qa'ida and ISIS (Islamic State and Iraq and Syria) have been claiming the legitimacy of use of force against their respective state authorities and extraterritorial use of force against foreign states. They claim that Islamic law authorizes them to use defensive force against aggression by non-Muslim states which constructively resort to aggressive force for their benefit and often collude with the rulers of Muslim states which abstain from exercising their political authority to declare defensive use of force in such situation. In addition, these groups also claim the legitimacy of use of force against the Muslim rulers who they accuse of aiding and even supporting the non-Muslim powers that exercise unlawful influence on the Muslim countries and as a result subjecting God's command to them. In this way, the armed non-state actors have claimed legitimacy of their recourse to internal and extraterritorial use of force. In other words, when the use of force by and against armed non-state actors is generally categorized as a matter of domestic law, non-state actors argued for the extension of such use of force to include extraterritorial use of force within the purview of Islamic law. As a result, their claim of the legitimacy of extraterritorial use of force creates a vital link between the use of force by and against state authorities and the latter's collusion with foreign powers. This vital link has become strong based on the argument made by armed non-state actors that Islamic international law does not allow collusion with another state, whether Muslim or non-Muslim, to cause internal disturbance and persecution. On the contrary, state authorities reject this claim made by armed non-state actors on the basis that the use of force against them is a legitimate authority of states in Islamic law, and inviting a foreign power to intervene is legal in Public international law. Examples of intervention by invitation and collusion with foreign power include the military influence and intervention of the powerful states or their allies in the internal affairs of a Muslim state such as Russia's intervention in Syria by invitation from the Assad regime and the ongoing airstrike in Yemen by Saudi Arabia with the request from the Yemeni government. Whereas this evidence strengthens the claim of the legitimacy of extraterritorial use of force by armed non-state actors against the invited or influencing foreign powers, there is evidence to suggest that non-state actors may also receive a supply of arms and military support from foreign powers, such as the Libyan rebels were supported by NATO in 2011 against the Gaddafi regime and Houthi rebels of Yemen have been receiving a supply of arms and military support from the Iranian authority. This type of foreign aids to armed non-state actors is illegal in Public international law. In these circumstances, non-state actors' claim for the legitimacy of use of force lies in Islamic international law as opposed to Public international law and state authorities' claim of the legitimacy of collusion with foreign powers lies in Public international law as opposed to Islamic international law. In these contrasting claims of the legitimacy of use of force, the question of legitimacy reaches a vantage point where it culminates to the question 'where does the legitimacy lie—Public or Islamic international law?'

Whereas the elite and powerful states have answered the legitimacy question from their institutional political position, the Muslim states and armed non-state actors functioning within those states have answered it based on religion and politics. The justification of religious and political arguments for the legitimate use of force at the vantage point invoked discussions about the nature of the legitimacy debate. This debate questioned the relegation of Islamic law at the state level and inter-state level. At the state level, it has been argued that Public international law has left the treatment of non-state actors in the hands of their rulers or governments which often use violent force against them. At the inter-state level, it has been argued that collusion of the Muslim rulers and state authorities with foreign powers and the resulting persecution is illegal in Islamic international law. It has also been argued that this collusion with foreign powers gives rise to the legitimacy of defensive use of force by armed non-state actors against their rulers as well as the foreign powers. These are extraordinarily strong claims that are being made by the armed non-state actors in Muslim states, which questioned the legitimacy of the political doctrine of 'sovereignty of states' and blurred the distinction made by

Public international law on the use of force between international and internal armed conflict. This is because while the sovereignty of states and classification of armed conflict to international and non-international are recognized in Public international law, this is not so recognized in Islamic international law. Islamic international law recognizes the sovereignty of God only, and in that sense, it supports the sovereignty of the entire Muslim community instead of one or more Muslim states. As a result, both Public and Islamic international law have reached a vantage point where these two legal systems questioned each other's legitimacy on the use of force.

Public international law recognizes the legitimacy of recourse to defensive force by a state in response to an imminent threat of armed attack by armed non-state actors (pre-emptive self-defence). In response to this defensive use of force the ruler of a Muslim state is left only with one of the two options, namely (a) to invite a foreign power to control the non-state actors or (b) to face intervention under the banner of pre-emptive self-defence. In this situation, a ruler of a Muslim state is likely to choose to invite a foreign power so it can still protect its political authority within the state. However, the same option may be available to armed non-state actors who may receive assistance from the foreign powers, which is illegal in Public international law but can be legitimate under the principle of humanitarian intervention or responsibility to protect as discussed in Chap. 1 of this book. As a result, armed non-state actors in Muslim states often choose to exercise their right of self-defence against foreign interventions that are backed by invitation from their rulers. These situations have given rise to a common dilemma between the legitimacy of use of force in Public and Islamic international law. For instance, on the one hand, the elite and powerful states claim the legitimacy of intervention by invitation despite the existence of legal uncertainty about the consent, humanitarian intervention or responsibility to protect, and use of force in pre-emptive self-defence in Public international law; on the other hand, Muslim states and armed non-state actors functioning within those states question the legitimacy of these claims as they are opposed to Islamic international law. As the Muslim states have signed and ratified the UN Charter, they are only bound by those provisions which are legally allowed by the charter but not any extra-Charter use of force under the auspices of legitimacy. On this footing, the author argues that anticipatory and preventive uses of force in self-defence are illegitimate due to their flagrant violation of the UN Charter, repugnant to Islamic international law, and not adopted in the state practices to become customary international law. This argument extends to the use of force without authorization from the Security Council as discussed in Chap. 2 of this book. However, there are valid claims of the legitimacy of pre-emptive use of force due to the customary nature of such use of force and their potential to become customary international law. In addition, the right of self-defence is legally available to both state and armed non-state actors alike as *jus cogens* of Public international law and general principles of Islamic international law on the use of force.

Both Public and Islamic international law prohibit intervention by invitation without valid consent and extraterritorial use of force by armed non-state actors. However, Islamic law limits the legitimacy of consent to the ruler, or the persecuted people in the absence of a ruler, or an undisputed Muslim leader where the ruler colludes with a foreign power to persecute its people. On the contrary, Public international law limits the legitimacy of consent to a legitimate ruler or government. In other words, it does not allow extraterritorial use of force by armed non-state actors and leaves this matter within the ruler or government under the political notion of sovereignty. As a result, Public and Islamic international law have rules of legitimate consent that are conflicting with each other. In this setting, Public international law allows intervention into the internal affairs of another state with an invitation from the latter's ruler on the one hand and prohibits extraterritorial use of force by armed non-state actors against the foreign powers on the other. However, Islamic international law does not recognize intervention by a non-Muslim state into a Muslim state whether by invitation or otherwise unless no Muslim state is willing and able to accept the invitation. In these circumstances, Muslim rulers and regimes that invite foreign powers to suppress armed non-state actors within the state promote persecution (*fitna*) of the people whom they are legally bound to protect from any persecution. These situations give rise to illegal intervention according to Islamic international law. Although intervention by invitation of a foreign power is legal in public international law, it is not legitimate due to its conflict with Islamic international law. As a result, where intervention by invitation involves a Muslim state, that intervention must follow the Islamic international law. Whilst Islamic international law imposed a limit on the use of force, that must be followed by an intervening state, whether Muslim or non-Muslim. In other words, merely claiming legality of intervention in Public international law as a power-conferring instrument that violates Islamic international law would result in illegitimate use of force.

While urging to recognize Islamic law it is conceivable that conflicting claims of legitimacy may be made by Public international law. In other words, the use of force may not be considered legitimate simultaneously by Public and Islamic international law. Similarly, whereas certain use of force is claimed to be legitimate in Public international law it is quite the opposite in Islamic international law. These conflicting claims of legitimacy on the use of force may occur concerning extraterritorial use of force in self-defence, and humanitarian intervention by states and regional organizations. For instance, on the one hand, Islamic international law allows extraterritorial use of force to protect people from persecution, and on the other hand, Public international law requires authorization from the Security Council or state consent in such circumstances. In this setting, when a state uses force in the territory of a Muslim state without obtaining authorization from the Security Council or state consent, the latter sees this use of force as illegitimate. The same applies to 'intervention by a non-Muslim state with an invitation from a Muslim ruler', which is legal in Public international law but illegal in Islamic international law as discussed above. The argument for justifying the intervention that such use of force is legitimate in Public international law suffers from legitimacy deficits as it does not consider Islamic international law on the use of force. In response to this argument, the attacking state questions the legitimacy of the application of Islamic international law in the decision-making process. These conflicting claims have resulted in the legitimacy deficits of both these regimes.

People of Muslim states often perceive Public international law as illegitimate due to relegating Islamic international law at the international level. Despite the acceptance of Public international law by the Muslim states as a valid source of law and applicable to them, the former does not recognize Islamic international law as a valid source of law irrespective of having the provisions for doing this about the use of force. As a result, Public international law still suffers from a legitimacy deficit in the descriptive sense, where the people of Muslim states, who are severely affected by the use of force so far in the twenty-first century, must perceive such force as legitimate. Overcoming the descriptive legitimacy deficit is vital for Public international law to prove that it is not relegating another major legal system such as Islamic international law.

In these circumstances, the author argues that the legitimacy of Public and Islamic international law does not lie in either of these legal systems as an exclusive body of laws. Islamic international law should recognize the legitimacy of use of force in Public international law to the extent that Muslim states have agreed to the UN Charter and as far as it is consistent with Islamic law. Similarly, Public international law must recognize Islamic international law as a valid source of law and apply this body of laws at the international level particularly in respect of any decision involving one or more Muslim states and armed non-state actors from those states. This coherent approach would overcome the legitimacy deficits of Public international law on the use of force by becoming more objective, neutral, and universal.

Islamic international law on the use of force has taken a coherent approach by adopting Public international law as a legitimate framework by signing and ratifying international treaties such as the UN Charter and becoming active members of international institutions such as the Security Council. Moreover, Islamic international law has maintained its legitimacy by creating the legal-political legacies in line with the Shari'a, which has been evolving as a living mechanism since the formative period of Islam. These legal-political legacies can complement Public international law in finding and recognizing legitimate use of force from the illegitimate ones. Furthermore, Islamic international law has been keeping up its legitimacy with the changing and ever-evolving international legal and political spectrums through the exercise of Ijtihad, which applied Maqāsid al-Shari'a, pragmatic eclecticism, and masalahah. As a result, Islamic international law has made the space for Public international law to be legitimately applicable to its subjects. Therefore, the time has come for Public international law to adopt a coherent approach by recognizing Islamic international law as a legitimate source of law and apply this body of laws in the decision-making process at the international level as well as in international courts and tribunals not least where any such decision would affect one or more Muslim states and non-state actors. Legal provisions are available in the Public international law framework to recognize Islamic international law as a valid source of law and apply it in the decision-making process at the Security Council, international courts, and tribunals. For example, the United Nations Charter, Statutes of the International Court of Justice (ICJ), and the Rome Statute have legal provisions for the application of Islamic international law in the decision-making process at the Security Council, the appointment of judges from experts in Islamic law in the

International Court of Justice (ICJ) and International Criminal Court (ICC), and formally recognizing Islamic law as a source of Public international law. This coherent approach can overcome the legitimacy deficits of both Public and Islamic international law on the use of force. The modern world has made a demand for the legitimacy of use of force, and that demand must be met by adopting the coherent approach between Public and Islamic international law. There is no place for hegemony and monopoly by the elite and powerful states at the international level due to their lack of legitimate authority to manipulate Public international law on the use of force by political and military power and to exclude or relegate Islamic international law from functioning at the international level.

Glossary of Non-English Terms

Ab initio From the very beginning
Al-mustadafin The oppressed socially weak Muslims
Bid'a Innovation
Caliph Leader of the Muslims
Caliphate Islamic empire
Casus belli An act or event that resulted in war
Dar al-'Ahd Abode of Covenant/Truce, territories/countries that have treaties of nonaggression or peace with Muslims, agreeing to protect Muslims and their clients in that territory and often including an agreement to pay (receive) tribute
Dar al-harb Abode of war, territories/countries that do not have treaties of nonaggression or peace with Muslims and where Islamic law is not in force
Dar al-Islam Abode of Islam, region of Muslim sovereignty where Islamic law prevails
Dar al-Sulh Abode of reconciliation by treaty
Da'wah Call to Islamic faith
Fath Conquest
Fi sabilillah For the sake of Allah
Fitna Persecution
Fiqh Knowledge of Islamic law derived through juristic interpretation
Hajj Pilgrimage to Mecca

M. Z. Sabuj, *The Legitimacy of Use of Force in Public and Islamic International Law*,
https://doi.org/10.1007/978-3-030-77298-7

Harb War
Ijma Consensus of opinion
Imam An equivalent to Caliph, spiritual and political leadership of the Muslim nation (ummah)
Ijtihad Exertion of intellectual reasoning
Isnad Chain of transmission
Istihsan Juristic preference
Istislah Public interest
Jihad Literally, "struggle" or "effort"; in Qur'anic contexts it denotes striving and struggling in the Path of God.
Jihad al-nafs Struggle against the soul
jus ad bellum A set of criteria that are to be consulted before engaging in war, in order to determine whether entering into war is permissible; that is, justifications for resorting to war
jus in bello Rules regulating the conduct of war
Jus cogens Established principles of international law that cannot be set aside
Jus gentium Principles of international law common to all nations
Kafir Infidel or apostate
Madhahib Different schools of legal thought
Maqasid al-Shari'a The spirit and purpose of Shari'a
Masalahah Public welfare
Ma'sum The inerrant Imam
Mufti Jurisconsult who is capable to exercise legal reasoning independent of the schools of law
Mujahid A person performing Jihad
Mujtahid A jurist exercising *Ijtihad*
Pacta sunt servanda Treaties and agreements are binding and must be kept
Qitāl Fighting
Qiyas Analogy
Qur'an The primary source of Islamic law that was revealed from the God
Quraysh A Meccan tribe which held political control in the city in the early days of Islam
Shari'a Islamic principles (legal and religious) developed from the primary sources such as the Qur'an and sunna
Shura Public consultation

Siyar Practices and transactions between Muslim states or Muslims and non-Muslim states
Sunna The narrations of the conduct and sayings of Prophet Muhammad
Takfir Excommunication
Ummah Islamic community
Usūl al-fiqh Legal methodology

INDEX[1]

[1] Note: Page numbers followed by 'n' refer to notes.

M. Z. Sabuj, *The Legitimacy of Use of Force in Public and Islamic International Law*,
https://doi.org/10.1007/978-3-030-77298-7

The manufacturer's authorised representative in the EU is Springer Nature Customer Service Centre GmbH, Europaplatz 3, 69115 Heidelberg, Germany. If you have any concerns regarding our products, please contact ProductSafety@springernature.com

Printed and bound by CPI Group (UK) Ltd, Croydon, CR0 4YY
30/09/2026
02225698-0004